D0120186

RICHER THAN GOD

RICHER THAN GOD

Manchester City,
Modern Football and Growing Up

DAVID CONN

Quercus

First published in Great Britain in 2012 by

Quercus

55 Baker Street

7th Floor, South Block

W1U 8EW

A CIP catalogue record for this book is available
from the British Library

HB ISBN 978 0 85738 486 7

TPB ISBN 978 0 85738 487 4

10 9 8 7 6 5 4 3 2 1

Text designed and typeset by Ellipsis Digital Limited
Printed and bound in Great Britain by Clays Ltd, St Ives plc

For my wife, Sarah, and my daughters, Isobel and Emily

and for my brothers, Alex Conn and Raphael Conn,
with love, always

Sport means nothing without belief
Simon Barnes

CONTENTS

CHAPTER 1

IN THE HEART OF EUROPE

Wednesday afternoon, 14 September 2011: grey cloud, a linger of summer in the sunshine but a wind with a winter foretaste; a day when the weather, as they say in Manchester, can't make its mind up. A month into the Premier League football season, I am dropping down over the Pennine hills from Yorkshire where I now live, to see Manchester City, the club I grew up supporting, whose floodlit wonders illuminated the nights of my Manchester childhood. Tonight the all-star squad, bought and paid lavishly from the oil fortunes of City's far-fetched owner, Sheikh Mansour bin Zayed Al Nahyan of Abu Dhabi, are playing Manchester City's first match in European champions football since the finest team in the club's history lost to Fenerbahce on a fearsome night of flares and fireworks, forty-three years ago in Istanbul.

They did things differently then, of course. Fans paid shillings to watch, mostly to stand on the groaning Kippax Street terrace running the length of Maine Road, City's old, brooding ground in Moss Side. No sponsor's name competed on the players' chests with the ship and red rose in the badge on the sky-blue shirts. The team which outfought United by two points to the 1968 Football League championship was drawn from the young lads of Manchester and English football's minor provinces, not the furthest international reaches of a billionaire's wallet. The illustrious threesome in City's backbone – fine, upstanding Colin Bell, barrelling Francis Lee, skiddy Mike Summerbee – had been bought from Bury, Bolton Wanderers and Swindon Town respectively. United, naturally, had to go and win the European Cup the same month, ten years after eight of manager Matt Busby's players were killed in the Munich air crash, so attaining English football's greatest-ever achievement. That was a story we grew into as boys, its basics inhaled with the Manchester air, and little was ever said about City's sole League championship since the war, claimed by a beaming Lee at a 4–3 victory away at Newcastle United. I was three then, so too young to see City in those two years, 1968–70, into which they compressed a golden age, winning the League championship, FA Cup in 1969, European Cup Winners' Cup and League Cup the year after. Into the 1970s, though, City were still a top team, superior to United, who were relegated in 1974 in the overhang from Busby's retirement. In formative years for my generation, City played enlightened football, won the League Cup at Wembley with a wondrous Dennis Tueart overhead kick in 1976, and played in European competition on those starry midweek nights.

Collapse, when it came at the end of the 1970s, was self-inflicted, and then the decades passed, mostly in gloom and several shades of cock-up, endured by supporters with stolid patience, the mood lightened briefly by taking inflatable bananas to the match. Yet City, of all clubs, are now, suddenly, the richest club in the world, or to be precise, the club with the richest owner, oil having gushed into the inheriting laps of Sheikh Mansour and his family, rulers in Abu Dhabi since the eighteenth century. When he decided to buy Manchester City, at the end of August 2008, the club was staring, not for the first time, at financial ruin. City had managed to tumble into that hapless predicament from a gift of outrageous fortune: a new, 48,000-seat stadium, built for the 2002 Commonwealth Games with public money – £78m from the National Lottery, £49m from Manchester City Council – which was converted, its athletics track ripped up and a new stand built, all at the public's expense, for City to occupy thereafter, on very generous terms.

When Sheikh Mansour bought City, he said – or rather, a statement in his name said – that he intended to 'build a team capable of sustaining a presence in the top four of the Premier League and winning European honours'. So far, in the three years since, he has committed around £1bn to pull off that football wish. To show he was serious at the beginning, as a 'statement', he instantly paid £32.5m for the Brazilian international Robinho, although he turned out to be a little too much in love with the good life, and too little with the Manchester weather, to play a manful part in the project. Sheikh Mansour's money, and the professional expertise he has introduced, has since wholly overhauled the new Manchester City: a new office block has been built, bars and an entertainment square for supporters, the Carrington training ground revamped. The cost of such solid improvements, though, is droplets, compared with the £452m of Sheikh Mansour's oil inheritance spent on buying twenty-two new players (average price £22m each) and paying wages gross enough to lure them to City – the highest-paid – the Argentinian Carlos Tevez, is paid £198,000 a week, or £10m a year, basic. The total committed is already more than a billion pounds, on one football club, in just the three years since City, then owned by the former Thai Prime Minister, Thaksin Shinawatra – who was accused of being 'a human rights abuser of the worst kind' but still allowed to buy the club – finished ninth in the Premier League in 2008. These millions shelled out on so vast a scale have brought a squad of new players to City, who combined to win the FA Cup in May 2011 – the first trophy in the thirty-five years since that 1976 League Cup victory – and finish third in the Premier League. That qualified present-day, Abu Dhabi-owned Manchester City, on target according to the business plan, into this first European Champions League night.

In the car on the way to the City of Manchester Stadium – just renamed the Etihad Stadium, after the Abu Dhabi airline which is paying £350m to have its name for ten years on City's shirts, stadium and new, £140m training 'campus' – the BBC radio news is unremittingly grey. Unemployment in Britain has risen to its highest since the banks' negligence crashed what passed for our economy into a slump. More than two and a half million people are out of work, and the City of London, whose most respectable of brass-plate names made a bonfire of their billions, are now predicting 2.75m people unemployed in 2012. The 'benefit', or dole, an adult over 25 receives for body and soul when he or she is out of work, is £67.50 for a whole week. Young people aged 16–24 must survive on £53.45. The Labour opposition, who were in government for thirteen years culminating in the banking collapse, is accusing the Conservative–Liberal Democrat coalition of choosing wholly the wrong course in the financial crisis. The new government is drastically cutting public spending, on schools, hospitals, 'benefits,' and money to local councils, a policy they claim will pay off national debt, and will put 700,000 public workers on the dole. Within the overall rise in unemployment announced this month, 77,000 are people under 25, meaning that almost a million young people have no work. There are fears that in Britain's towns and cities there will be a 'lost generation' of young people who will never recover from years of unemployment at the youthful start of their work-age lives.

The unions, what remain of them, have just voted to strike over the government seeking to save more money by extending public-sector workers' retirement age until 67, and making workers contribute more towards their pensions, which will nevertheless be worth less when they retire. The euro is in crisis as Germany, which still has a powerful, working economy based on manufacturing, struggles to prevent Greece, the sun-dried country which lived almost entirely off debt, from defaulting and dragging other industrially hollowed-out European countries with it. The headline above the leader article in tomorrow's *Guardian* newspaper, which I write for, urging the British government to do something positive to promote, or re-create, a proper, industrious economy, will be: 'Bleak, bleak, bleak'.

I come off the M60 ring road at Middleton, close to grand, grumbling Heaton Park and the north Manchester suburbs of my youth, then turn left towards the city centre, 'town', at Cheetham Hill. Always Manchester's first port of necessity to waves of ragged immigrants, including my own great-grandfather who washed up here with other persecuted eastern European Jews in the early 1900s, now people from India, Somalia and again eastern Europe bustle in the poor neighbourhoods and hope to make their way to the leafier suburbs up Bury Old Road. Take a left into Queens Road, and you wind round once-industrial neighbourhoods towards 'Sportcity', the concrete cluster of elite facilities including the stadium, for which the council attracted massive public funding a decade ago, in the hope of resuscitating the city's sunken east.

Openshaw, Miles Platting, Beswick, Collyhurst, Gorton – these exhausted areas formed the mucky engine-room of Victorian Manchester, the world's first industrial city, to which travellers were drawn to wonder at modern economic production, and grimace at its harshness. These areas, right around Sheikh Mansour's Etihad Stadium, remain Manchester's poorest and some of the very poorest in Britain. For all the chippy talking up of the city, the music of the late 1980s and 1990s, the ephemeral twenty-four-hour party heyday of the Hacienda club which no longer exists, the publicly funded major works to inspire 'regeneration' and the top-flight, foreign-owned football clubs, Manchester remains the poorest city in Britain. The money there is, in loamy Alderley Edge and other Cheshire havens where new-model footballers build their mansions, lies outside Manchester local council boundaries. Inside it are miles of stubbornly deprived tracts, where no reliable work has ever replaced the hard, grimy industry on which the north was built. The factories, mines and works died, were allowed to die, steadily from the 1920s, and seemed even to be helped on their way in the 1980s by a Conservative government which thought that the old industrial cities were too much trouble, and that a sustainable future could be shaped largely from 'financial services'.

Today, almost half of Manchester's neighbourhoods, 45.6 per cent, are in the 'most deprived' 10 per cent in the country, according to the Office of National Statistics which collates the figures. Of these, 19 of Manchester's areas, broken down to 2,000 residents, are among the most deprived 1 per cent. Collyhurst, the sleeves-rolled-up district close to City's £127m stadium, millionaire players and trillionaire Sheikh, is the second-worst neighbourhood in the country measured for 'income deprivation affecting children'. It is fifth-worst for 'health deprivation and disability', which includes how many fewer years people would live on average compared to more comfortable areas, and the numbers of people on medication for depression. The top seven in Manchester's list of most deprived areas are all former industrial and working-class neighbourhoods in the east, around the Etihad stadium: Bradford, Miles Platting and Newton Heath, Harpurhey, Gorton South, Charlestown, Ardwick and Gorton North.

Driving through, the grey gradually wearing down the sunshine, I sense the usual bleakness in the characterless housing estates: a solitary mum pushing a pram uphill, a huddled-up Bengali woman waiting at a bus stop, the odd shabby corner shop and bookies, until the gasometer in front of the stadium heaves into view. Here, very close to it, there is some new housing, wood and chrome and glass, an outward sign of the regeneration the stadium was intended to bring. The park, Philips, one of Manchester's first, created in 1846 to give the factory workers a breath of air and some green, and neglected for years following the cuts of the 1980s, has been spruced up at last. And there is the Asda supermarket, whose arrival in 2002, offering some jobs to local people, was hailed as a true landmark and sign of recovery for the area.

I pull into the stadium, in front of the Manchester branch of the national tennis centre where, with the greatest of respect, I have never seen anybody playing tennis, park, then walk up the ramp. When they moved into the new stadium, City plonked the shop right there at the top of the ramp, so the fans mostly have to pass through it on their way to the match. City's retail minds have refined, over the years, the art of locating the emotional g-spots in supporters always close to bursting with sentiment. When I once found myself upstairs in the shop, lingering too long, and actually welling up, over a limited edition boxset devoted to Colin Bell memory worship, for which the City Store wanted £125, I realised they knew exactly which buttons to press.

From childhood, I loved playing and watching football and by a moment of fate I grew up supporting City. Years later as a journalist my education into the realities of the game, its great clubs' volunteer origins, the organisation, ownership and ethics of the Premier League, began with Francis Lee's return to City, as a businessman taking charge, in 1994. He promised salvation from our sour, vinegary chairman Peter Swales, who had seriously outstayed after the 1979 madness, but Franny, as we all called our hero, propelled the club to yet more mountainous peaks of cock-up. That experience jolted me from football lover and loyal supporter, who had learned to see some humour in City's myriad miseries, to investigating the very history and founding purpose of football and its clubs, and how in modern times they had been transformed into corporations with 'owners' hungry for profit.

A course of investigation into modern football opens out into a tour around many unexpected aspects of the world at large, the most globally popular sport reflecting the times in which it is played. When Sheikh Mansour acquired Thaksin Shinawatra's fleeing, desperate Manchester City in August 2008, I knew nothing of Abu Dhabi or its bottomless reserves of fortunate wealth, nor understood the new power of such oil-rich countries compared with the post-industrial hangover of ours. I assumed that buying an English Premier League football club was an image-massaging play, a glamorous, western-attracting front, for the Sheikh from a ruling family in a country lacking democracy. Roman Abramovich's 2003 purchase of Chelsea had been an education into what happened in Russia under Boris Yeltsin, that a very few men, including Abramovich, had fastened themselves close to the president and emerged after a rigged process having bought most of the country's assets, at a fraction of their real value. Sheikh Mansour's first front man, the representative of his City purchase, was Sulaiman Al Fahim, an extremely unconvincing chap from Dubai, who bragged for three days about his backer's 'very deep pockets', and the stars City could now afford to buy: Fernando Torres, Cristiano Ronaldo, Cesc Fabregas, in some rich kid's trolley dash through the Panini football sticker album.

Very quickly, Al Fahim disappeared from representing Sheikh

Mansour and has never been heard from again in connection with Manchester City. Khaldoon Al Mubarak, a senior figure in the strategic shaping of Abu Dhabi's economic direction and image, took over as the public face of the Manchester City venture, and became the club's chairman, the most unlikely successor to Peter Swales. After that, as Abu Dhabi began to spend huge money and overhaul Manchester City in all areas, they were different to deal with, more open than all the previous occupants of the directors' box I had tried to come to terms with. They said they had nothing to hide, and were prepared to answer questions, and that turned out to be hearteningly true, up to a point. It is difficult to spend time with Sheikh Mansour himself, or the Al Nahyan family, who are represented with an always remarkable degree of his-Highness-style reverence by Al Mubarak and his lieutenants. At City and in Abu Dhabi, though, Al Mubarak proved himself engagingly willing to open up and explain the outsized spending, what they are up to, why Sheikh Mansour bought the club and what he wants out of it, how they are reshaping the club, what their philosophy is, and what it all signifies.

With Etihad Airways, and the Abu Dhabi Tourism Authority ('Travellers Welcome') slapped all over east Manchester's football club as an advertising vehicle for the gulf desert emirate itself, I had told them I was fascinated by this Abu Dhabi element of the City story. What on earth made a young Sheikh, lounging in unthinkable oil fortunes, decide he wanted to spend a portion of it buying and funding an English football club he had seen only on television? Rather than stonewalling and being hard to reach, as Thaksin and his men had always been, they invited me to go and see for myself. I interviewed Al Mubarak in Manchester a year, and £200m of player purchases, into his City project, at his home on a quiet street in swelteringly humid Abu Dhabi. That was a surreal journey, from being taken down to Maine Road as a boy in a bobble hat by my dad in 1970s Manchester, via my first interview with a Manchester City chairman, when Francis Lee had offered me five minutes in the poky old chairman's office at Maine Road.

For this game, City's first European champions match for forty-three years, enabled in just three by the Abu Dhabi oil money, I have been invited to meet in the chairman's lounge and watch from the directors' box with Al Mubarak and the men who now run the club. I told them I was writing this book, about the extraordinary journey of the club I supported myself, from the Third Division at Maine Road as recently as 1999 to this extravagant incarnation. The Abu Dhabi ownership has been contemptuously condemned around English and European football, where, apart from in the upper reaches of the Premier League, clubs are still mostly owned by local businessmen or their own member-supporters, not absentee sheikhs in faraway lands. The spending, to buy an entirely new squad of the best footballers, save for just two young survivors, is widely attacked as contrary to the traditions of football, where teams have been gradually built. The president of tonight's opponents Napoli, the film producer Dino de Laurentiis, would sneer after the away leg at the whole idea of a club buying its way into the Champions League, saying the sheikh will soon tire of City and buy himself 'another toy'.

European football's governing body, UEFA, whose competition this is, introduced a rule, to be enforced from 2014, to try to stop clubs spending far beyond their true means and falling into financial trouble, as so many have during what should be football's best of times. Under the 'financial fair play' rules, between 2011 and 2013 clubs will be permitted to make losses of €45m in total, at most. If they are flagrantly in breach and rack up huge losses, Uefa's ultimate sanction is to exclude that club from European competition, unthinkable for Sheikh Mansour's Champions League-aspirant project. City's losses for 2010–11, the year just before their finances come to be assessed for the financial fair play rules, was £197m, the greatest loss ever made by an English football club. It was more than five times the total City will be permitted to lose over the following two years, and so made it look impossible that they could be anywhere near breaking even by the deadline, without Sheikh Mansour's bankroll.

I wanted to understand what the Abu Dhabi regime is doing with Manchester City, and why. What is it all for, and can it possibly be decent or sustainable to spend so vast an amount of money on a football club? I wanted to investigate the effect this is having on what used to be termed, fondly, the people's game, and what it signifies for Manchester and Britain. Also what does Manchester City, so changed from the football club which first captivated me, mean to me now? They always said they would talk it through, and tonight there would be people in the chairman's lounge, including Al Mubarak, I would find it valuable to meet. So, with that degree of openness, they invited me into what football club directors have customarily called their 'inner sanctum'.

The first time I ever heard that phrase in a football context was from Freddie Pye, a scrap metal dealer, former Stockport County owner and City director with a resemblance to James Cagney. He told me that shortly after Francis Lee's takeover, he had confronted Franny face-to-face about some perceived loss of face or privilege, in the toilets within Maine Road's 'inner sanctum'. The inner sanctum in the Etihad Stadium of the new Manchester City is a touch more plush than Pye enjoyed in his time. You are ushered in by a train of smiling women, through satin-curtained inner corridors bearing huge images of City's best bits, including a stunning, iconic photograph of Colin Bell in his gilded 1960s youth. At the door of the sanctum itself they smile again, welcome you in, relieve you of your bag and coat, and serve a drink of your choice from a tray of welcome.

Inside, there is no trace of doubt about the rightness of the project. In the far corner of the snug, rectangular room, across tables laid with crispest linen and wine glasses standing to attention, sits Al Mubarak. He comes to Manchester City with friends and family from Abu Dhabi; while he coolly conducts his business of global football acquisition, they take in the whole English Premier League experience with a kind of dazzled rapture. Sheikh Mansour has been to Manchester only once to watch the team he has bought, whose millionaire wages he is paying, and Al Mubarak, busy with his sovereign portfolio, makes flying visits to the Etihad. He uses his time, including the ninety minutes of action, to satisfy himself about the project's developments and what further must be done to satisfy its ambitions. Graham

Wallace, City's chief operating officer, responsible for the inner details of the financial operation, is there, as is Simon Pearce, an Anglo-Australian expatriate who is Al Mubarak's communications and business strategist in Abu Dhabi, and a key City director. I see Al Mubarak take Brian Marwood, City's 'head of football administration' – effectively director of football, an appointment the new City have determinedly stuck with, for which they are being consistently vindicated – to a side room, for a quick meeting. Marwood, the small, wiry former Arsenal winger, bears the face of a schoolboy called to see the headmaster when he hasn't quite finished his homework. Out watching the match, I sense Marwood sitting uncomfortably through City's halting performance against the adventurous Italians, next to Al Mubarak on the front row of the directors' box.

The midweek matches of City's European run in the 1970s lit up my Manchester nights: rushing back from school, uniform off, getting down to Moss Side, half-running through the dark terraced streets, then through the Kippax turnstiles and up the dingy steps, to see the pitch and an altogether more splendid world. I was there when City played the great Juventus of Turin team, who I recognised even then, aged eleven, were operating at a level of professional efficiency beyond our heroes' nevertheless talented endeavours. In the final flourish before our self-destruction, in the winter of 1978, manager Tony Book's team treated us to a wonderful run, beating AC Milan – who were they, then? – 3–0, and drawing with them 2–2 in an afternoon game played while we were in school. The most dazzling European night of my memory was a 4–0 victory over Standard Liège of Belgium the round before that, when Peter Barnes, City's left winger, ran with so much burning speed past his full back he made the defender look, honestly, as if he was running backwards. I was thirteen then, and went with my older cousin Alan; he is from Glasgow and was studying in Manchester, and I would get the bus from Salford 7, where we lived, or scrounge a lift with someone whose dad was driving, and meet Alan there. We paid £1 or whatever it was, and found a place quite low down towards the right-hand side of the endless Kippax, where I could get a decent view. The floodlights highlighted the brilliant green of the pitch, and the players came out and wove wonders. Even now, when Alan and I meet at family occasions, we still always talk about it.

Thirty-three years later, out in the directors' box of the Etihad Stadium, they have blue-cushioned full-body seats, like the ones you see manager Roberto Mancini and City's substitutes sitting in, down in what used to be called the dugout. Al Mubarak takes his place with Marwood and other City directors in the front row. Opposite them, in huge capital letters, and in Arabic translation, is a banner some City fans from the Bluemoon website clubbed together to buy after a year of the Abu Dhabi investment; it says: MANCHESTER THANKS YOU SHEIKH MANSOUR. No rebel yell against an absentee owner, that. Certainly not compared with the furious campaign waged by United fans against theirs, the Glazer family from Florida, who bought Manchester United in 2005 with £525m of borrowed money and have since drained out £480m from the club and its fans, to pay the interest, bank fees and other charges on their own borrowings to buy the club.

Ten minutes into the match, with Napoli not overawed by facing the Manchester City of such expensive construction, I realise the seats in the directors' box, in the stadium Manchester City Council built, are heated. As mine warms up, I find it quite a strange and intrusive sensation. It makes me wonder who decided on this as an integral feature of the City of Manchester Stadium, and how the instructions were given to the architects: Oh – and don't forget the under-seat heating for the directors' arses.

In a surprisingly understated atmosphere for City's first-ever Champions League game, and with a smattering of empty blue seats around the stadium's bowl, Napoli, playing in purple, are marshalled in defence by Paolo Cannavaro, brother of Italy's former World Cup-winning captain Fabio, and the Uruguayan Edison Cavani is dashing up front. City, after an early surge, find themselves confounded. After half-time crème brûlée, petits fours and coffee in the chairman's lounge, during which I have a brief chat with one of Al Mubarak's very charming Abu Dhabi friends, who feels his country must strive to carve a modern identity not solely characterised by having piles of money, Napoli come out and score. During fifteen minutes of adventurous football when they attack City, Cavani finishes with glee after an under-hit backpass from Joleon Lescott, the elegant defender City signed for £22m in 2009 from Everton. They are the blue club of Liverpool, less successful than the reds, to which City were always compared before the council built City the new stadium and all this happened. A not-in-the-brochure quiet, mixed with the age-old grumble 'Come On, City!' imported from Maine Road, spreads around the stadium, discomfort seeps into the directors' box and seems to me to settle over the sunken head of Marwood, who has overseen the spending of so much of the Sheikh's money on these very players.

It is one of the less celebrated, Aleksander Kolarov, who cost just the £19m from Lazio after playing for Serbia in the 2010 World Cup, who equalises five minutes later, with a curling, dipping free-kick, and City fans rouse themselves. They sing their anthem, 'Blue Moon', which used to be mournfully rendered in Second Division underperformances by inadequate City teams made edgier by the weight of history and the fans' unfulfilled expectations: 'You saw me standing alone / Without a dream in my heart / Without a love of my own.' At full-time, City's names, Yaya Touré, David Silva, Sergio Aguero, have not quite justified the petrodollars spent on them or their monthly direct debits, but the overwhelming emotion is relief. Manchester City's new life in the European Champions League did not culminate in embarrassment, as so many of their new dawns did in the thirty years before Mansour.

Back in the lounge I briefly see Al Mubarak, who has been busy working. He tells me he believes Mancini is now happy that he has pretty much got the squad he wants – two top-quality or even world-class players in each position, which was part of their written, documented business plan agreed within 100 days of the takeover. Pearce and his small team – who work in the Abu Dhabi Executive Affairs Authority, the strategic arm of the government, for Al Mubarak, and ultimately for his boss, the Crown Prince , Sheikh Mohammed bin Zayed Al Nahyan, Sheikh Mansour's brother – are relaxing, talking and laughing. Marwood, looking relieved, is circulating, with Wallace. Brian

Kidd, who scored for City against Juventus in 1976, the only game my mum ever came to with me (she thought there was too much swearing, even in the Main Stand), is now Mancini's coach, and he makes an appearance in his tracksuit. In that pure Mancunian accent hewn in Collyhurst, then a strong working-class area, where he and a number of other former top footballers were born, most notably United and England's Nobby Stiles, Kidd explains the team's difficulties against Napoli: 'I told the players,' he says, 'Europe is a very different education.'

In a quiet corner of the bar at the centre of the room – nobody from Abu Dhabi drinks alcohol – I see Colin Bell, Tony Book, City's former captain in the glory days, then manager in the good times which followed, and Tommy Booth, a centre half from the 1970s who was physically engineered to head footballs. I go, tentatively, to talk to them. I tell them I grew up a City fan and watched them as a boy, and they are clearly accustomed to starstruck fortysomethings approaching them with tearducts of nostalgia. I do my best to ease back on boring them with the extent to which I held them in awe, and how much just seeing them right now instantly evokes memories of my happy childhood. My two brothers, me the middle one; even, very visually, the lovely house and garden where we grew up, my bedroom wall emblazoned with City – before their heyday was past, the 1980s set in, we moved to a gloomy old place and my parents split up. How they in themselves evoke the sky-blue blessing which football, and Manchester City, bestowed on a boyhood.

Instead, I keep myself together as best I can and have a

conversation like a grown-up. Bell, looking well and content, says he believes City fans are the best in the country, because they still treat him with such generosity of spirit. (Basically, everybody who watched him, loves him.) Booth, at 61, has a good laugh, talks about drinking, and smile wrinkles appear in the corners of his eyes. He's just got back from a golfing trip to Spain with 'the lads', he chuckles. Book, still forever known around City as 'Skip' – for skipper, captain – and famous for having been a bricklayer, only joining City aged 29 from Plymouth, but soon lifting football's topmost trophies, does look old now – silver-haired, bow-legged, and smaller than you'd think.

He is shyer than Booth and Bell, then he nods across to Al Mubarak and the Abu Dhabi group, who are gathering to be driven straight to the airport. And Tony Book, part of the furniture at Manchester City for more than forty years, says:

'They're first-class, they are. They are marvellous with the old players.'

Over the years under the ownership of local men, even those who should have been heroes, the former greats of City's past – and there are not too many of them – were not always treated well at all. Now these three are embraced and making a living at City again, working the corporate rooms, in an operation headed by Summerbee, to ageing fans like me, who are made instantly happy by recalling their own heydays.

Booth reminisces about that Fenerbahce match; he was only seventeen, he says. He and Bell shake their heads, and laugh. It was truly frightening in Turkey, they say, the flares and the fireworks and a wild, wild crowd. 'I really thought we might not get out of there alive,' Bell muses.

It's all a bit different now, I say, and Booth says: 'Oh yes.' Then he sighs, shakes his head. 'It's mega money now.'

By that, I know he means what all former players mean: it is mega money for players' wages, which they never earned in their day, and here they are, still having to earn out of their past deeds, unlike the new lot out there who are made for life. I understand that, but for me it means more. It is mega money, which has not only changed football in the obvious ways for supporters – the seats, the players and managers from all over the world, the corporate feel, the safety and comfort, the expense – but also sanitised and quietened the experience. It has, as I have found on my journey of discovery, shaped and penetrated the very heart and soul of English football and its clubs. Not just money itself, but the obsession with it, and the personal greed for it, in ways you can trace powerfully in the extraordinary story of Manchester City.

The Sheikh, at home watching the new team he paid £800m for, bought my club, and paid to take it where all fans are presumed to want their club to be. We are told these clubs are the same institutions they always were, and all English men must support their football club all their lives, as a badge of identity. Yet for me, in my heart, a great deal has fundamentally and irrevocably changed with 'mega money', and with all I have learned about the game and its clubs, including my own. When I stood next to my cousin against a crush barrier in that cold midwinter at Maine Road aged thirteen, the floodlights illuminating our sky-blue footballers, up close on the brilliant green, it never occurred to me that Manchester City was a *company*, that somebody could *own* it. If I'd thought about it, I'd have said I believed it was a club, like it always said it was, and so it belonged to us all.

CHAPTER 2

SKY BLUE

In any story, when you think about it, there are two beginnings. There is the real-life start, the actual, factual history, and then there is where you came into it. Manchester City's real-life story, like most of the English football clubs which have burgeoned remarkably to global fame, began with a bunch of lads in the smog of the nineteenth century, playing the sport as a release, for air. Football had been played by the rich pupils of upper-class schools while their working-class counterparts were thrust into factory or mill work. Then, with the game's rules defined by the Football Association in 1863, it began to crop up in the north and midlands. Anna Connell, with her father, the vicar at St Marks' church, in the industrial smoke-stack of West Gorton, east Manchester, helped form a football club in 1880, to provide local youth with more wholesome ways to spend their time than battering each other over useless scraps of stinking territory.

Then there is the real-life story of Manchester itself, handily placed in the north-west of England for maximum drizzle, whose origins the history books dutifully root to a chilly Roman fort, Mamucium, in AD 77. The history really began in the

1800s, though, when the city became the world-famous cradle – too gentle a word, really – of the shock and awe of industrial revolution. Travellers came to wonder at, and be horrified by, the efficiency and brutality of the factories, engines, mills and newly powered transport. Some observers, like the Japanese, wanted to become as technologically developed, but to do so in a more evolved way, without the cruelty and savage inequality. Friedrich Engels, middle-class benefactor of Karl Marx, lived a comfortable German expatriate life in Manchester, working in his father's spinning mill, but became the most important chronicler of the city's chaotic development, in his classic *The Condition of the Working Class in England*, published in 1844.

Engels, shocked at the state of the poor in industrial England, went into and described the slums of the working classes, 'the grimy misery' around the city's commercial centre, where great fortunes were being made in exporting cotton and engineering, around a world which would never be the same. Manchester's tragedy is that its wider population never shared fairly the rewards of its triumphs, and the deprived areas Engels described almost 170 years ago have had their problems ever since:

'All Salford and Hulme, a great part of Pendleton and Chorlton, two-thirds of Ardwick, and single stretches of Cheetham Hill and Broughton, are all unmixed working people's quarters,' Engels wrote. He concluded his not-very-grand tour of the filth, stench and ruin of these places with a damning description:

'If we briefly formulate the result of our wanderings,' Engels wrote, 'we must admit that 350,000 working people of

Manchester and its environs live, almost all of them, in wretched, damp, filthy cottages, that the streets which surround them are usually in the most miserable and filthy condition, laid out without the slightest reference to ventilation, with reference solely to the profit secured by the contractor. In a word we must confess that in the working men's dwellings of Manchester, no cleanliness, no convenience and consequently no comfortable family life is possible.'

The middle classes, he said, could live their whole lives without seeing any of that 'hell upon earth'. They could take the straight roads into town from the altogether pleasanter places where they had their homes: 'The middle bourgeoisie in regularly laid out streets in Chorlton and the lower-lying portions of Cheetham Hill; the upper bourgeoisie in remoter villas with gardens in Chorlton and Ardwick, or on the breezy heights of Cheetham Hill, Broughton and Pendleton, in free, wholesome country air, in fine, comfortable homes.'

The people of Manchester did not take all of this without fighting, and they established another, counter-tradition, of which many are still proud: that of protest. On St Peter's Field in the centre of Manchester in 1819, when the city's development was accelerating, eleven people were killed and 600 injured when the King's Hussars and other armed soldiers on horseback charged and struck out with swords at a demonstration of people gathered to listen to Henry Hunt, a campaigner for all adults to have the right to vote in parliamentary elections.

'All men are born free, equal and independent of each other,' Hunt had declared, urging Manchester and Lancashire radicals to sign up and send a message to the ruling power.

'Truth and justice are too deeply engraven on your hearts,' he wrote, asking people to come, peacefully, to that meeting on 16 August.

The troops were sent in to arrest Hunt before the meeting started, then reinforcements knocked over a mother and child, killing the child, on the way in. The slaughter became known as the Peterloo Massacre, ingrained in the folk memory of Manchester as a struggle by the people against inherited privilege and brutal power.

In 1844 in Rochdale, Lancashire, twenty-eight weavers and other artisans, tired of the adulterated and expensive flour they were forced to buy in the mill-owners' stores, clubbed together to buy proper food and open their own shop. That was the start of the co-operative movement, of which football clubs' supporters trusts, holding shares mutually and voting democratically, would become a branch many years later. Trade unionism took hold in Manchester as workers agitated for greater dignity in the crucible of work, and the first general meeting of the Trades Union Congress took place in the Three Crowns pub in Salford, in 1868. There were always strong roots in Manchester for the Labour Party and its forerunners, seeking to represent Engels's oppressed masses, around the time the world's first professional football league was formed at the city's Royal Hotel in 1888.

Of course, from whichever latter day you are born, you can live your whole life a Mancunian, and choose Manchester City as your team, without knowing much at all of the city's bloody backstory or the football clubs' founding purpose. As football fans, we support the first team we see, and are educated in the game's and clubs' history, and our city, only in vague, inherited atmospheres.

Looking at the geography of Engels's Manchester, it was not that different when I first blinked into it, in 1965. Salford and Hulme were having their slums cleared and smog lifted, but their Coronation Streets were still for the working class. I was lucky, born in a 'fine, comfortable home' in Broughton, although, leafy as it still was, we did not breathe 'country air' and nobody described Cheetham Hill any longer as 'on the breezy heights'.

My dad was a solicitor, with an office on Deansgate next to the Green Shield stamp shop; he was quite well known around town, especially, in the 1960s, by the villains. My mum was a journalist working for the local Manchester Jewish newspapers; later she wrote for some of the nationals as a freelance and ultimately, when we boys were older, worked for the BBC on Oxford Road. When we were little she kept her hand in writing a weekly column for the *Jewish Telegraph*, and the clackety-clack of her typewriter, industriously filling the house when she was on deadline, was a backing track of my childhood.

To say that football is a modern religion is, of course, simplistic. With its weekly attendance, collective worship, devotion to the cause and icons, it is unquestionably religious. But as somebody brought up with both, I would go further – football is a stronger religion than religion. Perhaps in ancient times, when churches or temples were the only great buildings in a land of woad, where there was little music, colour, smells or mystery outside places of worship, they must have been awesome experiences. But modern-day religion, in draughty buildings needing appeals to maintain, with ageing congregations assembled out of a sense of duty, belonging or guilt, finds it hard to compete with the thrills and glories of the stadium.

We grew up quite observant, keeping to the festivals and holy days. The extended families and just about everybody around us in Salford 7 were Jewish and I was taught the Old Testament bible stories, and that God had a black book, in which he could see all of us little boys and would mark us down, gold stars when we were good, black stars for naughtiness. It was strong propaganda; I used to feel strongly in the toilet – I think, looking back, they must have been the only times as a child I was ever alone – that he was watching me, an old man with a grey beard, as I did a wee.

I was fortunate in many things: two brothers, Alex and Raphael, two grandmas round different corners, a lovely house with a garden front and back, conker tree in the back one, neighbouring children to play football with and Broughton Park in touching distance. I feel I was also blessed with a natural inclination to take the best from the religious stories. I'm not sure I ever actually believed in it, the word of God and him having created the world in six days with poor Eve supposed to have done something paradise-shattering, just for having a bite of an apple. I read them as stories, I think; always liked Samson for having one final go after they cut his hair off, and found something faintly funny in the episode of the golden calf. Moses was furious, I always felt, not so much at everybody worshipping the false idol of gold and money, but because he found them all partying, while he had been doing all the hard work of going up Mount Sinai and lugging the ten commandments down. I liked belonging to a community, in which people knew each other and the old people looked kindly on us kids, but I always rejected the tribalism, the separateness, the us-and-them of religion. I tended naturally to see good and benevolent messages in it all. A teacher in primary school once told us the famous story of a great rabbi, asked to sum up the whole of Jewish teaching while standing on one leg. The rabbi missed out all the strictures about what you shouldn't eat, what you shouldn't do on a Saturday, and boiled it down to a single moral purpose: treat your neighbour as you would like to be treated yourself. And I thought then as I do now: that'll do for me.

Given all this, the hemmed-in closeness of where we lived, the weight of rules, the omnipresent feeling of being outsiders, a minority, with persecution in the past and the threat of it still drummed into us, it is difficult to overstate how important football was to the Jewish men of Manchester. The game is passionately loved by millions, everywhere, and for the same reasons, the blessed release, and so it was for us. Playing it, hungrily, at every opportunity, and watching it, supporting your club, was the greatest of escapes from routine and the everyday, through the clanking turnstiles and into that land of excitement J.B. Priestley described so unbeatably in the 1930s as 'an altogether more splendid life'. I think, too, that Jewish men felt a sense of belonging, to the wider community, when they rubbed shoulders in the vast crowds at the football. The game was in the air we breathed, and City and United were intermingled with it. United's 1968 European Cup win, and the Munich air crash of ten years earlier, drifted into becoming something we knew without our ever realising how, like knowing Neil Armstrong had walked on the moon or Yvonne Goolagong had won Wimbledon. You had to support one club or the other. When I grew up the two clubs were equals and I, fatefully, was always blue. It wasn't a matter of family heritage or any grown-up influence, as far as I remember. My dad was not a football fan. He had grown up in Bolton, where my grandfather had pitched up from the East End of London to sell clothes in the dire struggle of the depression. Dad did go along to Burnden Park to watch Wanderers, he said, and he was there in 1946, aged thirteen, when thirty-nine people were killed in the crush, my grandma frantic with worry about where he was before he turned up safe. He went to Wembley with a few pals for the 1953 'coronation' FA Cup Final when Bolton lost 4–3 to Stanley Matthews's and Stan Mortensen's Blackpool. But although he told me about that, and big Nat Lofthouse who played up front for Wanderers, and we did go to Burnden Park a couple of times, when they had wooden seats and flooring, somewhere along the way he had decided he didn't really like football.

Because he was not a fan, and my brothers weren't interested, the classic working-class inherited path to being a football supporter always seemed impossibly romantic to me, the initiation described by Noel Gallagher, of his father taking him to City, of being passed as a boy over people's heads down to the front of the Kippax, while his and Liam's dad went for a pint. In the Gallaghers' family life in Burnage, which was not a happy one, with the drunk and abusive father, the way Noel has told it, going to City, experienced together like that, was their oasis.

My path to blueness is a vague memory, like a dream, of it being down to my older brother, Alex, even though he was never interested in football his whole life. I think that one day, when I was about six and he eight, he pinned me in the tiny airing room upstairs off his bedroom, and challenged me to say who I supported. In my mind, I think we had open a centre spread of the *Manchester Evening News*, which had a feature on each club on opposite pages. I was only a little boy and it was the badges which did it. On one side was United's, with a red devil, horns, tail and three-pronged trident, which I have always felt to be an awful symbol for a football club. On the other was City's badge with its images of Manchester: the rose beneath, and the ship above. It was far more seductive. I told him I supported City and from that moment, I really, actually did. There would be no Fergie and Giggsy and Scholesy for me, no treble, no Hughesy scoring in FA Cup semi-finals or Whiteside winning the cup in the years they class as unsuccessful. Because of the Manchester badge and the sky blue of the shirt, it would be Peter Swales and relegations and City till I Die for me.

We even went to United first, to Old Trafford, with 50,000 in the swaying, singing crowd, George Best still playing, but I was already a City fan because of those five minutes with Alex in the airing cupboard. A family friend, who was a football fan, took us along, and I will never forget my initiation, the vast crowd singing and bouncing in unison, Best up against David Nish, so it must have been Leicester City, the feel, palpable even to me, of end-of-an-era about grand Old Trafford with Busby gone and Bobby Charlton growing too old. But I sat in that scene already firm that this was not my club or my place, and at Old Trafford I was always an outsider.

I must have been taken to Maine Road before the first game I really remember, the enrapturing 4–0 midweek victory over United in the League Cup, because that did not happen until 12 November 1975, when I was already ten. I know the date because I have always kept the programme; I fished it out of the garage and have it next to me as I write – it cost 15p. So it is odd that I can't remember a game at Maine Road before that. My first clear memory of watching City is not seeing them live, but on television, on a Sunday afternoon, my dad sitting in his armchair reading his newspaper. I have this feeling we were in another family's house, although I can't imagine where everybody else would have gone. The game was against Norwich City, and like all our public memories it is up on YouTube now, so I know it was the 1972–73 season and I was eight. Shown on ITV's *Kick Off* Sunday highlights programme, City scored a goal of audacious brilliance, a free-kick, twenty-five yards out, conjured by our trio of talents: Bell, Lee and Summerbee. Franny Lee, blond, thickset, scampered over the ball and towards the right of the Norwich wall; Bell took the free-kick, passing the ball into the feet of Summerbee, back to goal, who was marked tightly but flicked it first time to his left, to Franny. That was the genius of it, you suddenly realised, with the force of revelation: they'd known Norwich wouldn't track Franny after he ran over the ball, and he was now in open space, unmarked, far into the Norwich penalty area. Franny took a touch to control with his right foot, and one with his left to finish under the goalkeeper, Kevin Keelan, who knew, even as the ball rolled under him, that they had all been made to look pedestrian. It was dazzling, and the television captured the three City greats together in one shot afterwards, breathing a confidence born from years of winning. Franny and Summerbee, who looked like mates, shook hands and grinned at the cheek of it. Bell ran across, dedicated, undemonstrative as ever, shaking their hands at a job perfectly done.

In that living room, whosever's it was, I remember I was absolutely beside myself. I jumped up, threw both arms up into the air, roared '*Yesssssss!*' then got down on the floor, crawled on all fours up to the telly, and kissed Franny's face. I can still remember the feel of the static of the telly on my lips.

My Dad, sitting in his armchair, must have looked down from his newspaper at his eight-year-old son, and been unable to believe what he was seeing. 'Get up!' he barked at me, furiously.

'What?' I asked him innocently, my passion for Franny interrupted.

'We don't do things like that in this family,' he shouted. 'That's just silly!'

He did get used to my rapture, though; when we finally did go to that League Cup fourth-round derby against United in November 1975, I had a woollen blue and white scarf round my neck, two Junior Blues (I joined up) 'silk' scarves, one on each wrist, a City bobble hat with badges my mum sewed in for me, and a bedroom bedecked with pictures of the players.

Dennis Tueart's overhead kick wins the 1976 League Cup for Manchester City, 2–1 against Newcastle United

City, with Tony Book now the manager, were rebuilding the team, carefully, sensibly, ruthlessly, trying to do what Liverpool did and United hadn't. They moved the old legends on as they matured to fade, bringing through excellent young players to replace them, or signing developing stars from other clubs. As a child, I didn't understand the heartbreak and cruelty involved, the hurt pride and careers being ended in their early thirties at a time when footballers did not earn hugely. Franny was sold to Derby County in 1974, and we'd all seen him on *Match of the Day* make his personally triumphant return, scoring for Derby at Maine Road with a marvellous, far-corner goal, rendered into TV immortality by Barry Davies's ecstatic commentary. 'Interesting,' Davies warmed up as Franny took the ball and began sprinting directly at the right-hand side of City's penalty area. Then, as Franny stroked the ball with the outside of his right foot, and the ball floated across Joe Corrigan and into City's net, 'Very interesting!' Barry Davies screamed. Franny trotted back, blond, more overweight than he used to be at City, absolutely beaming, and Davies almost verbally applauded: 'Just look at his face!'

Summerbee left for Burnley in June 1975, while Colin Bell stayed on. Looking back, you realise of course that football was about money back then too, and City must have been one of the richest clubs, with the 1968–70 success banked, regular 40,000 crowds at Maine Road, and some time to go before Swales's act of self-destruction. I was innocent of knowing it had anything to do with money though; I just loved that team, stars playing at the heights of football. I did not know who the chairman was, or that we had a chairman, and I never would have conceived of Manchester City as a business.

They signed Dennis Tueart, Dave Watson and Mick Horswill from the splendid Sunderland team which had stunningly defeated Don Revie's all-white Leeds in the great 1973 FA Cup final; I'd watched it on telly, enthralled. We signed Asa Hartford, a Scottish international, from West Bromwich Albion, and Joe Royle, a centre forward wide as a fence from Everton, and Peter Barnes and Gary Owen came sprinting through, fit and ready from the youth team. City were a team mostly of internationals, for whom you looked at the top of the First Division, with Liverpool, Bobby Robson's Ipswich, Derby and Leeds.

Denis Law had played for City for a season or so in what looked to me then like his old age, and he famously helped push United down to the Second Division with the backheeled winner in a 1–0 victory at Old Trafford, in 1974. When City were drawn to play United in November 1975, United had shown my generation that they were truly a great club, drawing on crowds of 50,000 in the Second Division, and galloping straight back up with the team reconstructed by Tommy Docherty, including Steve Coppell, always a nuisance against us, Stuart Pearson and Lou Macari.

The night we played United my dad took a car-full to the match but I don't remember who else came with us; certainly it was just him and me who had tickets to sit together. The crowd that night was so vast, the traffic from town so slow and thick, we parked miles away on the far side of Wilmslow Road from Maine Road, on some crescent in Rusholme I have never seen again. I remember getting out of the car into the night air and putting my blue and white scarf round my neck, then holding my Dad's hand and walking, trotting, through Moss Side towards the silver aura of the floodlights. I always felt, descending on Maine Road, that we were intruding on the houses there, the two-up, two-downs whose front doors opened straight onto the street and whose lights never seemed to be on.

Without being too nostalgic about one of the greatest occasions of my own childhood, beating United on a floodlit school night in midweek, it was pure football. The tickets for Manchester City v Manchester United had cost my dad next to nothing and the match was the absolute, whole experience. It was not twinned with a look round a 'store' first. We did not eat anything or stare at a screen in a concourse. There were no mascots to entertain me and I would not have noticed them if there had been. Hand in hand, we joined the streams of people hurrying to the floodlights of the derby.

The truth was, though, that Dad had not taken me all that often and if he did we had usually gone with somebody else, and he did not know Maine Road very well. I remember him not being sure where we were going, stopping to peer at the tickets which he had bought for the wooden bench seats in the Platt Lane end.

'Come on, David,' he said, deciding. 'Up here!'

So we ran up a staircase, a long, high climb, and as we scurried up the endless steps, you could hear the match had kicked off, so we hurried up and got right to the top of the stand. There, you could see the pitch, gleaming in the silver light, the two teams already playing. Men at the back where we were had not sat down yet and I was standing on my tiptoes when Dennis Tueart scored. I could hardly see, but everybody was roaring and celebrating and I asked my dad if it was true and he said yes, it really was: City had scored against United in the first minute. Then when they all sat down, finally, he found a steward in a luminous coat and the bloke looked at the tickets and told him we were in completely the wrong place. It was only because we had gone up the wrong staircase that we had seen the goal, and my dad, who was not, in truth, enjoying himself very much, always remembers that too.

So we went back down and up another staircase at the back of the Platt Lane stand and found our proper seats, and I sat next to Dad in the sheepskin-coated embrace of a disbelieving Maine Road, seeing City, my club, my team, skip around and beat United 4–0. Tueart scored again, as well as Asa Hartford and Joe Royle, top players in this second wave of City excellence. I do not remember too many details except the overall magic, all this wonder set before us. I must have thrown my arms around my dad, and I'm sure he wouldn't have moved much or jumped up for any of the four goals, but he always said he enjoyed watching me so involved. I must have skipped all that long way back, once he remembered where he had parked the car, and when we got home my mum would not have been really interested in what had happened, but she would have said she was glad for me, it was nice that City had won.

In that match – still one of the most glorious in Manchester City's history – Colin Bell, generally agreed to be City's greatest-ever player, suffered the knee injury which ended his career. Martin Buchan, United's captain, crunched into Bell just below the knee and the agony, etched in a cruel grimace across Colin Bell's usually impassive face, was captured by photographers for ever. I do clearly remember the hush falling over the crowd, the long halt to the match while they crouched over him, and then Colin Bell, that most upright of footballers, being carried off lying on a stretcher, to an assembly of applause.

Sport's cruelty, and its enduring hold, is that the game goes on. They carried Colin Bell off, and everybody was sorry; a substitute came on – I see my dad helpfully wrote on the back of the programme beneath the team sheet in blue biro that Tommy Booth was number 12 – and they all resumed as if Colin the King had never been there, orchestrating City's and England's midfield for ten years. Colin Bell's shredded ligaments, ruining a majestic career, were a footnote in the reports of a triumphant performance by Tony Book's Manchester City.

On reflection, the fact that Colin Bell sustained a career-ending injury in the midst of one of City's greatest nights – he did come back, fully two years later, on Boxing Day 1977, but never properly recovered – was a profound lesson delivered by supporting Manchester City. It goes beyond some of the attempts made through the gloomy years to characterise City's misfortunes – cups for cock-ups, which has the slapstick about it, or 'Cityitis', coined by Royle when he came back as manager, which to me always referred to the defensive yips nervous City teams suffered under pressure. There is something more profound in it, the nestling of misfortune deep in the bosom of triumph. You had to learn, even as a ten-year-old boy skipping back to the car with his dad, that even in the most gleeful of times, the very worst can happen.

Dad promised me one day, talking about football, that if City ever got to a cup final, he would take me to Wembley. That season, we did, all the way in the League Cup after beating United, and I went to every game, including the semi-final home leg against Middlesbrough, which City also won 4–0, Royle and Tueart scoring again. City were at Wembley, so I said to my Dad, 'We are going, aren't we?'

And he scoffed: 'I didn't mean the League Cup final!' he said. 'I meant the FA Cup final.'

So we never did go. City went to Wembley and beat Newcastle 2–1. Peter Barnes scored the first, sweeping it in at the far post with that darting speed which thrilled us so much. Tueart, of course, scored the winner, an overhead kick of still astonishing athleticism, a public display of confidence, daring and skill. Like a generation of City fans, I had the picture on my bedroom wall: Tueart, framed by the frozen Newcastle defenders, his back perfectly parallel to the ground, his head up and eyes fixed on the ball, right foot about to strike it down over his head and into the far corner, to win the cup for City. I stared at it so much as a kid it may be the image I have studied more than any other in my life.

Once we reached ten, many of us started playing the game properly, for teams, in kit, and we found out how different it was out there from the beautiful game we watched on telly or from the stands. Somewhere in my football journey, I think it was much later, when I began to write about the game as a journalist, some wise man – I have a feeling it was Allen Wade, the former head coach at the Football Association, whom I interviewed about the governing body's paralysis – said with absolute conviction, as a statement of fact: 'Of course, it is always vastly more enjoyable to play than to watch.'

It did not feel like that for years, comparing the intense star-filled dramas of the First Division, in crowds of 40,000, with the games we played in real life. Out in north Manchester beyond my nice back garden and homely Broughton Park, football was played in the mud and rain, the changing rooms were dark, freezing and stank of piss, and there was the ever-present threat of violence, more visceral the more we progressed. I made my debut as a ten-year-old in an orange kit on a pitch at Drinkwater Park in Prestwich, a place whose desolation could hardly be made up. So remarkably bleak was Drinkwater that it was captured, I discovered in more recent years, in a famous picture by the photographer John Davies, whose speciality was godforsaken industrial landscapes. In his great picture, you can see the four enormous cooling towers of Agecroft power station, litter and tipping in the foreground, a man with a horse, and out in the muddy middle, just make out little figures scampering on frozen-looking football pitches, the goalposts askew, with four people watching on the touchline. That was us. Davies captured in his image the unending grey and also the looming grandeur of Manchester.

You can feel the cold and cloud in his shot, but even he couldn't get the whole experience in. Drinkwater was also overlooked by a cemetery on the side opposite the power station, where Davies was standing, and the changing rooms were below him, out of picture. It was a breezeblock cube, lit by one weak light bulb, stinking, which the KGB would surely have turned down as unfit for interrogating dissenters. I can remember us all being shocked that this was where our dream, proper football, was played in Manchester.

Agecroft Power Station, with the football pitches of Drinkwater Park, Prestwich

Still, we, the U11s, playing our first proper match, shivered, and put the kit on. We waited as the team was read out, and I was in it. I remember we were all standing up and it was wet on the floor of the changing rooms, and you could hardly see. Then our manager, Julian Rosenberg, a tall dad with a deep, kindly voice, gave us my first-ever team talk.

'Boys,' he said, soothing, passionate about the game, 'I want you to go out there, and play football.'

So, we did our best. You would get big lads on motorbikes scrambling down from the hill which led up to the cemetery, riding across the pitch while we were playing. There was a slow slime of a river, some water anyway, running right alongside the pitches and a decent clearance from one of the bigger defenders would send the ball in and there would be a long, windy hold-up while a manager or dad wondered how to retrieve it. Once, in the winter, when the water was frozen and we were playing entirely in goose pimples, I looked up from the wind of the game and saw our manager, Brian Hymanson, walking away, his trousers wet, water up to the midriff of his sheepskin. It turned out some kids had been skating across the ice, one had fallen in, and Mr Hymanson had run across, waded in and rescued a boy. He got in the *Jewish Telegraph* for that.

I wasn't one of the most naturally talented or quickest of players, but I was determined, and I dug in to the hard work of improving, competing, trying your best. I always loved the game, and still do, yet the idea, back then, that it was actually more enjoyable to play at places like Drinkwater Park, Hough End's mudbaths, waterlogged Heaton Park or hilly Frederick Road, with rudimentary post-war facilities which are still much the same now, than to watch your team of internationals, was fanciful.

I remember musing about this to my dad in the back seat of his car on the way to playing one of our matches.

'Do you know,' I realised, 'I feel more excited when City score than when I score.'

And he replied, without hesitating: 'Well,' he said, 'that's very strange.'

But it wasn't. When Tueart or Royle or Brian Kidd scored at Maine Road, 40,000 people erupted together, roaring their release, a stunning collective experience of belonging to a football club, which you could not replicate anywhere else in modern life. When I scored for my team, the end result of earnest collective endeavour, a dad or two might applaud, if there were any watching. Your team mates might say well done, as we all trotted back, and they might even be ecstatic if it was an important goal against opposition with a bit of needle in the game. Nobody would jump on each other, on a windy mudbath, nobody hugged or kissed, like the professionals did on telly. It all combined, after a goal, in that moment of triumph, almost to exacerbate the loneliness, the small group solitude, of playing football out on a lost field, in the frayed edges of municipal Manchester.

CHAPTER 3

ABU DHABI UNITED

At the back end of the summer of 2008, Manchester City, always written up as the people's club, in contrast to United's corporate greed, by those who do not know the club very well, were owned by the fugitive former Prime Minister of Thailand, Thaksin Shinawatra. He had been accused of murderous human rights abuses, convicted of corruption, and the club was hurtling towards ruin, yet City fans had largely embraced him. The last Manchester-based major shareholder, John Wardle, who with his partner David Makin had led the sale to Thaksin the previous year, was funding City out of his own pockets again. With Thaksin on the run, wanted in Thailand, and his assets frozen in the country, City were haemorrhaging losses and up to their limit with the banks. So Wardle had been tapped for £2m, which he loaned on three different occasions, to 'help with cash flow'. People working at City at the time told me they did not know if they were going to be paid at the end of the month, and feared the club might fall insolvent and collapse into administration.

When the news broke on an Arabic news website that Manchester City had been bought, saved, it took some time for the reality to be accepted. After so many false promises over so many years, news of a revival in Manchester City's fortunes has to be taken with a pinch of scepticism. It did not help that the new owners were called, somewhat unfortunately I have always felt, Abu Dhabi United. Their front man was a paunchy, publicity-loving minor celebrity in Dubai, Sulaiman Al Fahim, who was the face of the property development bubble in the emirate and had hosted Dubai's version of *The Apprentice*. He did a lot of talking about Manchester City, about how rich Abu Dhabi United was, how very, very much money they had, how deep their pockets were. They had signed Robinho on the first day just to let everybody know it was for real and, Al Fahim promised, they could sign all the best players in the world, whoever they wanted. But then we all frantically googled Sheikh Mansour bin Zayed Al Nahyan, who Al Fahim said was behind Abu Dhabi United, and we suddenly had in focus a new world of gulf states, the United Arab Emirates, the Al Nahyan sons by the several wives of the previous long-term ruler, Sheikh Zayed. There was one underpinning fact: he truly did have enormous wealth from the vast fields of oil. Three years on, with twenty-two players very expensively bought, City in the Champions League, the FA Cup on the honours board, it still feels faintly unreal and profoundly unlikely, that the Sheikh who bought Manchester City did not turn out to be fake.

Sheikh Mansour bin Zayed Al Nahyan has never, so far, given an interview to an English journalist. His true character and personality behind his public face remain an enigma. His reasons for buying an English Premier League football club, and choosing Manchester City, are explained by his appointed

executive, Khaldoon Al Mubarak, City's chairman, as primarily a sound business decision, but there seems a great deal of
whim in it too. Not much is known, really, about the young
man with two wives who controls billions of pounds of his Al
Nahyan family wealth, and has decided to spend some of it
buying an English football club.

His profile at the Al-Jazira professional football club in Abu
Dhabi, which he owns and has funded to buy new players, a
kind of home-worked prototype for what he has done at Manchester City, states that he was born in 1970, and went to
university in America, where many young emiratis of his generation were sent, gaining a degree in international public
relations in 1993. He has several official roles in the country
his family rules; one is to be the chairman of the emirate's International Petroleum Investment Company. That is one of many
funds tasked with finding some way to invest the limitless oil
fortunes which have sprung from the Al Nahyans' portion of
the Arabian Gulf since the 1950s. The IPIC sinks it into oil,
gas and industrial projects around the world. At 30 June 2011,
the date of IPIC's most recent accounts, the fund had $62bn
of assets.

It may seem a puzzle to understand how Manchester City –
no trophy since the League Cup of 1976, in the third division
(now renamed League One by the Football League) as recently
as 1999, sitting in the post-industrial husk of east Manchester
– fitted into this world-view of almost incomprehensible riches.
Yet Mansour's takeover of a Premier League football club produced more publicity, more public exposure of him, than all
the multi-billion-pound deals done in his name. Oil and gas

may be what make the world go round, but football, particularly English Premier League football, interests people very much more.

In those first days of Al Fahim bragging, the authorities in Abu Dhabi realised Manchester City had suddenly become the most prominent outpost for the carefully cultivated image of the country itself. Introduced to front and oversee it properly was Al Mubarak, an executive from the officer class, a trusty of the Al Nahyans. Tall, calm, also US-university educated (at Tufts, in Boston, where he studied economics and finance), Al Mubarak is the chairman of the Executive Affairs Authority, which provides strategic advice to the Abu Dhabi government, and of Mubadala, another investment fund. On 30 June 2011, the date of the most recent accounts, Mubadala, investing in aluminium, aerospace, property and other interests around the world, had £29bn under investment. That is why he is a busy man, why his visits to Manchester are flying, why, while his friends and family polish off the petits fours in the chairman's lounge, Al Mubarak is using his time to rifle through meetings and even sign players – Lescott, for £22m, was sealed in a series of phone calls from the chairman's lounge during the first match of the 2009–10 season, at home to Wolverhampton Wanderers.

Al Mubarak was formally introduced as Manchester City's chairman, succeeding, in a line going back to 1973, Peter Swales, Francis Lee, David Bernstein, John Wardle and Thaksin Shinawatra. On the day the takeover was completed and negotiations finalised, 22 September 2008, an open letter was written to City supporters, in Sheikh Mansour's name.

The letter was addressed to 'Dear fellow Manchester City fans', which still rather grates. It was a mix of ingratiating flattery – 'you are the greatest fans in the world'; a setting out of initial plans – 'this involves a lot of listening'; a corporate explanation of why and how Sheikh Mansour bought the club, and a statement of unrestrained ambition.

'Like you,' it said, 'we are excited about the future of the club, and we hope the securing of Robinho as a Manchester City player during the transfer window is seen as a signal of our very real intent.'

As such takeover assurances of good faith and benevolence go, the letter was noticeably well-judged, sensible, it didn't overpromise, and stressed a respect for the club, its supporters and its history. On returning to the letter, you find, importantly, it has largely survived the test of time; they mostly did what they said they would, and quite spectacularly. They did not over-claim a sentimental, football-supporting motive for Sheikh Mansour, as the Glazer family did when taking over United with all that borrowed money in 2005. In the only interview any member of the family has given about United since, to the club's own in-house MUTV television station, one of Malcolm's sons, Joel, born and bred in America, claimed to be an 'avid' United fan. Two other Americans, Tom Hicks and George Gillett, turned a similar trick to the Glazers when they bought Liverpool in February 2007, after their eyes glinted with the prospect of TV multi-millions which Premier League club ownership could earn them. They promised in their official offer document that their approach to owning one of England's and the world's most legendary football clubs was 'a multi-generational commitment' by their families. It turned out on inspection that they were buying the club with £174m borrowed from the Royal Bank of Scotland, on a twelve-month loan, and they made the club itself responsible for paying the interest on it.

'I am a football fan,' said Sheikh Mansour in the letter – and unlike the Americans, who grow up, mostly, utterly oblivious to 'soccer', that is likely to be true. Abu Dhabi is a former British protectorate, and there is a tradition of football there for which the men, wrapped in Islam, nourish an escapist love.

'And I hope that you will soon see that I am now also a Manchester City fan.' There was in that a fairly modest request for acceptance from the absentee billionaire, to fans who had followed City for decades, with bloody-minded and grumpy loyalty but little joy or reward, over land and sea – and Stretford.

'We know a little of the history at City,' the letter continued, which suggested they knew the club's history was important to it, and how the club might be improved, an awareness lacking in many English businessmen who have bought their local clubs over the years brimming more with self-importance than wider understanding.

It was also made quite clear, twice, that although Sheikh Mansour is a member of the improbably rich Abu Dhabi ruling family, and occupies senior roles including minister for presidential affairs in the UAE and chair of the eyewateringly wealthy investment funds, he had bought City himself. There was a clear separation, which Al Mubarak has always stressed, between City and Abu Dhabi government or financial interests.

Although most people do not see it this way, with City wrapped in Etihad and other marketing for the country of Abu Dhabi, it is clearly important to them politically to state that Mansour owns it as an individual.

'Despite what you may have read,' the letter said, 'I have bought the club in a private capacity and as part of my personal business strategy to hold a wide portfolio of business investments.' In an official biographical note about Sheikh Mansour, released by City at the same time, in which he was described, simply, as 'Owner', that was emphasised again:

'Although he holds a number of official positions within Abu Dhabi and the UAE, Sheikh Mansour's ownership of Manchester City FC is a private interest.'

To explain why on earth Sheikh Mansour of Abu Dhabi had bought Manchester City of Beswick, the Premier League and the world, the letter tried to frame it as a rational, good business acquisition. The language of this does jar:

'In cold business terms,' it said, 'Premiership football is one of the best entertainment products in the world and we see this as a sound business investment.'

Describing football, which flowered in the muck of industrial England and has deep social and emotional roots, as an 'entertainment product' has offended the soul of the game since the very beginnings of professionalism in the 1880s. Then the FA framed rules aimed at retaining its sporting integrity, to keep its clubs as clubs and not see them become mere entertainment venues, like cinemas. Football clubs grew into temples of belonging, belief and lifelong loyalty, and to see them described as 'a sound business investment' still hurts, despite the Premier League years of 'mega money' in which it has come to be accepted.

Whether buying a Premier League football club really was motivated by sound business judgement of it as a good investment, rather than impulsive escapism, a means to have fun, a status symbol or, as clubs are now hideously described, as a 'trophy asset' of a rich man, only Sheikh Mansour bin Zayed Al Nahyan actually knows. Whether Sheikh Mansour really will make money, or be proved to have made a 'sound business investment' by sinking £1bn and counting into transmuting Manchester City into a European Champions League club, particularly with Uefa's financial fair play rules threatening his whole overspending strategy, seems doubtful.

More convincing, given what they have achieved since then, was the approach they outlined in the letter about how they would go about their Manchester City project. Al Fahim went and with him the idea they would instantly lure a bunch of superstars with outlandish wages to a historically underperforming club. Instead, they promised to take time to listen, even research the club in its fullest sense, then come up with a considered plan (obviously backed by supertankers full of money) to develop Manchester City into a top football club. 'We really need to sit down with the manager [Mark Hughes, to whom they pledged a vote of confidence], executive chairman [Garry Cook, whom they also inherited, and who they likewise kept on] and key staff, and put together plans that will, over time, get the club to where we want it to be.

'That is the stage we are entering now, and as anyone who runs a business knows, this involves a lot of listening, and a lot of talking to many stakeholders, and research and discussion, before plans can be announced.'

We never heard that from most of the English owners who bought the club before.

'As part of that, we will absolutely spend time listening to you, the fans, about what you think about the future of the club. We are very aware that without you there would not be a club to buy.'

That, of course, was true, and well said, and in fact the new regime did take time to learn about the history of the club and the culture of the fans. Once they read into it, as people used to living in a world of money, in which projects are continually brought to fruition – a Formula One racetrack in the Abu Dhabi desert, for example, for which Al Mubarak was also the executive responsible – they were surprised by the expectation of failure they found ingrained in the fans. Years since the glory days of my youth had been savaged by Peter Swales's 1979 watershed, followed by relegations, the snatching of chaos from the jaws of stability, had produced fans convinced everything would all go horribly wrong and whose main collective song was a bleak profession of loyalty:

> *City till I Die*
> *I'm City till I Die*
> *I know I am, I'm sure I am*
> *I'm City till I Die.*

A song about a fan's relationship with his football club, which does not celebrate glory glory or marching on together, but simply states that he is loyal, and then he will die, with nothing to celebrate in between. A fixation on the fan's own death, in a football song? That did rather puzzle the Sheikh's can-do men.

'We are ambitious for the club, like you,' the letter in Sheikh Mansour's name said, 'but not unreasonably so and we understand it takes time to build a team capable of sustaining a presence in the top four of the Premier League and winning European honours.'

This was sensible: they knew it would take time, even with all the money in the world. Next was the reference to Manchester City's history. This was not the club's great founding story, which they did come to appreciate subsequently, that City was formed originally by the daughter of the vicar at St Mark's church in Gorton, to give the deprived young men of the area something healthy, wholesome and constructive to do. At this stage in their understanding of the club, the reference to the history was about City's tradition of bringing through young players – 'local discoveries' as they used quaintly to be called – and it was a statement of intent that the Sheikh's City were not just going to sign ready-made stars.

This was a genuine tradition, nurturing good young players, which is recognised to create a more bonded team spirit, woven by men who have grown up in the area and feel an emotional connection with the club. Seeing your own young lads play undoubtedly cements the bonds of loyalty and connection with fans – certainly it always did with me. The great 1960s team had been peopled by Neil Young, Glyn Pardoe, Tony Coleman and the composed Alan Oakes, Mancunians or drawn from nearby. In the 1970s team I watched goalkeeper Joe Corrigan, whose improvement was an inspiring marvel, Peter Barnes and Gary Owen sparkled. After the 1979 meltdown, there were two dreadful generations: the first when City's young players, Paul Warhurst, Earl Barrett, Neil Lennon, Gerry Taggart, were barely given a first-team chance before leaving to enjoy long and successful careers elsewhere; then after Alex Ferguson arrived at United, when City's operation slumped, Ryan Giggs famously leaving because nobody had offered him a contract. Boys who came through, and whom we all loved watching as our own: Paul Lake, David White, Steve Redmond, Andy Hinchcliffe and Paul Moulden, beat United 5–1 in that landmark moment of 1989, but United would soon be stocked with their own youngsters, Giggs, David Beckham, Paul Scholes, Gary and Phil Neville, Nicky Butt, and dominate the 1990s, while City imploded again.

By the time Sheikh Mansour bought City, the academy had recovered, under the stewardship of Jim Cassell, who had been at Oldham Athletic, scooping up Warhurst, Barrett, other City rejects and hopefuls from elsewhere to provide the basis for blatant overachievement under the manager, Joe Royle: FA Cup semi-finalists in 1990 and 1994, members of the top division from 1991 to 1994, including becoming a founder member of the Premier League in 1992. The team Sheikh Mansour took over included, among the overseas players signed in instalments under Thaksin, several young City graduates: Stephen Ireland, Micah Richards, who had come from Oldham aged fourteen, goalkeeper Joe Hart, signed from Shrewsbury Town, Nedum Onuoha, Ched Evans, Michael Johnson and Daniel Sturridge.

'We know a little of the history at City and whilst we want to bring in the best players in the world, we also want to see the academy continue to develop talent and give Mark Hughes the chance to bring home-grown players into the team.

'We are building a structure for the future, not just a team of all-stars,' the letter continued, in direct contrast to the fevered all-star ramblings which had previously frothed over their takeover.

Then they talked about the club's community work, which has won awards for taking projects into schools in difficult areas of Manchester, with an anti-drugs and healthy eating message to young people more prepared to listen to people sprinkled by the magic dust of football than teachers pleading every day. Again, the new owners did not over-claim, but maintained they wanted to be good neighbours:

'We are aware also that the club has a significant role in the community going back years. As newcomers, we don't pretend to understand all of this yet, but we will make sincere efforts to back these initiatives and ensure that Manchester City loses none of its role in Manchester beyond football, and we want the club to continue to contribute to the community it represents.'

That was a fair enough statement of intent, on which the future actions of the new owners could be judged.

Sheikh Mansour's final sign-off paragraph is perhaps the one which in hindsight looks the least fulfilled – his assurance that he would actually turn up to the odd match. He made his excuses for the first one, down at Portsmouth, where the following year Al Fahim would become involved during a financial crisis. The club, after a former overseas owner, Sacha Gaydamak, withdrew his funding, would be the first Premier League club to fall insolvent.

'Unfortunately I cannot be at the game against Portsmouth on Sunday,' said the Sheikh. 'But be assured I will be cheering the team on.' Al Mubarak had his orders, though: 'The club's new chairman will be there and I ask you to welcome him. I will be at Eastlands soon and am really looking forward to sampling the famous City atmosphere.'

He did that for the first and so far only time almost two years later, on 23 August 2010, taking his place finally in that directors' box. He looked surprisingly young, slight, sheepish, even delicate, the rich Arab prince with his inherited fortune, in his suit rather than traditional Arab dress. For his colonels, captains, lieutenants and footballers, there was relief in a 3–0 home win over a Liverpool running into financial cataclysm due to the debts loaded on to the club by Hicks and Gillett. I interviewed Micah Richards a few months later; his huge frame and wide smile squashed and folded around a desk at Carrington. He grinned about the owner's visit:

'It made all the boys perform a little bit better, because the real boss was here.'

Al Mubarak, it turned out, did fly to Manchester and was shown around the City of Manchester Stadium, the staff offices and facilities, and the Carrington training ground, before going to Portsmouth for the first match since the takeover. He was, he said later, seriously unimpressed with what he found of the state of the club in the multi-million-pound, watched-all-over-the-world Premier League.

'I must say I was extremely surprised,' he told me. 'I took a tour with Mark Hughes and he showed me Carrington and I couldn't believe what I saw. It was not the level of infrastructure which is the minimum for a top-tier club.

'Immediately I remember leaving that trip and going back to Sheikh Mansour and showing him some pictures of the facility and he was very straight to say this is unacceptable.'

Hughes had been recruited from Blackburn Rovers to become City's manager by the football agent Kia Joorabchian, a deal-maker best known in England as the representative of the unknown investors who 'owned' the economic rights of the Argentinian international striker Carlos Tevez when Tevez arrived in England. Joorabchian, under Thaksin's ownership, had developed an influential involvement at City, and had also been key to the appointment of Garry Cook, who had been a senior executive at Nike when Joorabchian was involved in Brazilian football with the Corinthians club. Corinthians had had Tevez and the Argentinian midfield enforcer Javier Mascherano playing in the team before both players moved to England, on loan to West Ham United, in 2006.

Hughes had left a stable club owned then by the executors of the estate of Jack Walker, the Jersey tax exile who sold a Blackburn steel business and funded Rovers to have Kenny Dalglish as the manager, sign Alan Shearer and other stars and win the Premier League in 1995. That was the first Premier League real-life fantasy football project, before Abramovich and Sheikh Mansour, when an owner threw money in to buy football success. Before that, club 'owners', referred to as chairmen, were mostly criticised for never spending money on their clubs.

Walker died in August 2000, his executors reluctantly continuing to fund the club while trying to sell it, and Rovers were known for their well-appointed training complex and academy in rural Lancashire, soundly managed finances, and tight organisation, performing, overall, well above their true station. Hughes had not managed City in a single match when Thaksin, the owner of the club, went on the run, and Hughes said later that what he had found at City, 'wasn't exactly what was described and sold to me'.

After the chaos of Thaksin's convictions and the scramble at City to cope with financial meltdown, Hughes found out about the Abu Dhabi takeover while he was playing golf at the Marriott Hotel in Worsley, Salford. He had seen it was real via Sky television, and then gone to Abu Dhabi effectively for an interview for his own job, in the grounds of Sheikh Mansour's palace. He impressed both Mansour and Al Mubarak with his approach, at first, and they put their faith in him. When Al Mubarak came to Manchester before the Portsmouth match, he and Hughes went for a meal at a restaurant, Stocks, where they talked City, plans and football, and Hughes said he needed great improvements to the structures at the club.

'Khaldoon came to Carrington,' Hughes said later. 'We showed him the training ground, which, to be perfectly honest, was not fit for purpose. Very quickly, he realised the failings I had in terms of what I had to work with, and we went for quick wins: changing the environment, the whole aspect and atmosphere of the training ground.'

Under Thaksin, there was little investment in the fabric of the club. There were deals to buy players, and millions of pounds in agents' fees, but the stadium remained largely the grey concrete bowl handed over by the council. Carrington was stagnating, and the staff worked downstairs in the stadium, in offices which had no windows. While the fortunes Sheikh Mansour has sanctioned on players and their wages have been vast, it is notable that he has also invested in the club itself. Simon Pearce, Al Mubarak's lieutenant at the Executive Affairs Authority who became an influential director at City, recruited a long-term contact, Jon Stemp, to oversee improvements to the infrastructure, beginning with Carrington. They spent £300,000 modernising the gym, and £750,000 for a medical centre and rehabilitation facilities for injured players which, with advice, they upgraded to a quality they believed was the best in the Premier League. They also spent £650,000 improving the pitches, and around £1m at the academy complex back at Platt Lane, near to where the Maine Road ground used to be, which includes facilities used by the neighbouring community. For the staff, Stemp oversaw the construction of a new office block on the acres of car park which ring the stadium – complete with windows.

They did, also, actually take time to read into and understand the history of the club, and the culture of City fans, to reassure them they value them, want them to feel at home, be part of the ride, as well as explore their financial limits as consumers in the City Store. Cook, the former Nike man on a salary of £1.6m, who had announced himself to the media with a hideous statement about Thaksin being 'a nice man to play golf with', became obsessed with the story of Anna Connell, the vicar's daughter, and the founding Christian values of

Manchester City. He seemed to want to believe that his modern-day mission, involving as it did paying £10m a year wages to footballers like Tevez in the same impoverished area of Manchester in which the club had been founded, could be on the same moral and historic path as Anna Connell's, because they were supporting the community work and trying to do things properly. At least, unlike previous local owners of Manchester City, he knew the club's story.

Famously, Cook moved the advance ticket office indoors at the City shop because he could not bear to see supporters queuing up bedraggled outside, at the lines of booth windows, in the world's rainiest city. In the concourses around the stadium, the club dressed and decorated blank walls with effectively a supporters' exhibition, entitled 'My first match', a series of reminiscences in words and pictures which, with their stories of dads now gone, the old sights, sounds, smells and former players, prods the sensitivities of the tearducts. That made the people from Abu Dhabi the first to recognise that Eastlands, the gleaming stadium they were handed by Manchester City Council in exchange for mournful Maine Road, was a characterless architect's bowl which did not feel like a home and struggled to generate atmosphere.

After agreeing to buy Robinho for £32.5m before they had actually completed the takeover, Sheikh Mansour and his executives, and Mark Hughes, had not been able to indulge their appetite for buying players. The opening of the transfer window in January 2009 was their first opportunity to do so. They spent £50m on the first wave of players for Hughes. Not Torres, Ronaldo and Fabregas, but goalkeeper Shay Given, £7m from

Newcastle; left-back Wayne Bridge, £12m from Chelsea; striker Craig Bellamy, who cost £14m from West Ham; and they paid £17m for Nigel de Jong, a bull terrier in human form who prowls midfields.

'The balance within the squad was extremely erratic,' Al Mubarak explained, 'and it was very important to add depth in every position. The additions we were able to bring in were excellent and what we needed; that helped us get to the end of the season and be able to do the transformation which was needed in the summer.'

That first season, the newly richest football club in the world lost to Manchester United in both derby matches, 1–0 at home, 2–0 away, and to Middlesbrough, Portsmouth, Bolton, Fulham and 3–0 at home to Nottingham Forest in the FA Cup third round in January. With £82.5m spent on players and the inflating of the wage bill, they finished tenth, a place below where they had been the season before, under the incongruous partnership of Thaksin Shinawatra and Sven-Göran Eriksson.

In the summer of 2009 they went on a more dedicated spree, spending £137.5m in total, bringing the amount Sheikh Mansour paid just to sign footballers in his first year in east Manchester – not pay them the wages that lured them to City – to £221m. Hughes was authorised to sign Gareth Barry from Aston Villa (£12m); Roque Santa Cruz from Blackburn Rovers (£17.5m); Emmanuel Adebayor from Arsenal (£25m); Kolo Touré, also from Arsenal (£16m); Joleon Lescott from Everton (£22m), and Carlos Tevez.

They bought Tevez from the 'third-party' investors represented by Joorabchian. United had had him, only on loan, for two seasons. Sir Alex Ferguson had said he was willing to buy Tevez permanently from those unnamed owners for the £25.5m option price, but at the crucial time, Joorabchian had gone missing. The representative of the owners of Tevez had found, across town, an unfeasibly rich owner, who was willing to pay a great deal more. The price City paid, never disclosed in public, was, according to reliable sources, £45m, although Joorabchian disputes the figure.

So Carlos Tevez signed for City as the talisman of the mon-eyed revolution, the City owner's second landmark 'statement of intent'. They decided to blare his arrival – and theirs, really – on a billboard positioned at the beginning of Deansgate, the gateway to the city, over the Irwell bridge and opposite the cathedral. It was a boast about having gazumped United for the signature of Tevez, a recognisable football superstar. The £45m fee was paid by an Abu Dhabi sheikh to an unnamed company, which owned the player's economic rights, based in the British Virgin Islands, a tax haven which ensured secrecy about who owned the company, and an escape from having to pay tax on the profits.

The billboard, in sky blue, had a picture of Tevez in a City shirt, arms outstretched, and it proclaimed: 'Welcome to Man-chester.'

CHAPTER 4

'THE JOY WAS JUST COMING'

It was just coincidence that Manchester City's tumble into decline began in 1979, the same year Margaret Thatcher's Conservatives were elected to rule Britain, and hastened the decimation of Manchester itself. The Conservatives were voted in, as governments mostly are in Britain, not because people positively wanted what they offered – swingeing cuts to public services and privatisations – but because enough voters were tired of the serving (Labour) government and wanted it out. The 1978 'winter of discontent', during which several public-sector unions went on strike and uncollected rubbish piled up in the streets – there is a celebrated photograph of City's glamour signing, Polish captain and World Cup star Kazimierz Deyna, standing next to piles of it in Manchester's Albert Square – persuaded sufficient people that change was necessary. There was a public appetite to curb the power of the unions, which the Conservatives proceeded to do, brutally.

The Thatcher government came in with plans to celebrate 'business', in the form of banking, the City of London, individuals owning shares, then they oversaw the wholesale collapse of the country's actual industrial businesses. Manchester, whose

economic foundation had been wrapped around cotton, suffered the terminal ruin of that industry in the 1920s and '30s,
due to the failure to invest and improve processes in the face
of cheaper competition from overseas, particularly India. Vast
redbrick Victorian mills, empty, derelict, or hosting the odd
sad carpet business, were vacant presences across my 1970s
Manchester childhood.

Now the factories, chemical companies and engineering works
of industrial Manchester teetered, also underfunded, on the
threshold of a new watershed. The policy of abandoning them
to a global market, scorched by high interest rates, led to a historic collapse. Around 150,000 manufacturing jobs in Manchester
were lost between 1978 and 1984. The docks of the Manchester
Ship Canal, which had steered the city's industrial economy for
decades – and given the city, and City, the ship of its badge –
were already history, the cranes petrified statues to the past. Great
companies, including GEC, Metro-Vicks, Ferranti's, some
founded by Manchester entrepreneurs and vital inventors in the
nineteenth century, laid people off in the tens of thousands.

'Firm by firm, there were savage cut backs,' writes Professor
Alan Kidd, in his excellent *Manchester, A History*. 'The 1970s
and 1980s were decades of national industrial decline in which
the Manchester region more than played its part. The inner
industrial belt of factories, workshops, canals, railway depots
and row upon row of terraced housing, which had once been
a lively, dirty but exciting place, betrayed the symptoms of inner-
city decay.'

Town, whenever you went in during those years, was coming
like a ghost town.

It always felt, because of the confrontational disputes (most bitterly the miners' strike) that marked Britain's industrial collapse, and the Thatcher government's determination to 'win' them, that this permanent ruin to the basis of the economy, particularly in Manchester and industrial places like it, was allowed to happen too easily. It was almost trumpeted as progress, a march to a cleaner, modern future. Now, thirty years later, in the depths of a crisis caused when the bubble of banking burst to reveal far too threadbare a real economy beneath, and limp talk of somehow 'rebalancing' Britain back to manufacturing, we seem only slowly to be realising how wrong and illusory it all was.

Yet Thatcher's brand of state-shrinking, not investing in industry, venerating the Stock Market and City of London as good in themselves, at least arrived when it did because an election was scheduled for that year. Manchester City, under Peter Swales, just happened to choose that time to self-destruct; he could have done it anytime.

Or, as all the supporters knew, they should not have done it at all as there was no need for it. City were not a paradigm of Manchester's wider problems, just as now, the two clubs are prospering, in 2012, while the economy is mired in slump. The club was flourishing, not failing. Deyna, in his polo neck, was an image of success and aspiration, next to the refuse in the city's main square. After Dennis Tueart won the 1976 League Cup for the blues, City, managed by Tony Book, finished second in the First Division, to Liverpool, in 1977, with Maine Road crowds averaging over 40,000.

Gary James's encyclopaedic history of the club, *Manchester the Greatest City*, a true labour of love, details that the following season, 1977–78, the most expensive Maine Road season ticket to watch one of the finest teams in English First Division football was £37 (equivalent to £188.70 in 2012, according to the Bank of England's comparator). Thousands of fans bought the season ticket for the Kippax, priced at £11 – £56.10 at today's prices – which accounted for the teeming presence of young people, teenagers, and football justifying the term 'the people's game', for all social classes to enjoy.

That season, the team whose pictures I still had on my bedroom wall included Joe Corrigan, an England international goalkeeper by then, the achingly classy Willie Donachie, Dave Watson, Asa Hartford, Tueart, Joe Royle and Peter Barnes. They finished fourth, behind Liverpool, Everton, and Brian Clough's miraculously championship-winning Nottingham Forest. Clough then took Forest to two European Cup victories, a climb to the greatest heights from the nether end of the Second Division which now, in the age of 'mega money' – it has cost Sheikh Mansour £800m to take City from ninth to challenge for top spot – can never be repeated.

The stricken Colin Bell made his return, trotting on after half-time in the Boxing Day game against Newcastle United in 1977, two years of work, rehabilitation and running up and down the Kippax steps after his knee had been savaged. I was down at the front of the North Stand that half-time, chatting to my friend Ric Demby and his brother, Neil, when a rolling rumble of applause began; we thought it was just welcoming the team back on until we realised its profound depth and saw Bell striding out. City won that game 4–0, too, as they had against United when he had been carried off, but he could never fully recover from his injury and played haltingly through the convulsions which followed until he was forced finally to retire in 1979.

City had finished above United for six years out of seven in the 1970s, and Peter Swales's stated ambition was to make that superiority permanent. I dimly remember him promising that Maine Road would become as grand an arena as Old Trafford, redeveloped all the way round, and that City would be the top club in Manchester. For thirty years fans have cursed what he did next to achieve that destiny; it became a formative trauma, still featuring centrally in pained recollections by forty- and fifty-something City fans in the venerable City fanzine, *King of the Kippax*.

City did have a dip before that, prompting Swales to think he had to do something. Tueart had left, for the star-filled meteor of American soccer which was the New York Cosmos, and Mike Doyle, Manchester grit rendered human, was allowed to go too, to Stoke. The replacements were not always successful and Deyna was disappointing, and through the winter of 1978 we watched the unfamiliar sight of City struggling. I remember feeling it seemed undignified for Asa Hartford, such a busy craftsman in a good side, to find himself overrun.

The great European nights were the floodlit relief, City playing with a freedom and relish they could not muster in the league. All City fans remember that the away leg against AC Milan in the San Siro stadium was played during the afternoon because the match had been fogged off the previous evening. So we were at school, on Thursday 23 November 1978, and I can still remember the classroom we were in, the brown desks bruised by fossilised ink, the greyness of our uniforms. Somebody had a radio, and that was how we found out that in technicolour Milan, Manchester City had drawn 2–2, having led 2–0. Later we saw the game, played in cold Italian sunshine, the goals scored by Brian Kidd and, after a run of endless energy, Paul Power. It was the return leg I stood with my cousin on the Kippax to watch, City ending the finest period in their history, before Swales's masterstroke, by beating AC Milan 3–0.

There was, then, no crisis to solve, with crowds of 40,000, a decade of attractive players and unparalleled stability achieved after the golden two years. What was required, when you reflect on it, was steady stewardship, shrewd succession planning, of players and managers, for the club to keep its head as the second wave of excellent players were reaching maturity. Instead, Swales flapped, and decided to take a headlong, showy leap for glory.

I think it was only then, because he did something so dramatic, that I even became aware that Manchester City had something called a chairman and his name was Peter Swales. Always sour-seeming, with his combover hairstyle and much less charisma than he thought he had, Swales reached for the future by recalling the glories of the past. In January 1979 he supplanted Tony Book, who had all the fans' respect, with Malcolm Allison, the coach to Joe Mercer when City had harvested their late 1960s glories.

The idea was that Allison, who had fetched up at the end of the decade back managing Plymouth Argyle, had the innate genius to magic back the golden years. What happened was a decline so unnecessary that many balding middle-aged blokes are only now beginning, haltingly, to recover. It was City's crisis, so may seem to some an obscure and domestic saga now, but it is surely not overstating to say it was without parallel at any top English football club. Allison, without the wise, older Mercer who had helped channel his coaching talents in the 1960s, seemed even to me, at fourteen, drunk with a sense of his own genius. Perhaps too many awestruck people at City had told him how brilliant he had been; City were in the Second Division when he and Mercer arrived, only winning promotion in 1966, and within two years they were champions. Swales, seeking later to explain why he brought back a man who had had a brief time managing without Mercer, in 1972–73, seemed to suggest it was other directors who were a little besotted with Allison and his aura.

It was the fate of my generation to be too young to know Allison when he really did conjure acts of genius, to see that remarkable rise from a desolate Maine Road in the Second Division to the winners of Bell, Lee and Summerbee. Bell, in his autobiography *Reluctant Hero*, pays great tribute to Allison's motivational powers, saying simply:

'In my opinion, Malcolm Allison is the best coach that has ever been.'

Yet we only knew Allison when he came back without the restraining guidance of Mercer, and sullied his own story. He proceeded to simply clean out all our favourites, without seeming to take time even to watch them. Gary Owen, one of the very successful young players to advance and replace ageing stars, was sold to West Bromwich Albion, his dad famously saying that when he took him there, Owen was miserable, like a dog being driven to be put down. Then Allison sold Barnes and Hartford, Brian Kidd and Dave Watson. Royle, Tueart and Doyle had already gone. It was almost a whole team of excellent, beloved international players dismantled, but Allison believed they could be replaced, and he told us that the players he had his eye on introducing would be better. I believed these men, Peter Swales and Malcolm Allison, until it was clear it had all gone dreadfully wrong and the emperor was naked, and that was a very salutary life lesson.

From a team whose narrative included afternoons in the San Siro stadium, City began suddenly to write themselves into football's outlandish alternative history, the club for cock-ups. The overspending by Allison and Swales is still legendary today and no less ludicrous with the passage of decades. Michael Robinson went on to be a rampaging centre forward admirably for Brighton, played thirty games for Liverpool, then went to Osasuna in Spain where he learned fluent Spanish and became a renaissance man and Spanish television personality. But there was no need for City to lose Kidd and Royle and pay £750,000 to Preston North End for Robinson who had played only forty-eight games in the Second Division. Steve MacKenzie, who we liked, although he was never up to the standard of players we were brought up on, was an excessive £250,000, having never played a first-team match for Crystal Palace.

The excess which has stood the test of time in football lore was the unfortunate Steve Daley, a talented central midfield player for Wolves, who now does a turn on the after-dinner circuit talking about how Peter Swales and Malcolm Allison came to blow £1.4m on buying him. I talked to Joe Royle about this period, which obsesses all the former players and everybody who worked at City at that time, as well as the fans of my generation who experienced it as a bewildering chapter of adolescence. Royle gave a hollow laugh, and said:

'They took a silk purse and made a pig's ear of it.'

I always remember my first home match of the 1979–80 season, after Allison's great purge. We had been on holiday to Torquay, where it had rained and been endlessly uneventful until Stoke City turned up at our hotel on a pre-season tour. Alex was obsessed and disgusted by the fact that one of the Stoke players had – he claimed – brushed his teeth and gobbed it all back into the hotel swimming pool. Nevertheless I persuaded both my brothers to go to Torquay United's Plainmoor ground to watch Stoke play a friendly on the Friday night, where there was a good crowd of bored holidaymakers from all over the country, waiting for the new season to start. I missed City's opening game, and at the first fixture back, I met Ric Demby in the Main Stand and he had to tell me who all the players were, because we had almost a whole new team. Ric, an innate enthusiast, pointed out Robinson – 'He's brilliant' – MacKenzie, and some of our own young players, including sixteen-year-old Tommy Caton, whom Allison had promoted painfully early, declaring they were ready.

Swales, an obsessive generator of publicity for City and himself, was forever allowing the cameras behind the scenes at City, most famously for the ITV Granada documentary mini-series, *City!* When you see it now, it is an excruciating fly-on-the-wall witness to Allison's vainglory, Swales's self-regard for his own leadership qualities and the poor young players' overpromoted helplessness. The scene where Tony Book tells the cameras the chairman has decided to demote him in favour of Allison is still painful to watch. The faces of the survivors Booth and Corrigan, who were sharing a dressing room with international performers just a year earlier, are a study in pent-up bewilderment. In one televised episode, Allison grouped his young players together on the training ground and pointed them out one by one. There was Caton, tall, blond, frizzy but looking already careworn; steady Ray Ranson, game Nicky Reid, Robinson and MacKenzie. These were his young stars, Allison declared, who would be as good as the players he had discarded, and one day, he proclaimed, all five would play for England.

In 1979, after half a season of Allison managing and Tony Book diminished beneath him, City stumbled to fifteenth. The following season, with so many players gone and good young lads thrown in too early, City finished seventeenth and were knocked out of the FA Cup 1–0 by Fourth Division Halifax Town, in the cloying mud of their ground, The Shay. It was the sort of football humbling we did not previously know could actually happen.

In just a year, Malcolm Allison's peculiar brand of genius and unique eye for a footballer, supported by Peter Swales's reaching for the stars, had transformed City from a club which needed to steady itself to a hollowed-out team bottom of the league. Swales finally realised that there was no grand mystique to Allison's judgements, no miracle waiting to reveal itself, saw that he had been howlingly and devastatingly wrong, as all sane onlookers and supporters knew at the time, even fourteen-year-olds waving sad goodbyes to one admired foot-baller after another.

So Swales sacked Allison, his coaching wonders of the 1960s tarnished for my generation by the wreckage he bequeathed us for the 1980s. Allison's exit was delivered with characteristic exhibitionism, filmed for all time by Granada in the *City!* documentary:

'The joy was just coming,' Allison lamented, of himself, at the club he'd transported to the bottom. 'I was going to get some of the pleasure, and now I'm not going to get any of the pleasure.'

The pleasure he left was to be all ours.

'I'm sure you'll be successful in the future,' he told the players, as they were forced one by one to line up in front of the cameras and shake his hand. That prediction came true, but only for one of them, Paul Power, who did enjoy success, but only when he finally left City and won the league with Everton.

There was a bright, windswept interlude before we went down, one last gasp of the big spender. Swales appointed John Bond next as the manager, his interview also filmed by Granada, who must have been unable to believe their luck, as City welcomed them in to document for ever the insides of a once-great football club's chapter of serial embarrassment. Referring to the players, Bond told the directors solemnly that 'I ain't going to have people who are going to be pissing about and flouting the image of Manchester City'. That seemed to impress them greatly as plain speaking, but I remember even as a young teenager it seemed a pretty crappy way to talk about taking on the job of managing Manchester City.

Bond understood the need to have some experienced players and he brought in Tommy Hutchison, a skilled winger whose better days had been seen at Coventry City, Gerry Gow, a Scottish midfielder specialising in extreme tackling, and Bobby MacDonald, a left-back who could score headed goals from corners. With Power, a meticulous gentleman footballer we never appreciated enough because his prime came after the stars had left, and Kevin Reeves, for whose signature Swales had somehow found another £1m, City made it to the 1981 FA Cup final.

I was sixteen by then and went to every round. I had drifted away from religion and have not really stopped drifting since. There was no great internal conflict or crisis of faith about it, no intense reading of great texts on the origins of the universe. It was more a shedding of rules which acted as restrictions from a world of rich attractions. There were, in a nutshell, girls, lovely girls, at parties in someone's house, two buses away. I went to school in Bury, so there were parties in Bolton and Bury and Rochdale and other Lancashire outposts we walked and walked to find. There was music, and on Saturdays, when the Jewish religion was enjoining you not to drive, not to do anything much except walk to synagogue, there was football. I played for the school in the mornings, then it'd be Maine Road in the afternoons, maybe on the bus from Heaton Park's Grand Lodge entrance, maybe a lift from someone who also had a scrounged ticket going spare, maybe paying £1 to stand on the Kippax, to watch Bobby Mac and Tommy Hutch with our willing lads play their way to Wembley while heading inexorably down.

So I left the synagogue for ska, snogging and smoking, not after some great search of the soul, but shuffling the prohibitions off to get to freedom. Years later I watched a documentary about Israel, where these debates, religion versus a secular society, are a raging, central feature of contemporary life. One man, I remember, smiled and explained to the interviewer:

'I used to be religious,' he said, 'but life is sweeter without it.'

And I thought that was right. Take the positive messages of religion, or, really, of universal human values, the notion that there is such a thing as right and wrong; of justice, that you should stand up for what is right, fists clenched when necessary; understand we are all born equal. Try to live by those principles, but out there in the world, not restricted to a small community, defining yourself by an artificial difference. Treat your neighbour as you would like to be treated yourself, as that rabbi once said, standing on one leg, and get yourself down to Maine Road.

I remember Goodison Park best, of course, the FA Cup quarter-final, standing down in that narrow, hostile terrace, behind the fences which surrounded all top football grounds as a response to pitch invasions and hooliganism. I saw Everton's Trevor Ross punch Paul Power full in the face in the first half, then, after an age of misery, with Everton 2–1 up, when Power scored his remarkable equaliser six minutes from time, we all went wild and I found myself for the first time hugging a complete stranger on a football terrace. Kevin Ratcliffe was sent off for an upwards head-butt on Hutchison who was wasting time in the corner, and afterwards, as I made it back to the car with friends old enough to drive by then, it was mayhem, with crowds of casual Everton fans tearing down the road, attacking City fans on foot and even in cars.

City won the replay 3–1 and in the semi-final at Villa Park against Ipswich, I could just about see from the Holte End terrace as Power revealed he had been hiding all this time an ability to score from curling free-kicks 25 yards out. I went to both the FA Cup finals against the Tottenham Hotspur of Glenn Hoddle, Garth Crooks, Steve Archibald, Osvaldo Ardiles and Ricardo Villa, the 1–1 draw on the Saturday at Wembley, when Tommy Hutchison scored for both clubs, and the great replay on the Wednesday when City fans all went down to London again. I still have the programme, 80p. I don't remember what we paid for the tickets to stand in the City end; it was £4 or something. It was certainly not £90, as some of the tickets were when Sheikh Mansour's Manchester City finally reached the new Wembley for an FA Cup final again, in 2011, thirty years later.

The first final had been grey and cloudy, and a drab game after Tommy Hutch's header. The replay was altogether more magical, down at a floodlit Wembley. I actually missed seeing Steve MacKenzie's tremendous volleyed equaliser because fans were fighting in our end and crowds of us were drawn to watching that. We had a whole curve behind a goal and everybody had bought white flags with a blue City logo on them – I still have mine, somewhere.

From the City end, we could not really see the Ricky Villa dribble which won the cup for Spurs and has been endlessly replayed every year since; up the steep banking, behind the greyhound track which ran around the Wembley pitch, the other end was a long way to see. I remember after that looking out at our curved end flowing with City flags and realising, as the minutes floated away, that we were not going to win. There was nevertheless a poignant beauty in the occasion, from the singing of 'Abide with Me' to the final whistle, the blue and the white, the green of the pitch and the silver Wembley flood-lights, the skills of Spurs and the true effort of our players. Then it was a long, dark journey back, and a stop at bedraggled Watford Gap services at two in the morning, which was crawling with thousands of City fans spilling out of minibuses, sodden with disappointment.

I remember one of the girls at school asking me the following day if I had been to the game, and she said she had watched it on telly. She said she'd enjoyed it, and that she had thought Glenn Hoddle had nice legs. And I remember that making me realise even then that football had a much wider potential appeal, as a spectacle, than the hard core of in-the-blood addicts to which a troubled game was starting to boil down.

School football on Saturday mornings was a good standard, playing the best young lads your own age on cared-for school pitches, a nice zip on the surface from the morning dew. I had graduated to men's football on a Sunday, and the school games were so much cleaner than the hardness of the Manchester amateur leagues, on the council's mudbaths playing who knew who, out in the middle of nowhere. Years of playing and training, taking football and fitness quite seriously when many of the more naturally talented boys were leaving it behind, led to me suddenly, dramatically improving. As a journalist, I interviewed the Bolton Wanderers and Liverpool midfield player Jason McAteer, who described a period in his growth when 'I found my engine', and a similar discovery happened to me. I developed stamina, more speed, and a better touch.

We had a new PE teacher at school who had played football to a high level in Staffordshire – he had played with Stoke City players Adrian Heath and Lee Chapman – and he invited a friend and old coach of his to watch us. He was a small, chirpy man with a busy authority, introduced as Alan A'Court, and he was, we were told, coaching at Crewe Alexandra. I didn't realise until looking him up later that he had been a well known professional footballer, who had played at Liverpool for Bill Shankly, in the early team with Ron Yeats, Ian Callaghan and Ian St John. He even played for England in the 1958 World Cup, against Brazil. And here he was, on a school playing field in Bury on a Thursday afternoon, organising us to play two-touch. It was the only time after years of working hard at my football that I had ever been watched by an emissary from a professional club, so I played in front of Alan A'Court with all my determination, controlling it, sprinting, leaving my marker, asking for the ball again. Afterwards, he approached me and another boy, who stroked a football very truly, to come down and play for him, the following Monday.

'Play for who?' we asked.

'For Crewe,' he said. 'Crewe Alexandra youth, against Liverpool youth, in the FA Youth Cup.'

It was an extraordinary opportunity, landmark recognition for my journey from being the slow but willing lad at thirteen, stuck at left-back because all the creative places were taken.

My dad arranged to drive down to Crewe, with a carload of my mates, to watch. Then over the intervening weekend Crewe sacked the manager for whom Alan A'Court was working, Arfon Griffiths; I'm sure we watched it mentioned on Saturday's *Football Focus*. A'Court was good enough to phone me, to tell me that meant he was fired, too, and so he could not see us selected for the Liverpool game at Gresty Road on the Monday.

My one chance to gain a breath of professional football was gone, but I was not too disappointed, and I have never thought too much about it. Dario Gradi, the great coach to young players, joined Crewe a year later, so you could idly wonder what might have been if you had been there when he arrived, but I never believed then or since I was good or tough enough to batter out a professional career. It has just always been exceptionally nice to know a football man of Alan A'Court's experience saw me as potentially good enough to play in the FA Youth Cup against Liverpool.

In 2003 I noticed that Alan A'Court had published an autobiography, *My Life in Football*, chronicling his ten years at Liverpool, and coaching career at Norwich, then Stoke when they were successful in the 1970s and where our teacher, John Potts, had known him. Page 119, very close to the end, is where you find him 'helping' Arfon Griffiths at Crewe, then being told he was not wanted by his replacement, Peter Morris.

'This time,' A'Court wrote, 'there was no reprieve. I really had finished my active connection with the professional game.'

I left a message for him via the publisher of his book, saying I had known him briefly as a boy and had become a football journalist, and wondering if he'd like to get in touch. Late one

Friday, when I was in the car off for the weekend with my wife and daughters, he called me. He said he did remember that day clearly, out on that windy field in Bury, desperately scouting for Crewe recruits. I told him how remarkable it was, the way people's paths can cross in each other's lives, that the lowest point for him, the difficult end of his noble career, will forever be the highpoint of my own football efforts.

City finally went down at Maine Road on the final Saturday of the 1982–83 season, to Luton Town, Raddy Antic scoring in the 81st minute, David Pleat, the manager, running on in his hush puppies, literally skipping with joy, to hug his beaming captain, Brian Horton. We, the many City fans of my generation, honestly did not know much at all about the Second Division. We'd only really thought about it when United went down there for a season. Our rightful place, as we had watched throughout the 1970s, was around the top of the First Division, with a splendid team of good or great players. Not getting relegated with a team ransacked by Malcolm Allison and Peter Swales, after a home defeat by Luton Town.

As we stood silently, watching Luton celebrate and City slink away – I had a season ticket in the North Stand by then – Neil Demby, my friend Ric's older brother, aged twenty-one, was crying. A lad in front of us – this is my main memory of relegation – was losing it. He flung the remains of his season ticket to the floor, then turned round, away from the pitch, and started to kick his seat in.

Those who believe the superficial view of Manchester City, that the fans through the years which followed relished being not United, that they embraced failure and endured it with gallows humour, only ever understood part of the story. City fans grew up watching a winning team, with truly great players, in the expectation of entertainment. They did not choose a club of no achievements, so there was always a sense, after Allison's return and the throwing of so many players into a skip outside Maine Road, that it was all an aberration. Even as it all turned into reality, with a new cast of players you wanted to appreciate, there was a feeling that it was all not really happening. There was always a yearning for success, for the golden days of our childhoods to return, beneath all the efforts to find something to laugh about in the 1980s.

Peter Swales, from then, was a man loathed and resented by the great majority of Manchester City supporters. I have always had the idea that I had grown up with the principle: love the club, hate the chairman. But I now realise that it wasn't the case. Looking back on all this now I realise I was completely unaware of Swales while the club ran smoothly, only understanding his role as the club's ultimate boss when he messed with our history and brought Allison back. From then, the cries of 'Swales Out!' at Maine Road weren't occasional rebellions, just a sign that the football season had begun again. It was not so much what he did; however disastrous and ill-judged it had turned out to be, people could understand that he believed bringing Malcolm Allison back could spirit success to the club again. It was that when it turned out to be so spectacularly wrong, he failed to take responsibility. He stayed on, he clung on, a personification of the failure to do the right thing, of the fans' idea that the chairman was too in love with his own position, serving himself while the fortunes of the club were wrecked.

It is odd, but even now, writing this, I can hardly believe it all happened. We're still in shock. There we were, before 1979, with Doyle and Corrigan, Watson and Tueart, Owen and Barnes, and the picture of the overhead kick in 1976. I do know for a fact that grown-up reality never did match up to the City of our bedroom walls, but a part of me still clings to that as City's untarnished reality. Ray Ranson, Nicky Reid, Michael Robinson and Steve MacKenzie had good, earnest careers, but Tommy Caton died terribly young, aged only thirty, and none of them ever played for England. So this all taught us that what you are told sometimes, even about something you believe in very strongly, and by people you trust, can turn out not be true in the end. That is a sad but probably important lesson of growing up. Yet somewhere in my consciousness, just as there is probably an unshakeable thought, still, that God really is watching over me when I am having a wee, lingers the conviction that Malcolm Allison was a maverick genius, that he could see in those players what nobody else could, that it would all work out. A part of me still believes those players will some day play for England, Malcolm Allison's plan will be vindicated, because it cannot possibly have been so misguided. And Maine Road will yet be developed into a super stadium, just like Peter Swales promised it would, even though it is now demolished.

CHAPTER 5

HIS EXCELLENCY THE CHAIRMAN

I first met Manchester City's Abu Dhabi-appointed chairman, Khaldoon Al Mubarak, in an enormous suite on some upper floor of the Lowry Hotel, an island of five-star opulence on the grey border where Salford meets Manchester. It is two miles from where I grew up, and there is something in the run-down red brick walls around the old Victoria bus station, the long-gone cinema on the corner of Chapel Street, and the high-rise flats as you go up Great Clowes Street, which will forever be Manchester to me. The Lowry, built in 2001 and Manchester's first five-star hotel, is, like the Selfridge's and Harvey Nichols which arrived after the IRA's bomb wiped out much of the city centre in 1996, a statement of intent for new prosperity. Amid Manchester's industrial decline, which was its story for much of the twentieth century, speeding up and forced into near-ruin in the 1980s, these are the Robinhos.

I was led out of the lift and into a waiting area with a selection of magazines on the table designed to reassure guests that they are metropolitan business sophisticates. There was a huge window at the back of the room, a wall of glass, giving out on the roofs below of neighbouring buildings. Al Mubarak was sitting in an armchair in front of it, legs crossed, the fingers of his left hand touching his temple, a thoughtful pose. He is young and cerebral, but he was framed there like a leader of men, to be respected.

The word people who had met Al Mubarak used most to describe him was impressive, and so he was, in a quietly intense way, always conveying the impression that he had thought about what to say before he spoke, and then saying it with conviction. When we met, it was the summer of 2009, after City's second spending spree, including the Welcome to Manchester purchase of Tevez. At the club which had been living off John Wardle's pocket money to pay its wages a year ago, Al Mubarak had been responsible for spending £199m of Sheikh Mansour's oil money in a year on transfer fees alone, to buy fully ten new footballers for Mark Hughes. He was calm, not flashy but studious, deep brown eyes behind silver-rimmed spectacles, giving the appearance of being in control even as he was pouring so much money into Manchester City and the bank accounts of some lucky footballers. His new role at the football club was, it turned out, just a small addition to his portfolio of major responsibilities.

He told me, in his perfect, natural English with just a slight Arab timbre, that he had been born in Abu Dhabi, one of the seven countries making up the United Arab Emirates. He had grown up and gone to school there, then done a degree in economics in Boston, USA, at Tufts, an expensive private university. That was the ordained route for an intelligent local middle-class boy to becoming a trusted pair of hands in the executive class of his country, assisting the ruling family in the planned investment of its limitless wealth. In Khaldoon's generation, the first after oil drenched the gulf with its fortunes, the sheikhs had moved on from solely employing foreign expatriates to handle the money and construct proper businesses. They had realised they should have their own young people educated, so they could come back and be the managers, reporting to the dynastic owners, and in turn employing the expats and professionals required.

'We send a lot of students on scholarships to top universities in the US and UK,' Al Mubarak told me. 'I was sent on a scholarship to the US.'

When he returned to his country from Boston, he said, 'I started my career in the national oil company.'

This is the Abu Dhabi National Oil Company (ADNOC), which was formed when the UAE was established independently from British influence, as recently as 1971. The company was founded to extract the vast reserves of oil and gas lying under the Al Nahyans' feet, and is the engine for generating the endless riches and consequent growth of Abu Dhabi from a desert emirate as late as the 1960s, to one of the world's wealthiest countries. Directed by the Supreme Petroleum Council, which is chaired by Sheikh Khalifa bin Zayed Al Nahyan, the president of the UAE, ruler of Abu Dhabi and Mansour's brother, ADNOC currently produces 2.7m barrels of oil a day. At around $100 a barrel, that is $270m gushing into the coffers of Mansour's family, just from the oil, investments aside, every day. I make that $98.55bn a year or, rounding it up, $100bn, real money, not leveraged banking-bubble nonsense, for a tiny country of only 400,000 native emiratis.

Al Mubarak sat in the hotel named after the artist who chronicled the matchstick men and matchstick cats and dogs of Salford's ragged past, and explained the course he had charted in his improbably rich country, as a bright young US-educated economics graduate. With advice from international oil companies, banks and expatriates, Abu Dhabi had established a structure of companies to try to invest, not waste, the vast windfalls from oil. With no democracy in the country, and a tribal, feudal structure to its social and economic hierarchy, the Al Nahyans, who had ruled the country since the eighteenth century, got to keep all the oil. They maintained acceptance of their authority by most of the emiratis following a process of modernising the country, and sharing out some of its riches.

'There is the government of Abu Dhabi,' Al Mubarak explained, 'which is the wealth of the government and people. That has various investment vehicles, including Mubadala, the International Petroleum Investment Company [chaired by Sheikh Mansour] and the Abu Dhabi Investment Authority [which did $1.3 trillion of deals in its peak year of 2007].

'I quickly worked my way up,' he continued, 'and I still run one of the biggest investment companies the government owns; I'm the chief executive. It is a company that over the last eight years has risen to prominence and now we are one of the most prominent companies in the region.'

The company he runs is Mubadala, chaired by another of Sheikh Zayed's twenty-one sons by several wives, the Crown Prince of Abu Dhabi, Sheikh Mohammed bin Zayed Al Nahyan, Mansour's older full brother. Mubadala's brief is to buy into diverse ventures around the world targeted at helping to solidify Abu Dhabi's wealth and power, in a future once the oil has run out. In 2009 the investments Khaldoon had overseen were principally in oil and gas, property, hotels and aerospace – increasing to 70 per cent the Mubadala holding in SR Technics, a Zurich-based aeroplane maintenance company which was the former maintenance division of Swissair. The company had recorded income that year of 17bn UAE dirhams – £3bn – and had total assets of 88bn dirhams, £15bn.

That was not his only day job, or indeed his main one.

'I also chair the Executive Affairs Authority,' he went on. 'That is my primary role. Through that I sit in the executive council of the UAE, that is the equivalent of the council of ministers, which runs the government affairs of the UAE.'

The EAA is a key branch of the Abu Dhabi government, providing strategic advice to the country, also reporting to Sheikh Mohammed, the Crown Prince. It is a kind of in-house government strategic think-tank, as Abu Dhabi seeks to harness its huge resources without antagonising any major groups internally, or countries in its location deep in the Arab world, or in the West. In the Al Nahyans' chosen path, to make the most of their enormous wealth while fostering social and political stability, the EAA has its eye on strategic positioning – it developed a 'brand' for Abu Dhabi in 2007 – and is entrusted with steering a course. Its responsibilities are to provide advice to the Crown Prince and government across almost all conceivable areas of Abu Dhabi life: economic and energy policy including developing a vision for the country's development up to 2030; diplomatic and international relations including with the UN, government affairs, legal issues, education, the physical development, including urban planning, of the whole country.

Which seems like it could get quite busy. And he has all of this in his several in-trays, responsibility for strategic advice to his country's development, and management of a £15bn investment fund, at the age of thirty-three.

A key self-description of its role by the EAA helps to explain how Khaldoon Al Mubarak, who is up pictured on its website as its chairman, titled 'his excellency', in traditional Arab robe and head-dress, came to be the chairman of Manchester City. The EAA is the government department involved in strategic communications – PR and image management – for the country of Abu Dhabi itself.

Khaldoon Al Mubarak, chairman, Abu Dhabi's Executive Affairs Authority and Manchester City

'The Strategic Communications Affairs Advisory Unit works closely with key public and private entities in the Emirate of Abu Dhabi,' it says, 'to provide advice and assistance in the planning and implementation of strategic communications programs that have the potential to influence the reputation of the Emirate.'

The global popularity of the English Premier League, shown and watched in 200 countries around the world, including by men sitting cross-legged on floors and smoking shisha pipess in Abu Dhabi bars, means that Manchester City, Peter Swales's cocked-up football club I grew up supporting, is a huge media phenomenon. Al Mubarak told me that the attention and coverage devoted to the takeover of City, worldwide, dwarfed anything they had ever been involved with. At the time, Mubadala had been concluding a partnership investment deal with AMD, a Californian company which is the second-biggest producer of microchips for computers in the world, has 11,000 employees and turns over $7bn. Yet that deal, which was worth $4bn, was specialist, geeky business, for the trade press, compared with the vast global attention devoted to buying a Premier League football club.

'Over the last eight years we have done some amazing deals,' he reflected, 'yet the exposure I got from being associated with the club far exceeds anything that happens with the business side. To be honest, I completely underestimated it. I knew it was going to be high-profile, to a certain extent, but nowhere near what it actually transpired to be.'

It was that, the teeming global following for football, which landed him with the job in the first place. In understanding how and why Manchester City came to be taken over by a young sheikh in Abu Dhabi, and what he wanted with it, it must always be remembered that his excellency Khaldoon Al Mubarak, this blue-chip executive occupying some of the highest levels of responsibilities in his emirate, was not involved at the beginning. The original front man, remarkably when you think about it, had been the bloke from Dubai who later turned up with insufficient money at Portsmouth, Sulaiman Al Fahim.

Al Mubarak and the others are always polite and diplomatic about Al Fahim; they do not explicitly say that those days of global media braggadocio were threatening to undo the decades of effort Abu Dhabi had put in to handle their gigantic windfall with an awareness of decorum. They have quietly amassed huge stakes in strategic businesses around the world, stockpiled the cash and sent up their skyscrapers, without strutting about, boasting too publicly about how much money they have, or how deep their pockets are. I asked Al Mubarak if Al Fahim's bragging had been an embarrassment to them, had begun to impact badly on Sheikh Mansour and Abu Dhabi itself, or paint the country in a garish light it had always made a strategic effort to avoid. He said:

'That was an important trigger, the realisation that when you buy an English Premier League club it is a totally different ball game, the public persona, the image, the public relations side of the deal, was very much bigger than the investment. That had been underestimated.'

Mark Hughes put it more directly, when I talked to him:

'Sulaiman Al Fahim was appointed as the spokesman for the group, and he came out with statements which were unhelpful.

They wanted to make an impact, and that is what they did with the signing of Robinho, but after that the statements didn't reflect Abu Dhabi in a good light, and that is when Khaldoon was asked to come in and take it over.'

Khaldoon in person was as precise as Abu Dhabi United had been in the public statements drafted in that open letter to City fans, that Sheikh Mansour had bought the club in a personal capacity. They have always been at pains to make that clear, to emphasise that this is no state acquisition of the club by the Al Nahyan family or the Abu Dhabi government itself.

'His highness Sheikh Mansour is a member of the royal family, is a minister for presidential affairs,' Al Mubarak told me, 'but he also has his own private wealth and the investment in Manchester City is a private investment by him. It has nothing to do with any of the government investment companies.'

Thaksin Shinawatra, on the run and convicted of corruption, had needed to sell the football club, which was being propped up with £2m loans from John Wardle. They had engaged an English broker, Amanda Staveley, to sell the club, and Thaksin's lieutenant, Pairoj Piempongsant, had contacts in the gulf. Al Fahim, whose name was made in the property bubble of Dubai, made the approach to Sheikh Mansour, the royal in Abu Dhabi who had already bought a football club there, and was known to be interested in a Premier League club. He bought Manchester City with some of the multimillions the scions of his father, Sheikh Zayed, have to spend for themselves. It was not a corporate or state-sponsored venture planned by the Abu Dhabi government or those investment companies straining to spend the oil miracle prudently.

Al Mubarak, explaining why, gave the same argument as they had in their letter to the fans, that it was for fun, because Mansour does like football and he fancied buying a club he could build and fund to win trophies, but it was an investment too:

'Sheikh Mansour is a huge football fan, he follows it very closely and I think he has always wanted to have a European club that he can take and build and become one of the top clubs in the world. There is an enjoyment that comes with owning it, a pleasure.

'But also he is an astute businessman, he also believes that you can create a value proposition in football that has not yet been accomplished. There is a pure football, emotional side of it, but there is also a big business side. I think that is what appealed to Sheikh Mansour towards acquiring Manchester City.

'It's a great ride, a great journey, but there is also a business sense that we can create a franchise, a business, over years, which will create value and reap a long-term return.'

So that, in effect, was the job Khaldoon had found himself tasked with. The real authorities in Abu Dhabi had seen that Manchester City, of all things, which Sheikh Mansour had bought personally, quickly, was the greatest international image-shaper the emirate had. Al Fahim was sullying that image and Khaldoon and his team from the EAA were sent for, the people who stepped in with their expertise, to provide advice and guidance in 'strategic communications programs that have the potential to influence the reputation of the Emirate'.

Simon Pearce, who became a director of City on a small board which included Al Mubarak and Martin Edelman, a trouble-shooting New York lawyer, is the director of strategic communications for the Executive Affairs Authority. He works across all of the responsibilities Al Mubarak has as chair of that body, but in particular he steers the image Abu Dhabi is striving to have reflected upon it, as it seeks to cement permanence in a volatile region and explosive world. Pearce had his signature on the development of the 'brand of Abu Dhabi', marketing the country itself. It appears to have two purposes: one, to reassure Abu Dhabi's own population that the traditional way of life was still being valued even as the money poured in and the place changed for ever, and two, to present a desired image of dignity to the world as the country went out to spend, invest and solidify its presence.

The brand quotes Sheikh Zayed, revered within Abu Dhabi and recognised around the world to have been a visionary leader for the UAE, that history must be honoured.

'A nation without a past is a nation without a present or a future.'

Explaining itself, the brand of Abu Dhabi, which is its own office and department, states:

'Abu Dhabi is a tolerant place with multi-denominational communities; it has resisted the urge to flaunt its prosperity and has carefully planned its investments to ensure a deep connection with its heritage, environment and its people.'

Pearce authored the document which set out the 'values' and 'essence' of the brand, which was termed 'respect', and the brand is said explicitly to be promoted in business, by the country's development plan to 2030, by Etihad Airlines, the Abu Dhabi Tourism authority encouraging visitors, and by the Formula One

Grand Prix and other 'world class hosting of major international events'.

So Manchester City has on its board a man whose professional duties include overseeing an image for Abu Dhabi itself, which would be shot through with the idea of respect, for the past and traditional values, while solidifying unthinkable wealth in an impoverished Arab region. Manchester City, two steps from ruin when Mansour bought it, was, like everything else they did, going to be part of enhancing the image of Abu Dhabi, not debasing it.

'We are acknowledging that this is telling a lot to the world about how we are,' Al Mubarak told me. 'It is showing the world how we are handling this project, the true essence of who Abu Dhabi is and what Abu Dhabi is about. There is almost a personification of the values we hold as Abu Dhabi, with the values of the club and the values we would like to stick to.

'This is something new, something we didn't really plan for, but it is becoming an important part of this.

'The values are loyalty, commitment, discipline, long-term thinking. You look at everything we do in Abu Dhabi; the respect side of it, the appreciation of history, understatement.'

It was Pearce who was sent in by Al Mubarak to inspect City down to its bowels, all around its botched edges, with world-class consultants Booz Allen and Co., to examine what needed to be done to make it, very quickly, as Sheikh Mansour had prescribed, 'a European club that he can take and build and become one of the top clubs in the world'.

The action resulting from the stocktake called for more than just throwing the £200m to buy a battalion of new stars for

Mark Hughes. There was, as Hughes had shown Al Mubarak when he first visited, the famished insides of the Carrington training ground which was refurbished with à la carte gym equipment and wholly new, high-class medical facilities.

'There were some quick fixes, quick wins,' Al Mubarak said, 'fixing the gym facility, the medical facility at Carrington – we had to do that quickly because it was simply unacceptable.'

The plan overall, worked up with Garry Cook, the chief executive whom they retained (to the surprise of many in football who believed he would go the way of Al Fahim), envisaged a similar overhaul in every area of the club: football structure, administration, executive and board level, coaching, academy, supporter relations, commercial, the lot. Cook, the ex-Nike man, saw City as a 'brand' itself which would have major sponsors and 'partners' and be sold and broadcast all over the world. Al Mubarak continually expressed amazement that the basics of a proper organisation were missing, that there was no personnel department, for example. People who worked there said they were given their jobs by whoever their boss was in that department, and there was a woman you gave your holidays to. But human resources was not a department with a name of its own at Manchester City.

From the beginning, they identified that they wanted a director of football position. They observed that the academy for young developing players, still based at Platt Lane, the one remaining Manchester City presence in the old base on Moss Side, was too separate, geographically and organisationally, from the first team. There was too little, for them, of a systematic way to identify kids coming through, and to help secure what the first team manager needed. They recognised that director of football was a title which had never worked in English football, because the traditional manager, always termed the boss, tended to see it as a curb and rival to his authority. Their idea was that the director of football would pull together all elements of the football operations, from youth to medical to multi-million-pound signings, support the manager by overseeing all the operations required for a successful first team, not dictate to him, and leave him free to coach.

Cook knew Brian Marwood, the former Arsenal winger (also capped by England, once), who after serving as chairman of the Professional Footballers Association union had been head of football in the UK for Nike. He had done sponsored boot deals for some young players including James Milner and Adam Johnson, and Cook believed Marwood could do the director of football job. To avoid the stigma of that title, they gave him the grand name of head of football administration. From the beginning, they identified that to have a winning team, capable of competing with United and the best clubs in Europe, given Uefa and the Premier League's squad limit of twenty-five, they wanted two world-class players in each position.

Al Mubarak explained what they had meant by spending £32.5m on signing Robinho even before they had actually concluded the takeover:

'We did want to make that statement,' he said. 'It was very important that we come in and show intent, and bringing in such a talented player as Robinho that made sure to the city, the fans, to the club, the Premier League, that we were serious. I think it was important that message came out clear.'

They regarded what they spent in January as the 'second wave of fixes', after the gym, medical facility, appointing Marwood, reorganising the board, executive structure and beginning to build the staff their own office block where there could be some natural sunlight. So to strengthen Hughes's squad, they spent £50m in January. Then in the summer Manchester City bought Barry, Santa Cruz, Adebayor, Touré and Tevez for another £115.5m. The wages they were paying to draw the players to Manchester City from clubs which had all previously been more successful were around £100,000 per week – much more in the case of Tevez, who was paid £198,000 a week in a contract which guaranteed him always to be the highest-paid thoroughbred in Sheikh Mansour's stables.

I asked Al Mubarak if this was his dream job, whether, after being so responsible for the multi-million-dollar serious work, it was great to be involved in football, of which he too is a fan.

He smiled: 'It would have been a great retirement job.'

He spoke with most conviction not about City, but Abu Dhabi, seeming deeply committed to his country and this idea they have worked out for it: to develop an economy and a future sustainable beyond oil, to be respected, and to adhere to their traditional values of family and a more liberal, liveable-with form of Islam. I had told them that I was very interested in this, the remarkable acquisition of Manchester City by a member of the Al Nahyan ruling dynasty in Abu Dhabi, and by the way they hoped the club would be a vehicle for, or reflection of, the best image they wanted to portray of their country. They said I should come, and that I could interview Al Mubarak there too.

'When you come,' he said, 'you will see the true essence of Abu Dhabi, what Abu Dhabi is about. And you will gauge it.'

He believed that what was happening, the involvement of Abu Dhabi with a club as homespun English as Manchester City, the clear improvements they were making, the banner greeting them in the stadium, the expressions of thanks and good will from the City fans, the lack of any animosity or racism towards them, could improve relations between the Middle East and the West.

'There is an element of bridge-building, of understanding, between the Arab world and here, and that has all come along as part of this journey. But it was never intended.'

Whichever way you asked Al Mubarak about the instinctive repulsion many people in football have for this kind of 'project', for a rich man with no previous connection to just buy a club then pour in as much money as it took to buy success, he did not so much defend what they were doing as fail to understand the question. If you told him that English football was never based on an 'owner' buying a club and throwing money in to buy a team of stars, you realised before your question trailed off that Jack Walker had done just that at Blackburn in 1995 and Roman Abramovich at Chelsea since 2003. English football was open to it. If you said football was not supposed to be about which 'owner' had the most money, so who could pay the most to players, thereby seducing them to their club, he wondered aloud how United had won the Premier League so many times, and how anybody could compete with them, without money. If you tried to argue that a club should be a club, belonging to the people who support it, that a sporting competition does not seem sporting if it is owned by one rich man spending whatever it takes to stockpile the necessary mercenary talent, you would be describing an abstract idea with which he was unfamiliar, and which did not match reality as it was, and as it was viewed from Abu Dhabi. From there, Sheikh Mansour bin Zayed Al Nahyan had watched the English Premier League become the most viewed domestic sporting competition in the world, overflowing with glamour and money, and he had seen that its clubs were companies, not supporter-owned clubs like Real Madrid and Barcelona, or the clubs in the German Bundesliga, and they were wide open for purchase by a menu of owners. United, Liverpool, Chelsea, Aston Villa had all been bought; Spurs was owned by the currency speculator Joe Lewis via the tax haven of Bermuda, while Arsenal was being fought over by a Russian and an American billionaire. To Mansour and Al Mubarak, this was more fun than oil and gas, but nevertheless an English football club was not very different from SR Technics or any other company the enormous financial reserves of Abu Dhabi were buying every day. It was a company, a business.

'I appreciate the argument about having so much money,' Al Mubarak said politely, although he did not seem to, really, partly because I had found it difficult to articulate the question clearly enough, there in the fat suite of the Salford hotel which is itself a monument to the desire for money. 'The way I answer it is: yes, this is a club, but it is a business, and in a business you are there to compete. There are big clubs and small clubs and some are richer than others and that is the reality. That is the eco-system of football.

'There is an opportunity we have identified and taken hold of, a mid-tier club will move to become a big club because of the financial resources we are able to make available. Because we see value in making that transition. And that is the bottom line.'

That was the first time they invited me to the chairman's lounge. They said they had nothing to hide – if I was interested in what they were doing, they would show me whatever I liked. Frankly, when I walked through the main entrance, allowed in by the beefy security men, welcomed up the stairs and smiled into that cocoon within the stadium that Manchester's cash-strapped council built, I was astonished at quite how plush it all was at Manchester City. The food was an unapologetic gourmet experience, lamb medleys and duck confits cooked up by a chef hired to improve another area they had clearly felt was below the required world-class standard. I sat on a table with Jon Stemp, the long-time friend of Pearce's who built and managed sports facilities, so had been rapidly recruited to oversee the swift overhaul of Carrington, moved on to the new office block, and became head of infrastructure, responsible for all the new City's physical developments. Edelman was there, silver-haired and urbane, looking, in east Manchester, very New York.

Al Mubarak brought friends and family, wide-eyed, to that game, too, and they sat and ate and pinched themselves while he was drilling deep into chairman's business. It was the first home match of the 2009–10 season, against Wolves, at which City rolled out their new billboard signings: Tevez, Adebayor, Bridge, Touré, Barry. I went out into the blue-cushioned seats of the stadium's directors' area, where I bumped into Ian Niven, a long-serving former director from the 1970s through to the 1990s. He was on the board when Swales brought Allison back, and had been always around the inner sanctum ever since. I interviewed him during one of the manifold crises, when City were down in the Third Division in 1998–99, at his flat in Didsbury. It was full of City treasures – old player contracts, including Francis Lee's, specifying a very modest weekly wage, and some magnificent ornate wooden panel he said had been chucked in a skip on the Maine Road forecourt – in Peter Swales's time they hadn't seemed to cherish the history too much.

Niven looked out on the stadium, the brand-new millionaire players trotting out for the first time, Al Mubarak and the Abu Dhabi-appointed directors taking their seats, the banner opposite, on which Manchester thanks Sheikh Mansour. And he spoke the sentiments of some City fans trying to make sense of it all:

'Well, it isn't the City I know and love,' he said, 'but if all this were going to happen to anybody, I'm glad it's happened to us.'

City, with this new unfamiliar team, did what they have done periodically since the Abu Dhabi money revolution began – thought they were going to win easily, because of who they were, and the money which had been spent. Adebayor scored after 17 minutes, Wolves, just promoted to the Premier League and playing the richest club in the world, seemed dazzled, and City had so much of the ball they played themselves into self-congratulation. After half-time Wolves, managed by Mick McCarthy, who appears shrewder as a manager than he did when we watched him artlessly heading balls a very long way from the middle of City's defence in the depleted 1980s, seemed to realise at half-time who they were and found their spirit. Kevin Doyle came on and was very tidy, and Andy Keogh hit the bar. The script, that Sheikh Mansour's £200m, invested with professional expertise, would raise Manchester City to the heights of the late 1960s, was touched by just a spirit of the 1990s, but City held on to 1–0, to much relief from the people who had spent all the money.

The BBC report of the match said: 'There is no disputing that Carlos Tevez is the new darling of City's fans after switching allegiance from Manchester United.'

Just two years later, only two players in that starting team would still be regulars: Micah Richards, the muscly lad with the deep determination and ready laugh, the one academy player to survive the signings, and Barry. The rest were sold or loaned off as they were displaced by the next wave of millions spent. Tevez, the darling, would become one on his own.

Back inside the chairman's lounge, Al Mubarak had been busy on his phone in a corner of the lounge, while his friends and relatives were tucking in to their away day in the Premier League. Pearce was in the room, off on an errand, out to the ground, back in. Later, it became clear what had been happening: while the other City directors, staff, their guests, owner of Wolves Steve Morgan and his party were polishing off their profiteroles, Al Mubarak had been concluding another signing. Joleon Lescott, the easy-on-the-eye centre half from Everton, was added to the collection, for another £22m of Sheikh Mansour's money.

CHAPTER 6

GHOST TOWN

It was in July 1986, the records say, that unemployment in Margaret Thatcher's increasingly divided Britain finally peaked, at 3.09m. Whole populations of jobs in manufacturing had been waved away, coal mines aggressively sealed up, and the country's future pinned instead to the national plan of shopping on the credit card. Manchester suffered dreadfully, as did the other former industrial cities. Its inner neighbourhoods, particularly in the east, where the factories and engineering works had been since the nineteenth century, became scoured by all the dereliction.

The city began to make a name for itself with music forged in reaction to this gloom, first by The Smiths, Joy Division and spiky punks, later, at the 'Madchester', ecstasy end of the decade, by The Stone Roses, Happy Mondays and other twenty-four-hour party people. The Hacienda club, itself built into the void of a disused industrial warehouse, across from some empty railway arches and near Central Station, which had been an empty husk for years, attracted worldwide coverage. These few bands, one main record label called, with ironic evocation of history, Factory, and a nightclub which never made a profit, even began to be written up as the engine of an economic recovery, as if Manchester could reinvent itself from mass employment's muck and toil, with a bit of creativity and fashion.

The local voters in Manchester, living, for all the hype, in some of the most run-down and wretched urban districts in the country, always vote for a Labour council, and it took a strategic decision, after Thatcher won her third election in 1987, not to fight her government's strictures any longer. I interviewed Graham Stringer, then the leader of Manchester City Council, in 1996, and he reflected that they had lost their anti-cuts campaign against the government, and had to accept reality:

'There was a realisation that the world had changed, and that within this country, she [Margaret Thatcher] was Prime Minister, whether we liked it or not.'

Manchester's council, with Howard Bernstein as the chief executive, accepted 1987 as a watershed, and decided it was in Manchester's better interests to play the game by the rules set under Thatcher's Conservative government. Councils' money was still capped at an asphyxiating minimum for local people and services, and as the decade wore on, the schools 93 per cent of young people attended – not the private schools paid for by the wealthy parents of 7 per cent – had leaking roofs councils could not afford to repair and too few textbooks. The National Health Service sagged in dismal and outdated hospitals, and due to the financial squeeze, the waiting list for major operations stretched into years. In June 1985 the Conservative government abolished wage councils for people under 21, which meant there was no longer a decent minimum which employers in shops, restaurants and hotels had to pay their young staff.

Wages of £2 per hour (£80 for a forty-hour week, gross) would remain normal for millions of people right up to the end of the Conservatives' eighteen years in power, in 1997. A clear memory of that election was Michael Portillo, the right-wing former Conservative minister, defending in a radio phone-in his opposition to a minimum wage being introduced, to end the years of such poverty pay. One caller after another came on to say they were paid £2 and £3 per hour. Portillo defended that as a 'market economy' working well, until the presenter, Ed Stourton, asked him directly:

'Michael Portillo, would you cross the road for £2 an hour?'

Portillo was stuck for words, momentarily, before saying that having people earn such wages gave them a foot on the employment ladder, and the chance of promotion.

If you played football, had kids or walked a dog, you saw the neglect grip the nation's parks, and not just in Manchester. Parks, sport and leisure are still 'discretionary' services for councils to provide – they are not compulsory, like social care and education, so when cuts bite, savings are always made to the sport and leisure budget. Many councils outsourced maintenance of parks to private companies offering to do the minimum for the lowest price. Park-keepers, tending the places, a fixture in Broughton Park when I was growing up, became folk memories. Their buildings fell derelict, as did most of the changing rooms and public toilets provided for teams playing football. In Manchester the parks and playing fields, mostly endowed in the late Victorian years of philanthropy, improved in the 1930s and refurbished in the '50s, fell into disrepair, as the council cut the budget to maintain them. My club played in the Manchester Amateur Soccer League in the 1980s, in the same Premier Division as FC Astro, the team from Moss Side with all black players which went unbeaten for four championship-winning seasons and nurtured many fine footballers for semi-professional and professional ranks, including Gus Wilson, who captained Astro and played for Dario Gradi's Crewe Alexandra. At that top level in Manchester amateur football, we played at Hough End, south Manchester's main playing fields, whose pitches were appallingly drained, and whose changing block had barely been touched for thirty years.

Councils in the nation's cities, their central government funding cut by £3.7bn in ten years from £12.2bn in 1976, were also prevented from raising more than a set figure from the local rates, in order to preserve services. This was known as 'rate-capping', and led to a further squeeze on schools, social care, housing and other services. For the first time in my generation's experience, homelessness became a central feature of urban life, with people begging on the streets and sleeping in doorways and under bridges. Bound in this vice, councils had to bid – the provincial, depressed cities usually in competition with each other – for specific stand-alone funds, from the government or European Union, to finance special projects. Manchester decided that they would serve the city better if they sought to play the game well, and did not fight the cuts any more, a political battle they had found unwinnable. Graham Stringer, describing this process, acknowledged that the council had to 'jump through hoops' to prove its suitability to receive the pots of money available for prescribed regeneration projects. Bernstein, who had worked at the council since he was a sixteen-year-old in the planning department, proved himself highly adept at it, and Manchester got in earlier than the other suffering industrial cities. They became better at bidding and proving their case, and began to transform the grim Arndale Centre-dominated crumble of a city centre with the Metrolink tram system, an arena, GMex conference centre in the body of Central Station, the Bridgewater concert hall, Castlefield and other rejuvenations.

Manchester City, still a pallid shadow of their former selves after the Swales–Allison debacle, nevertheless managed to win promotion in 1985, stepping back up to the First Division with a gleeful 4–1 win against Charlton. I was at university in York, and dragged a group of non-City-supporting friends over to the match; we decided on impulse that morning to make the trip across. I think the lads, leaving our college bubble in the small, pristine old city with its Roman walls and minster, were quietly awed by Maine Road, full to 40,000, the crowd's brooding frustration at a journeyman team rumbling beneath the celebrations. That month United, with Bryan Robson, Norman Whiteside, Gordon Strachan, won their famous FA Cup against Everton with ten men, after Kevin Moran was sent off. In 1986, back in the First Division, we beat Liverpool 1–0 at Maine Road, but, home for Christmas, I remember it nevertheless as a grey, scrappy afternoon.

Some of the staunchest defenders of English football's new direction dismiss any objections to its insatiable modern commercialisation as misguided nostalgia for the 1980s. They point out the grimness of that time as if critics of the present, who lived and supported the game through it all, are unaware of them. The Premier League chief executive, Richard Scudamore, paid £1.6m in 2010, including a £1m bonus for securing the 2010–13 £3.5bn television deals, put his name to an article in the *Guardian* some years ago, opposing the Football Supporters Federation's call for more matches to be played at 3 p.m. on a Saturday. To this modest request, so that fans could plan and know when their games will be on, and enjoy football at the time established over 120 years of league competition, Scudamore immediately presented the spectre of racism, hooliganism and unsafe grounds in the 1980s. His argument seemed to run that fans complaining of commercial excesses in the Premier League era have only today's football, produced by the TV mega-deals which fuel it, or be transported to the 1980s failures which led ultimately to Hillsborough.

This is a patronising and offensive argument because the fans who supported football through the 1970s and 1980s are very aware – more so than the bosses in the boardrooms who pay Scudamore his bonuses – how dark and dangerous watching the game was too often back then. Yes, there were no pay-TV billions washing through football but fans died at Hillsborough because of negligence by the South Yorkshire Police and Sheffield Wednesday Football Club, whose ground was disgracefully unsafe. Nobody is nostalgic for grounds which were neglected by the clubs and their chairmen, and turned out in the middle of the decade, at Bradford City, yet still at its end too, at Hillsborough, to be deadly.

But there is nostalgia, which has never gone away, for what

was good about football before the age of mega money, however much the cleansed merits of the present day have been
extolled for twenty years now, since the breakaway to form
the Premier League. Football in the 1980s was still accessible,
cheap, so people of all classes and crowds of young people
could go. Even people struggling in a dire recession could
afford to be at first division football, part of an event mainstream and high-profile enough to be shown on BBC
television. You felt a part of your club, that it still belonged to
you, you were involved in your soul with its story, however
mismanaged it had been. The middle of the decade, 1985–86,
saw the lowest crowds in a season since the league expanded
to four divisions after the First World War, although the total
numbers turning up to support their clubs in the most dire
and hostile conditions was still 16.4m. There were still 100,000
at FA Cup finals, and 53,000, a full house, turned up to the
1989 FA Cup semi-final at Hillsborough, a ground unfit to
host them.

My favourite year for watching City turned out to be 1987–88,
when the club's lightweight, cut-price team was back down in
the Second Division. I had left university, where I had read a
lot of books and played a lot of football, with a degree in English Literature, resolved that I wanted to be a writer, but not
sure how to go about it. I came back to Manchester to try to
work it out, and ended up spending a year, in the age of Margaret Thatcher's yuppies, labouring in factories in Rochdale,
Oswaldtwistle (in a dyeing – and dying – mill), and, for a time,
working in a once-posh restaurant in central Manchester. The
manager was a belligerent young guy from Glasgow, who once

retorted to a customer complaining about the awful food: 'Well, at least you can fucking afford it.'

My dad was some kind of hero to the family of one of the sous-chefs, because his own dad had moved in circles in which my dad had been talked about in awed terms, as a brief who could get people off – or bail, at least. They were, in the kitchen, all City fans.

In that fuzzy and confused stew, waiting for grown-up life to break through, City was a rock, a freedom and a pleasure. It became what supporting a football club evolves into for many in adulthood: certainty. It was irrelevant that the football was Second Division; in fact we all quite enjoyed it. The captivating childhood thrill of going to the match, seeing the floodlit pitch shimmering green on a black Mancunian night, gave way to a more mature sense of belonging. Whatever miseries happened all week, there it was on a Saturday afternoon, the familiarity of a public home, the seat in the stand, the team in blue, the feeling of continuity from wide-eyed childhood, a sense of who you were and where you were from, and the great game of football itself, so simple, so endlessly absorbing.

When you look back on it, you can hardly believe now that paying, loyal football supporters were forced to watch matches in those conditions, from behind fences, treated like criminals. If you were too low down and in certain seats, you simply could not see the game because the railing across the top of the fence was in your eyeline, but that was never acknowledged as a problem by the directors, comfy in their best seats in the ground. My friends and I tried to avoid or ignore all the obstacles to enjoying football, the fences, the fighting, which was virulently thuggish but not as widespread as the media and government portrayed it. I picture us stepping over all the horseshit spattered around Maine Road, walking past the touts openly selling tickets stamped COMPLIMENTARY outside City's official ticket office, then rattling through the turnstiles to get to the game and see the pitch.

A large part of the enjoyment that season was because a core of City's kids, who had won the FA Youth Cup in 1986, were breaking through to the first team. Of course, we know now they were thrown in, too early for most of them, because the club was broke, Swales having blown the 1970s treasure on the Malcolm Allison indulgence. Back then, few were as aware as now that money dictated football success; the newspapers mostly did not report football clubs' accounts, and back then I had not yet learned how to read them or delved into investigating it all. But I think we were all aware there was a financial element to it, that City were reduced to signing Jim Tolmie, from Belgian club Lokeren for £30,000, and Mark Lillis, straining the chequebook at £130,000 from Huddersfield Town, because the money for top players was gone.

Yet nobody ever thought to call for some rich man to 'buy' the club and throw money in to rescue us, fairy godfather style. The whole crowd wanted Swales out, but that was because he had personally overseen the wrecking of the club, and so his position had been considered untenable ever since. There was a sense when the young players came through – Steve Redmond, Ian Brightwell, David White, Andy Hinchcliffe, Paul

Moulden and, most talented of all, Paul Lake, playing always with his head up, like the spirit of Colin Bell – that this was a grand old football club seeking to recover on its own resources. And that that was how you were supposed to do it. We had overspent, and we had to work our way back, with youth, and with the money when we had some. There was no windfall from a sugar daddy and it never occurred to anybody that that was a solution – no overseas billionaires were coming to rescue English football clubs when the game did really need the money.

City's boys came in, they worked very hard, they meant it, they were ours, they were admirable, and their endeavours were a treat to support. Even though, I have always felt, they suffered because they had to do too much too young. City fans, getting on for a decade after the shock of 1979, began to find the spirit to laugh in the face of misfortune. The first edition of *Blueprint*, a City fanzine, had a feature on the back: our worst ever team. Then fans began to take inflatable bananas to the match, a piece of silliness not only to lighten City's own depths, but that of football support itself. Following the Heysel disaster of 1985 and nasty outbreaks of hooliganism elsewhere, Margaret Thatcher's government was preparing to introduce an identity card scheme, which would apply, uniquely, only to football supporters. The fences were up around the grounds and policing was heavy. Kenneth Clarke, a trusty Thatcher minister, said of her later that she regarded football fans as an 'enemy within', the phrase of chilling hostility she held for the miners whose strike the government, helped by the police, had crushed.

City fans stood in that landscape, and waved at impending disaster with blown-up bananas. When you see the photographs of the game which secured promotion the following season, 1988–89, at Bradford City's Valley Parade, rebuilt after its appalling 1985 fire, the City fans are celebrating behind fences which look more appropriate to a borstal. The absence of fences in front of Bradford's tragically neglected wooden main stand had saved hundreds of lives from the fire which had still killed fifty-six people, yet here they were, with iron railings topped by fierce spikes, in front of a stand. In the picture of Trevor Morley – a major signing for City at the time, £300,000 from Northampton Town, a portent of financial recovery – celebrating his goal, City fans are poking their hands through those fortress railings, one of them clutching a banana.

Ian Brightwell holds an inflatable banana aloft, as Manchester City win promotion to the First-Division, at Bradford City, in 1989

It was around this time that 'Blue Moon', City's anthem for the era, first emerged mournfully from the heart of the Kippax.

> *Blue Moon,*
> *You saw me standing alone,*
> *Without a dream in my heart,*
> *Without a love of my own.*

A song for the support of Manchester City: loneliness, heart-break, broken dreams. The second verse of 'Blue Moon' goes like this:

> *And then there suddenly appeared before me,*
> *The only one my arms would ever hold*
> *And somebody said please adore me*
> *And when I looked, the moon had turned to gold.*

'Blue Moon', although you would not know from the Kippax repetitions, is a song of love, redemption, ultimately a golden moon. Yet City fans have never sung this part of the song, seeming unaware of the happy ending. Only blue moon (never gold), and 'City till I Die', the vow to stick with City in con-templation of nothing decent actually happening between now and death. City fans did wallow in some self-pity and grim humour in the late 1980s, but observers who believed they embraced failure, were happy to be some 'real Manchester' alter-native to United's success, misunderstood the club funda-mentally. There always was, underneath, profound resentment that the club has fallen so far from the excitement we had all grown up supporting, and a deep anger towards Swales, for ruining the club with the 1979 madness, and then staying on.

Recovering, working their way back with the group of young players and whichever signings we could afford – Swales was no owner piling in cash to transfuse a club's fortunes, but had become a habitual pennypincher in his trademark raincoat – City raised the spirits with committed performances, speaking of potential. I had a season ticket, my rock of permanence, friendship and escape from the puzzles of real life, huddling together with the enduring faithful at a gusty Maine Road. One Saturday in November I had too much to do, and was forced to miss it, the only home game of the season I could not make. City played Huddersfield Town and they won 10–1, still the record league victory in the club's history, while I was away doing something else. In the rain of early winter, all the young lads played, with David White, Paul Stewart – a surprisingly good signing from Blackpool, who actually improved while he was at City, an unusual phenomenon to watch – and Tony Adcock, an £80,000 lower-division centre forward bought from Colchester United, all sweeping in hat-tricks. Neil McNab, the scurrying midfield engineer of these difficult years, got on the scoresheet too. It was all on ITV, Huddersfield seeming to be almost literally absent for the second half, somehow disappearing, in their yellow and black checked away kit, like football chameleons into the green and brown of the Maine Road pitch.

These were signs of progress for a shredded football club, and that team which brightened the horizon reached the quarter-final of the FA Cup, in March 1988. We were drawn to play Liverpool, still the dominant power in English football. They had engaged in no mad self-inflicted collapse, instead continually regenerating their team, this time by introducing John Barnes, Peter Beardsley and John Aldridge to replace retiring Kenny Dalglish and Ian Rush, the incisive striker who had gone for an adventure to Juventus. Admiring our youngsters' efforts against Huddersfield, Blackpool and Plymouth, to then draw the strongest club in the country, with whom City had genuinely competed in the 1970s, was a perspective we didn't need.

It is my quintessential memory of football in the 1980s. The quarter-final was played on a Sunday afternoon, because the small chinks of comfort we were deriving amid the weakened state of City were to be pitilessly exposed by live television coverage, all terrestrial then, so guaranteeing a massive national audience. I played with my club in the morning at Hough End, a full Manchester winter having relieved itself on to the pitches, which became rectangular churns of mud, the only grass clinging on in narrow strips along the touchlines. It was the highest standard of Manchester amateur football but I never enjoyed it greatly. The pitches were awful and it was always windy; I used to wonder if Hough End had been strategically placed in a south Manchester wind tunnel. The football was unremittingly hard and rivalry between the clubs was unfriendly, with ever-present physical threats and intimidation. The beautiful game whose skills we had grown up seeking to perfect in parks and gardens ground down to a saga of mudbath battling, with strength and 'bottle' more important than any of the skills we had worked on. There was satisfaction in trying to perform well, though, especially against the stronger teams with excellent players who played semi-professionally on Saturdays, and we did serious training in midweek, long runs in the dark all over Prestwich, and endless sprint competitions between spaced-out lampposts, which kept us fit and fast.

However caked in mud we were, however many slide tackles delivered or received, nobody showered after a game at Hough End. Serving hundreds of amateur players, there were some showers, I think, coming out in a trickle in the concrete block in the midst of the old brute changing rooms, but nobody in the 1980s braved the cold walk outside on to the freezing floor itself covered in mud, for a wash we were never convinced would be warm or even work. We just used to put our jeans on over legs encased in drying, flakey mud, and leave our faces spattered with it, until we got home.

This time, our captain, a strong athlete who could command the ball with the outside of his left foot even on those squelching surfaces, was going to the match, so he offered to take the City fans straight there in his car. Then, on the way out of Hough End, he dropped his car keys and they washed away, down a drain. Eventually, after we stood under the grey sky and realised all our other options were exhausted, three of us set off, mud on our faces, on our backs and on our legs underneath our clothes, to walk the mile or two to Maine Road. When we reached the periphery of the ground, there was trouble and bad air between City and Liverpool fans, officious police on horses and all the usual obstacles to actually watching a game of football at the highest level in England at the time. We had tickets in the North Stand, the fences were still up, 44,047 were in the ground for the sort of game we had grown up experiencing as our true station in football. Stewart tried his muscular best up front, Lake stood out, there was the usual indignation that Liverpool had the referee's instinctive sympathies when he waved on John Barnes after a handball which looked blatant to us, but Barnes crossed for Ray Houghton to smack the ball into City's net. Beardsley scored with a penalty, then reality descended, as Liverpool, who would win the First Division nine points clear with commanding performances that year, dispatched City 4–0. They went on to lose the cup final, though, 1–0 to Wimbledon, an outcome I never saw as romance, but a victory for the thuggish interpretation of football, as perfected by Wimbledon's 'Crazy Gang', which we put up with as a dispiriting routine, out on the public badlands, every week.

Some mates we met in the North Stand gave us a lift home, and we sat in their car, quiet, the mud now starting to itch and irritate, taking in the lesson Liverpool had provided, about where the revival, with our bright young kids and Paul Stewart, had really taken City in the football pantheon.

After a year back in Manchester of brooding on the future leavened mostly by City, playing on a Sunday and the few friends still around at home, I caved in to the realisation I had to make some serious progress. Feeling under pressure from my dad and some tired sense that it was no use fighting it any more, I enrolled on a law course leading to qualifying as a solicitor. I never wanted to do it, but was pressed into accepting that somehow it was destined. The Law Society-registered course for people already with a degree was offered at only a handful of colleges, and the one which had a late place, by the time I got round to committing myself to doing it, was Wolverhampton Polytechnic. There, in a town I felt comfortable in because it was like north Manchester but with the odd nice cafe, with a good group of law students, many of them also somewhat reluctant, we learned some very useful basics. That in English law, property is sacred; how a company is formed; the principle that its owners limit their own personal liability for the debts the company takes on, only to the value of the shares they have bought. How to read company accounts, how much money a company makes (its turnover), its debts, how to see whether it made a profit or loss, how much its highest-paid director got. And the fact that for a person to be convicted of a criminal offence, it had to be proved he intended to commit the crime. All of these building blocks were taught by nice, personable lecturers in an overcrowded classroom opposite the Molineux main stand. Wolves, at the time, had two sides of their historic ground condemned in their own 1980s collapse, but they had Steve Bull at centre forward and were thundering their way back up from the Fourth Division. When you went to a game, standing in the home end behind the goal, you could feel the depth of tradition in the support, that it was a proper big club, really.

So I was in the Black Country anyway when City fans made their legendary journey to the midweek away match at West Bromwich Albion; I just got the bus there with a mate off the course I dragged along. He was bewildered when we got in there, the festival of inflatables: bananas, hammers, dinosaurs, crocodiles, anything the fans had managed to nick from their kids. Somebody had brought a small paddling pool, and when another fan threw a dolphin inside it, everybody cheered. Then the song went up:

'Paddling pool, paddling pool, paddling pool.'

City lost, 1–0.

On 15 April 1989 I was staying with my mum at her flat in Manchester, back for the weekend to see friends and play Sunday football, when the news came on the radio that people were dying at the FA Cup semi-final between Liverpool and Nottingham Forest at Hillsborough. I felt that dread in the stomach football fans have spoken of since, that we all instinctively knew it could have been us, that we immediately understood the conditions in which we had been watching football, defiantly enjoying it, wedded to the game, were a disaster waiting to happen.

Since then, as a journalist, I have written for years about the grief and dignity of the bereaved families of the ninety-six supporters who died, and about their enduring campaign for those responsible to be held to account and for the real truth about the disaster to be accepted. I have investigated the extent of the South Yorkshire Police operation, which followed the disaster, labelled a cover-up by the families, seeking to evade culpability for their own fatal mismanagement, and lay the blame on the Liverpool supporters. How Sheffield Wednesday's Hillsborough ground was deficient in safety in crucial respects, which led directly to more deaths. How the fences at the front of that vile Leppings Lane terrace with its 'pens', erected by football to separate itself from its own supporters, ended up finally killing so many of them. How the Football Association had commissioned Hillsborough as the venue for its semi-final without ever asking a single question about safety. Not even if Sheffield Wednesday had an up-to-date safety certificate which, as it turned out with shameful and disastrous consequences, it did not. The FA's request for Sheffield Wednesday to host the FA Cup semi-final inquired only about how many free tickets its dignitaries (eager committee men, including Peter Swales, who became chairman of the FA's international committee) could have, and how the money from the match would be divvied up. I have explored and written about how Hillsborough became the watershed for English football, how the professional clubs, given grants of public money to help rebuild grounds into all-seater stadiums, then raised ticket prices hugely, in contravention of the Taylor Report into the disaster. How the top clubs and their shareholder 'owners' then proceeded to make fortunes for themselves from football's commercial revival, while the grief-stricken families were left betrayed by the legal processes, fighting for justice.

Yet one small observation I have never recorded. Over the years I have watched a lot of film of what happened on the day, including footage taken by the police, who still somehow failed to recognise the lethal overcrowding, which was obvious to the naked eye of those watching helpless from the other sides of Hillsborough. In among the crowd on the day an FA Cup semi-final ended in death and disaster, you can see a small bunch of inflatable bananas. There they were, brought along by high-spirited Liverpool fans, waving the idea that football was rightfully a people's carnival, while drowning in the Leppings Lane end, at the funeral of English football's bleakest decade.

CHAPTER 7

RICHER THAN GOD

Sheikh Mansour's men said come to Abu Dhabi at the end of August 2009; the weather would still be smotheringly hot, with 100 per cent humidity, it was Ramadan, but there would be plenty happening, to give an illuminating insight into how the country was developing. I could come and seek to understand Abu Dhabi and how buying Manchester City fitted in, interview Khaldoon Al Mubarak in his own country, perhaps even see Mansour himself. In Britain our economy, whose supposed regeneration in the thirty years since industry's collapse had been based on the financial miscalculations of the City of London and massive personal borrowing, had imploded a year earlier. The banks, including some of our great and historic institutions, abused the faith and reverence invested in them, and failed to use their freedom to support company innovation or research and development. Instead, they had turned inward. Looking for new areas from which to reap corporate fees and personal bonuses, the banks in America had begun lending money to poor people in their own country, for mortgages to buy houses they could not afford to repay. In England, time had been called on the party six months earlier, in

September 2007, with the insolvency of Northern Rock, the one-time building society which stood for solid saving and steady mortgages. It had been floated as a bank on the Stock Market during the craze for 'demutualising', sunk itself eagerly into novel US mortgage markets, and left its reserves nakedly short. The very English image of middle-aged people forming orderly queues to withdraw all their savings from Northern Rock prompted the government to realise it had to nationalise the bank, at a cost to the public purse of £25bn.

America's economy was sinking, Greece, Portugal and Ireland (hailed in the 1990s as an economic miracle country from which Britain should learn low-tax lessons) would have to be financially bailed out, and the euro would require constantly applied adhesive to keep it together. In Britain, the Conservative–Liberal Democrat coalition, elected in 2010, would declare its determination to cut the 'structural deficit' of government debt within four years, which they would do by raising only 22 per cent of the extra money from taxes on companies and the rich. The remaining 78 per cent would come from cutting back on public spending, by £83bn, the greatest slashing ever to be undertaken by any government. The money for schools, hospitals, social care and all other public provision would be savaged. Labour in its time had tried to promote investment in industry through regional bodies such as, for Manchester and Liverpool, the Northwest Development Agency, and the coalition scrapped those within weeks of taking office. From the public services, 710,000 people doing an honest job would be put out of work. Councils across Britain in 2010 would say they could no longer afford to keep libraries open. By November

2011, unemployment would be around 3 million again, a heart-sinking repeat of the 1980s, with adults who had worked all their lives signing on for jobseeker's allowance 'benefit' of £67.50 for a week. The fear of 'a lost generation', who might never know what it is to work and lead a productive life, was being voiced by those who cared.

In Abu Dhabi they literally have more money than they know what to do with. Al Mubarak and Sheikh Mansour and his other ruling brothers have set up 'wealth funds' and huge investment companies whose job it is to find somewhere to sensibly invest the riches relentlessly gushing into their hands. The statistics pile up to attest to the country's riches, real money, for the most powerful of commodities, oil. Abu Dhabi has 10 per cent of the world's known crude oil reserves, and therefore accounts for much of the UAE's $247bn Gross Domestic Product in 2010. That works out at $50,000 each per head of the 5 million population, but its distribution is fiercely unequal – just 1 million, 19 per cent of the UAE's population, holding the vast bulk of the wealth, are emiratis, and 440,000 of them are in Abu Dhabi. Of the other 81 per cent, made up of expatriates doing much of the work, 50 per cent are estimated by census to be migrant workers from south Asia, who are paid a relative pittance. In October 2008, when Barclays Bank was also wobbling on the edge of needing a government bailout, Sheikh Mansour helped to save it by investing £2bn in the bank for an 11 per cent stake. Just seven months later he sold that stake, making a £1.5bn profit. In October 2010 he made a further £750m selling financial instruments he had also bought as part of the deal.

Al Mubarak's Executive Affairs Authority had suggested that to get a feel for Abu Dhabi, and its capital city of the same name, it might be handy to view it all from a helicopter. Just walking from the hotel lobby to the little aircraft waiting in the gardens, my clothes and head were drenched in sweat. As you leave the universal air-conditioning in the buildings, the humidity hits like a broiling wall. In England, if you wear glasses, as I do, they steam up when you come inside a building from the cold. In Abu Dhabi, when you go outside in August, your glasses steam up. Almost nobody was out on the streets at any time of day. They were all in their new air-conditioned cars, mostly white with many 4X4s. They drive up to air-conditioned tower blocks, or shopping malls, then back in their cars and home to air-conditioned houses or apartments in towers. Almost the only people you see in the streets are the migrant workers, from Bangladesh, India and Pakistan, whose poverty pay and habitually abject employment conditions, while building the United Arab Emirates' palaces in the sky, have been the UAE's chief source of international criticism.

It was the first and still only time I have ever been in a helicopter. It was exciting, but I am not the bravest for heights, and being so high in so small a conveyance feels perilously unprotected, like dangling above buildings in a Renault 5. Yet as we travelled up and over the glittering towers of Abu Dhabi, the desert sun glinting off the turquoise waters of the Arabian Gulf, the corniche beach a strip of white sand below, I began to gaze and take it all in.

It is hard to get your bearings because Abu Dhabi, being so new, has been laid out to a plan, rather than grown and sprawled from a recognisable centre, like European cities. You would be told a certain area, the Al Markaziyah, was the closest you could get to downtown, then when you got there, nobody except a few Bengalis in green overalls would be on the streets, sweeping or building.

The country takes its name from the wildlife found according to lore on the island – Abu Dhabi: father of the gazelle. The Al Nahyan family were Bedouin who have ruled the country since the eighteenth century, securing their power through war and hunting. The main source of trade for centuries in Abu Dhabi came from diving for pearls in the gulf. The area had strategic importance because of where it is geographically and in 1897, although the British never conquered Abu Dhabi and its neighbouring states and pocketed them for its empire, they became British protectorates, under the arm, and arms, of Britain. After the truce between Abu Dhabi, Dubai, Sharjah and its neighbours Britain defined them as the Trucial States, by which they were known until 1971, when Britain withdrew. Sheikh Zayed bin Sultan Al Nahyan, Mansour's father, is generally revered in the country and recognised outside it as a statesman who saw, during a thirty-eight-year reign, how these emirates could strategically organise their fortunes and flourish peaceably together. Under his leadership and with the diplomatic encouragement of the British, the seven Trucial States formed the alliance, the United Arab Emirates, which has survived ever since, of which Abu Dhabi is the dominant state both financially and politically.

Perhaps the most astounding fact about Abu Dhabi does not nestle in the glass thicket of skyscraping wealth you can see below you on a brilliant day from a helicopter, but in understanding how recently it has all been built, since the oil. The first oil-drilling concession in Abu Dhabi was granted to the British-backed Iraqi Petroleum Company (later absorbed into BP) in 1939, but it was a small-scale agreement, and the Second World War then interrupted development. It was as late as 1958 when the huge reserves were discovered in the sea off Abu Dhabi, and four years later that exports began. Until then, Abu Dhabi really was a desert land, with just a few scratchy settlements around its oases, barely any solid buildings, Bedouin scraping an existence in the elemental harshness of the heat and sand. It was only in 1961, the year the maximum wage for professional footballers was finally abolished in England, that the first paved road was constructed. The country was then accelerated into the fastest of lanes, bypassing a thousand years of the gradual, painful development which had ground through the gears of Europe. There was no agrarian revolution, no industrial revolution, and there has never been a political revolution; the Al Nahyan dynasty is still in charge. There was no building the country and society up, from desert to skyscraper, step by step, decade by decade, as it was in Europe, wrestling with social tumult throughout. Abu Dhabi rocketed from being a desert state, its people engaged in farming, travelling by camel and hunting with falcons, to unspendable riches and watching Premier League football on plasma screens in luxury hotels and skyscrapers, in the time it has taken to get oil out of the seabed.

Sheikh Zayed is credited as a visionary not only for his inter-emirate diplomacy, but also for his internal leadership of Abu

Dhabi, shaping the country's stable and peaceful enjoyment of its new wealth. His brother, Sheikh Shakhbut, lacked such sophistication, and under his rule from 1928, after the money flowed in, it did so unequally to the Al Nahyans. There was too little general development, in education, health or infrastructure, and the country stagnated, with too few of the great benefits shared among the general population. In 1966, the year Joe Mercer and Malcolm Allison took Manchester City back to the First Division, Zayed, whom the British had identified as a shrewd and promising politician, took power in Abu Dhabi via a bloodless coup. Shakhbut, who had reportedly become eccentric and reclusive, was escorted without violence from the country, never to return.

In 1971, when the seven states came together to form the UAE, it had just 180,000 inhabitants, who were largely Bedouin and living in tribes. Sheikh Zayed had no intention of introducing democracy, nor of widening power beyond his family – democracy was 'transitory and incomplete, engendering dissent and confrontation', he is quoted as having said – but he saw there was no peaceable stability to be had if he and his family were seen to be oppressive rulers. A key element of his regime was to dispense some of the wealth to the population – the emiratis – and to invest the profits from oil in hospitals, schools and dedicated planning of housing, roads, water, sewerage and utilities.

Abu Dhabi itself has been developed to a plan, the multimillions paying for the city to be transformed from huts and tents to towers and malls with no intervening phases of development, but the idea was that it should become an amenable place to live. The emiratis bought in from abroad both the professional expertise, Europeans and Americans who lapped up fat wages tax free, and, less admirably, the cheap labour from Asia to actually do the sweaty graft. Throughout the economic development, Zayed's propounded philosophy was to marry Abu Dhabi's new fortunes to a foundation of the country's traditional way of life and values. He promoted Islam as 'a civilising, humanitarian religion that gives mankind dignity', and although the men have several wives, and the religious rules are enforced, Abu Dhabi's sunni version of Islam, with women encouraged to play more of a role in public life, is considered liberal compared to the harsh regimes in force elsewhere in the Middle East.

'Those who forget their past, compromise their future,' Sheikh Zayed is celebrated for saying. You could read those wise words a few ways: as an injunction to a country to retain traditional religious values while careering into the modern world, to be aware of its precarious existence in the shadow of Iran, Saudi Arabia and other large and volatile neighbours – or as a justification for his own family remaining in charge, as they always have, and banking all the money. When he died in November 2004, aged 86, he was praised as a progressive, western-friendly Arab leader, and succeeded by Sheikh Khalifa, the most senior of his nineteen sons.

The deluge of riches changed life in Abu Dhabi from one which for hundreds of years had been about scraping subsistence, pearling and fishing half the year, farming in oases the other half, to seven-star air-conditioned luxury. They became immediately used to achieving whatever it was they wished to build or do, because of the extraordinary money at their disposal. Yet Zayed and his advisers envisaged from the beginning that oil, whose reserves are estimated to have 100 years left in them, will run out eventually. His stated policy was to invest the money in creating the foundations of an economy which will survive after that. To put it bluntly, when all the oil has been spent, they do not intend to return to the tents.

'Plan Abu Dhabi', a strategic vision for the country and city to 2030, summarises:

'Abu Dhabi is blessed by a rare abundance of fossil fuels. However, this finite resource will not create a windfall of wealth in perpetuity. The city needs to find new ventures and diversification for economic development.'

Another doorstep of a document, 'The Abu Dhabi Economic Vision 2030', seeks to flesh out how the country can build a convincing economy, diversified beyond oil which, at the current production rate of 250m barrels a day, constitutes 60 per cent of all the enormous wealth. In all other areas, the document says, Abu Dhabi is running a 'deep' trade deficit, importing $21bn more than it exports. Their over-reliance on oil also means, the document states, that they are vulnerable to the fluctuations in oil price, which can drop, sending the whole country's income suddenly plummeting.

'It is essential that Abu Dhabi creates a more sustainable pattern of growth,' the vision says, 'in which it can guarantee healthy economic development over extended periods of time, capable of softening the impact of external factors such as the oil price and other exogenous shocks.'

The document envisages eleven new industries to be developed if the economy can be broadened beyond reliance on oil wealth, including manufacturing, petrochemicals, aviation, transport and tourism. This is, then, a very genuine challenge, to find ways to spend the oil windfalls, which will build the country a foundation it has never had even while becoming super-rich. That is, in essence, the national project, as drawn up by the strategic arm of the ruling family's government. Manchester City is absorbed into that strategy, as an advert for the country, with Al Mubarak arguing the £1bn spent so far will eventually transform it into a sustainable 'business'.

At the back of this document Khaldoon Al Mubarak, chair of the EAA, is the fourth name acknowledged as an author. Simon Pearce, director of strategic communications for the EAA, listed down near the bottom among the expat professionals, is another Manchester City director who has had a hand in directing Abu Dhabi's planned future. The Crown Prince, Sheikh Mohammed bin Zayed Al Nahyan, has his name at the top. He heads the EAA, so it is to him, in all the areas they cover, including the strategic policy and communications work for the country's planned future, that Al Mubarak and Pearce report. These are the day jobs, and primary responsibility, for the people in charge of Manchester City.

The helicopter swung in the sunshine over the rearing glass and steel towers, then over Zayed Sports City and the main Abu Dhabi football stadium, to patches of desert marked out for new building, the migrant workers' dormitories sitting in the dust on the edges. Beyond was what they wanted me to see: Yass Island, where a completely new Formula One racetrack was nearing completion, in time for the first-ever Abu Dhabi Grand

Prix in November 2009, and a Ferrari visitor attraction next door. Overseeing this whole project, from the negotiations with Formula One boss Bernie Ecclestone to expand his racing circus here and build from sand the racetrack 'branded' with Abu Dhabi for the global TV audience, was Khaldoon Al Mubarak, another small task on his to-do list.

Hosting a grand prix, a punishingly expensive thrust of the economic 'vision' for Abu Dhabi, is one of the sporting and cultural projects, in which Manchester City is now also central, aimed at attracting visitors to Abu Dhabi, and presenting the country on the international stage, in association with world class events and excellence. The Yass circuit, built to host one race a year, is not even the most extravagant venture Abu Dhabi has launched to associate itself with high-quality culture and promote itself for tourism. From the helicopter, you could see the wide boundaries and early foundations of Jazeera al-Saadiyat – 'Happiness Island' – on which the Abu Dhabi government was said to be spending up to $27bn. It has paid for agreements with the Guggenheim museum, Louvre art gallery and New York University to open branches there, in Abu Dhabi on Saadiyat Island. The plans also include museums dedicated to Abu Dhabi's heritage and Sheikh Zayed, a maritime museum and arts centre, two golf courses and a marina. For such art and cultural holidays in the desert sun, the project envisages so many visitors will come that it has commissioned 29 hotels.

In 2009 Abu Dhabi also hosted the FIFA Club World Cup, the competition in which the champion club of Europe plays the equivalent champions from South America and the other

Fifa confederations. It is a competition which has never claimed great European attention or prestige but Abu Dhabi still considered it an important enough vehicle for building the country a welcoming, modern, successful image through the most captivating of vehicles: football. Chuck Blazer, the grossly overweight Fifa baron from New York, was, at the time I was there, wheeling around the marble acreage of the Emirates Palace Hotel, in town to inspect progress.

In the evening I went up to Zayed Sports City, the complex named after Sheikh Mansour's father, the first ruler of the modern nation. The stadium, Abu Dhabi's biggest, expanded to 42,000 to host the Club World Cup, is named the Mohammed Bin Zayed Stadium, after the Crown Prince, who is second in command to the son who succeeded Zayed to become the current ruler, Sheikh Khalifa. It is home to Al Jazira, the football club which Sheikh Mansour took over in 2000. He did a mini-City with it, pouring several millions in, so the club could attract noted overseas players with wages 10–15 per cent more than they could earn in Europe, and tax-free. That night the club was unveiling the latest signing: the Brazilian Ricardo Oliveira, who formerly played for AC Milan, had arrived from Real Betis to accept the sheikh's pay cheque. Up around the stadium were astroturf pitches, all occupied with energetic floodlit matches, testifying to the enthusiasm for football in the former British protectorate. Inside the stadium, in a conference room were 400 or so supporters, all young emirati men, hailing the new Brazilian. Sheikh Mansour appears to have enjoyed the experience of buying and funding a football club to success and so with Manchester City, when it arrived available and urgently for sale, he decided to try such a project on a grander football stage.

Back at my hotel that night, I met an American who had worked in Abu Dhabi for many years and seen the country develop. We got chatting and I asked what is probably a dumb question. In sight of the car park, surrounded by new, all-white cars, sitting patiently in the humidity, I was trying to make conversation, and there are also only so many ways you can talk about quite how much money is gushing around in Abu Dhabi. Dubai did suffer an economic collapse; it is the largest emirate with Abu Dhabi, and its ruling Al Maktoum dynasty is reported to have a traditional rivalry with the Al Nahyans. One of Sheikh Mansour's two wives is Sheikha Manal, the daughter of Dubai's ruler, Sheikh Mohammed bin Rashid Al Maktoum, interpreted by some as a marriage which aids diplomacy between the two ruling families. Dubai has no substantial oil reserves, and its boom based on property development did crash with proper financial casualties. In December 2009 there were serious doubts about whether Dubai could pay its debts, loans went in from the UAE central bank and Abu Dhabi-based banks, then Abu Dhabi itself lent its neighbouring emirate $10bn to help keep it solvent. So that suggests it was a bit silly to wonder, in a tired late-night conversation, whether Abu Dhabi had been affected by the recession.

He did not pause to think about his answer. 'My friend,' he said, 'we're richer than God.'

The principal criticism levelled against Abu Dhabi during its period of breakneck development has not been the lack of democracy or its religious strictures. There is an architecture of army and secret police, but Sheikh Zayed's distribution of money and housing, enabling the emirati population to live well and comfortably, has kept them largely content, although there are outbreaks of dissent, harshly repressed. The chief focus of attention has been on the treatment of the migrant workers whose labour has built the palaces, apartments and malls of the new Abu Dhabi. In 2006 the organisation Human Rights Watch produced a report, *Building Towers, Cheating Workers*, which found gross abuses of migrant workers in the UAE, including poverty wages, dreadful accommodation and effectively forced-labour conditions, with workers' passports confiscated from them upon arrival.

In 2009 the organisation produced a report specifically on the massive Saadiyat Island project in Abu Dhabi. Human Rights Watch spoke to eighty-five migrant construction workers, four security guards and five cleaning or kitchen staff among the thousands of men drawn to work there from India, Pakistan, Bangladesh, Sri Lanka, Nepal and Thailand. A further twenty-one foreign workers were interviewed where they lived in Abu Dhabi, in what were described as labour camps. It found that some progress had been made since 2006, with attempts to improve the overcrowded housing conditions, particularly on Saadiyat Island itself, and mandatory health insurance for all workers, a major civilising advance. Construction companies have to state that they do not engage in forced labour, although the report said that 'abuses continue'. Chief among the sources of oppression was that the workers had often been cheated in their home countries into paying a very expensive 'recruiting fee' for the opportunity to work in the UAE, of up to $4,100, an impossible amount for which some people had sold homes or borrowed at high interest from money-lenders. Then when they arrived, they told Human Rights Watch, the wages they received were lower than they had been promised, so they toiled all day in the heat only to dig themselves deeper into debt. The UAE's 'sponsor' system for foreign workers tied them to one company, a practice which, the workers said, was 'universal' on Saadiyat Island, and companies often confiscated their passports. Trying to organise into a union to fight collectively for better conditions, or going on strike, were not protected by law, and those who attempted to do so 'continue to face detention [in prison] and deportation', the report said.

In 2005 Abu Dhabi's government had introduced 'the most concrete reform', banning work during the heat of the day – between 12:30 p.m. and 4:30 p.m. – in July and August. However, after complaints from the construction companies themselves, the report said, that break was reduced to between 12:30 and 3 p.m. The workers, alone and far from their families, found themselves working up to twelve hours a day, 'often in extreme conditions of heat and humidity with temperatures often exceeding 100 degrees Fahrenheit (38 degrees Celsius)'.

The 'main complaint of migrant construction workers in Abu Dhabi', quite simply, 'was that they are paid low wages.' The men interviewed for the report 'received an average daily salary of around $8 a day, for 10 paid hours including overtime. Their estimated average yearly salary was $2,575. Some had received pay rises, 'usually around $5.45 per month', but this was less than the rate of inflation, including the price of rice, which had doubled in the year.

Human Rights watch found that in 1980, a federal law had required the UAE government to implement a minimum wage and cost-of-living index.

'Nearly three decades later,' it said, 'the government still has not done so.'

In a direct challenge to the self-image of the country and its marketing, Human Rights Watch took as the title of its report the name of this prestige project, calling it simply: *Happiness Island*.

I had been told that after sunset, when the dawn-to-dusk fast of Ramadan ended, migrant workers could come to the city's Grand Mosque, and be given food free for the breaking of the fast, iftar. Named after Sheikh Zayed, the Grand Mosque is an enormous temple of no-expense-spared wonder in marble, gold, ceramics, of 82 domes, 1,000 columns, a vast, hushed main prayer hall, lit by the world's largest chandelier. It was built by 3,000 workers at a reported cost of $545m. When I went down there, there were huge crowds of men taking advantage of the charity. Eleven vast marquees were set up, and inside men were sitting cross-legged on the floor. You could count 100 in a long line on one row, and there were eight rows in a tent – almost 9,000 workers eating with their hands from white boxes of goodies bearing the donor's name in blue: Armed Forces Officers Club and Hotel.

The men were friendly, welcoming and in decent shape. None of those I spoke to were construction workers on the big sites; they were drivers and shopworkers. Rijo Jakob, who said he was 34, from Kerala in India and working in Abu Dhabi as a limousine driver, showed me his meal: there were dates, salad, yoghurt, water, fruit, and a generous lump of meat on rice. It was, he smiled, camel biryani. The people I spoke to said they missed their families, but the wages were better than they could earn back home. Abdul Gafoor, 24, also a driver, said that on his salary, 2,000 Abu Dhabi dirhams a month (£349), he could not afford to eat such nice food if he had to buy it. The labourers, he said, make 600 dirhams a month, work outside in the heat and have poor accommodation:

'It is very, very difficult for them,' he said.

Umar Farooq, a shopworker, 32, also from India, said he missed being away eleven months of the year from his five-year-old daughter and son of eighteen months. He said he was living in lodgings shared with eight people in his room.

'It is very difficult,' he said. 'People are there from different cultures – I go there just to sleep and eat. Low-salary people come here for iftar; high-salary people, they can have iftar at home.'

Walking with his colleague in the hot evening up to the mosque to pray, to add his sandals to the massive pile left outside, he said: 'The money we earn here is very low. But it is good, compared to India.'

I did not come close to meeting Sheikh Mansour; I never have, and neither has any journalist from Britain. We know little of him and his family, really, who live as remote royals like our own. We know him now through these few public acts, most prominently his decision to buy Manchester City and spend whatever relatively small portion of the vast, inherited

Al Nahyan riches he needs to on enticing and paying the right players to buy it success. How we think of him depends to some extent on what we think of the project itself, whether a vanity exercise, vulgar and contrary to football's evolved traditions, from a young prince with too much money, or benevolence for which the City fans' banner justly thanks him.

Khaldoon Al Mubarak invited me to see him at his home, which struck me as very open and accommodating. It was so great a contrast it was almost funny, with the five minutes I'd had to fight for in my first interview with a Manchester City chairman, Francis Lee, 15 years before in the office of the old inner sanctum at Maine Road. It was more than remarkable, to think of the way Manchester City and English football have changed, as I walked down a dark, quiet Abu Dhabi residential street, in the humid night of the Arabian gulf, to see the chairman of Manchester City. Inside, the same crowd of men who had been with Khaldoon in the chairman's lounge at the City of Manchester Stadium were round his house, having a laugh and watching TV.

At Al Mubarak's, the scene reminded me of houses at home, in north Manchester, with a crowd of blokes sitting around a comfy leather couch, watching a decent telly, with football the great escape from work, family and the rigours of religion. It struck me again as it had throughout the visit, how similar the Arabs and Jews are culturally, in their manner and their religions. And in Abu Dhabi, they really, genuinely, do like football. I had seen the basic bars in the city where men in traditional dress, reclining on the floor, drinking fruit juices – no alcohol – smoking scented tobacco from shisha pipes, were watching live European football on big screens. Here as elsewhere all around the world when Britain had its empire and protectorates, the first football clubs were formed by the British expatriates, wanting to play their games of home in far-flung territories, then taken up enthusiastically by the locals. Al Mubarak himself said he grew up playing the game, and had been a fan for twenty years; they had all watched the Italian league, for preference, for years, but over the previous five years, he said, the English Premier League had 'taken off'.

We went to a sitting room to talk, over glasses of water. He had been on his exercise bike, and sat in his shorts and T-shirt. We discussed football, how City had dropped into his portfolio, but as at the Lowry Hotel in Manchester, he became most animated when talking about his country. He sees it as a civilised oasis in the troubled Middle East. He believes the culture, accepting of foreigners, less oppressive to women, western-friendly, is a role model for other Arab countries.

'People have a negative perception of the Arab world and Islam; a lot of problems have been created by poor education, poor governance, social issues which were not handled well,' he said, of the countries with much greater populations, where ruling elites hoarded the money, leaving the people poor, resentful and prone to revolutionary Islamism.

'The UAE has gone on to address the social issues, to reform education and health. Abu Dhabi is trying to set a good precedent for the whole Arab world, economically, socially and politically.'

Of their own scandal, the poverty and exploitation of the workers who have done the hard work for a country of billionaire sheikhs, Al Mubarak promised that reforms, and enforcement of the law, will come. He pointed to the health insurance reform, saying he believed that pointed the way towards decent treatment for workers; he had 'tremendous respect' for their sacrifices and discipline, he said.

'Mistakes have been made, and that is part of the evolution of the country,' he asserted.

He described himself as 'very confident' that the plans set out in Abu Dhabi's economic vision, in whose development he had been integral, would secure a solid future for the country. I said I could see it in transport, given the geographical position of Abu Dhabi, and if they could use the oil money to develop manufacturing, but I was struggling to believe it could attract mass tourism when you cannot change the weather. Surely, I asked him, spending so hugely on a racetrack for one grand prix a year could not be classed as sustainable, nor the massive expense on Louvres and Guggenheims too few western tourists may be tempted to visit.

'A sign of our confidence is that we have stuck with the plan even through the economic crisis,' he replied. 'All of it, the international museums, the racetrack, the universities – New York and the Sorbonne – it is all part of a long-term plan we are very confident in.'

He talked about the hectic intrusion of football into his working life, the flying visits to Manchester, the need to fix the place, spending £200m of Mansour's money on buying footballers for City. Dealing with agents he found 'very annoying', as they 'popped up' demanding 'huge fees', then more would appear halfway through a deal saying they had a stake in the deal too. Far from overpaying for the one (Robinho) then four then seven players they had signed in a year, he asserted:

'The market conditions worked to our advantage. The clubs have their own financial difficulties, so it was a buyer's market and we got good value.'

He said he had been shocked at how threadbare the internal organisation of City had been, repeating that there was no human resources department, no chief finance officer.

'One of the big surprises was how amateurish it was,' he said of City. 'I'll be frank, I expected it to be more structured and developed from a business and corporate perspective.

'I found it shocking in the famous Premier League, to be without such basic functions.'

From a country whose steps into the future, and important deals, are controlled and planned with corporate thoroughness, it is clear that the City deal was not. Pairoj Piempongsant, Thaksin Shinawatra's fixer, with the English dealmaker Amanda Staveley, who had contacts in Dubai through horseracing, had presented a knackered club to Al Fahim. He had taken Manchester City to Sheikh Mansour who, watching Premier League football like the other men in Abu Dhabi, knew it was one of the big clubs. A small infusion of his money had taken Al-Jazira to the top of football in the UAE, and he instinctively fancied the same adventure with another club, but in football's most glittering arena, Europe. No rules were in force at the Premier League to bar him from doing so, however much anybody complains or is turned off. He had watched the other English clubs, Manchester United, Liverpool, Chelsea, Arsenal, bought by owners from overseas, who also had no previous connections to the clubs. He was shown City's potential, the loyal crowd, the new stadium, although he would not have known the remarkably generous circumstances in which it was built, by Manchester City Council, for the club. He would be able to move straight to assembling a fantasy football team – buy Robinho straight away – not spend years building a new stadium, as any buyer of Everton or Tottenham Hotspur would have to do.

Sheikh Mansour fancied buying Manchester City, so he did. Al Mubarak stressed again, as they are always at pains to, it was Sheikh Mansour's own purchase, not one carried out by the government. Mansour used that portion of the Al Nahyan billions each member of the ruling family gets to call his own.

'It was a private equity deal by Sheikh Mansour,' he repeated.

Al Mubarak, and his sophisticated corporate and communications culture, was only called to become involved three days later. That was after Sulaiman Al Fahim, bragging to the world about Abu Dhabi United, was trampling the understated, respectful image Abu Dhabi has spent decades cultivating, even as oil transformed its ruling clan from Bedouin herdsmen to masters of the universe.

CHAPTER 8

SWALES OUT

Peter Swales, the Manchester City chairman with the famous combover hairdo and raincoat, who made his money in rented tellies, was finally gouged out of the club, at the onset of spring 1994. He had managed to cling on for 15 years after his recall of Malcolm Allison had crumpled the club into the misguided miseries of the 1980s. So there was a bitter symmetry in the way his end came, with an act of needless self-destruction, focused on the crucial position of manager for which, in all his time, he could never settle on anybody for long. But there was an unfortunate symmetry, too, about the way the fans turned for salvation by reaching back themselves to another hero from the golden years. Blond, cherubic Francis Lee, embodiment of those happy days before Swales turned the 1980s bleak, was going to lift us up where we belonged, back to the sky-blue joys of childhood.

Yet it had all been going surprisingly well. There had been an unfamiliar few years, a respite approaching normality, during which City had made appreciable progress, the young lads added to with more solid players the club could gradually afford. In 1992 City became founder members of the Premier League – formed by the twenty-two First Division clubs in 1992, all the

143

fuss and protests from the Football League a puzzle, because it looked the same as the First Division, with the same number of clubs, three, to be relegated to and promoted from the division below. City's team was robust, the club stable, unnervingly so. The prime source of fans' discontent was the blunt way a strong team played, more muscle than the dash of adventure which City fans always liked. I think we were also unsettled by the absence of anything tangible to be unsettled about. City worked their way back from the depths of penury with the loyal support of a grumpy, unforgiving crowd, and had stayed in the top division since 1989. The team was strengthened gradually, worked its way back steadily – with one freakish interruption: the day the kids, in their first season back, beat Alex Ferguson's expensive, stellar Manchester United 5–1.

True to my City supporting life, I was away, abroad, at a cousin's wedding. I heard the result on the World Service, utterly disbelieving. Then the highlights were on some channel that night, in which the honest triers who had won promotion delivered a magically enhanced version of themselves; as if Steve Redmond would always carry the ball authoritatively out of defence in the First Division, David White customarily cross perfectly first time, and Andy Hinchcliffe was forever sprinting with unerring timing into the penalty area to head a compelling fifth goal past United. As if this City team was born to have Bryan Robson, £1.7m new signing Paul Ince, Mark Hughes, the £2.3m Gary Pallister and the forlorn, failing manager, Ferguson, sloping defeated off the Maine Road pitch. Paul Lake, graceful, the upright ghost of Colin Bell, did, though, properly belong naturally in a result of that stature.

I went back to law student life in Wolverhampton, raving about the balance City's manager, Mel Machin, had fashioned, with Ian Bishop – a midfield signing who was actually good! – conducting the play, White, Lake, Hinchcliffe and David Old-field, the long-legged centre forward who had scored twice against United. When City were next in our area, I urged one of my football-supporting housemates, Mark, that he just had to see this team in action. So when City played away at Derby soon after, I dragged him all the way across the Midlands to see them. Mel Machin's City lost, 6–0.

I always picture Derby's striker, Dean Saunders, running delighted around the Baseball Ground, but I also recall that game for the nastiness of the away end. The terrace was low down, the view an insult, crush barriers too few, and for much of the match we found ourselves milled about, and squashed against a core of City's hooligan crew, who muttered conspiratorially throughout, about 'mashing' people up. When I think of the penned-in containment of football fans before Hillsborough, the abject lack of safety, I think of that away end in the Baseball Ground, even though this was a few months after the disaster. Lord Justice Taylor had said he believed the disaster could have happened at a great number of stadiums, which were in a pitiful state. He had recommended that all football grounds should be made all-seater, which was later amended to apply to just the top two divisions. At the time, having stood in a great heap of neglect and unpleasantness over the years, I did not lament the condemning of the terraces. Pride Park, built to replace the Baseball Ground, would become one of the first heralds of a safer game. At City, Swales, whose new Maine

Road roof and Platt Lane Stand would become permanent monuments to over-promising, faced his most substantial and expensive challenge yet: to build a seated stand along the whole length of Maine Road, where the Kippax had stood since 1923.

Machin, who had steered City to promotion, then the 5–1, then the 6–0, was sacked by Swales at Christmas 1989. The chairman appointed Howard Kendall as his eleventh manager in seventeen years, and after so much calamity, Kendall, who had won 1985 and 1987 League championships with Everton, laid on a demonstration novel to most of us: how to be a calm, sensible football manager.

City were bottom of the First Division when he took over, and although he quickly shuffled off players we had come to admire, including Bishop, he understood what made a convincing footballer. Kendall brought across some of his Everton trusties, including tough, scampering Peter Reid, and other men capable of what was necessary. Kendall proved he could recognise the essence of a footballer when he signed for £800,000 Niall Quinn, who had looked awkwardly stringy for Arsenal, but who developed at Maine Road a sureness of touch and that most admirable of qualities to a supporter: evident resolve to make the very best of the talent he had been given.

The World Cup in 1990, and the BBC's Pavarotti-sound-tracked appreciation of it, rehabilitated football's image, as a great sporting spectacle with operatic dramas, so soon after the disgrace of Hillsborough. I watched it in the middle of final law exams at our student house, next door to a stenching Black Country tyre factory. When England, with Paul Gascoigne, Gary Lineker, David Platt, played in the semi-final

– England! In a World Cup semi-final! – even the women came down to watch. After Chris Waddle wafted his penalty to England's defeat, I sat with Mark, shaking our heads, drained. Then I shuffled off for a final revise of divorce law.

Paul Lake, who had been selected for England's get-together squad but not for the World Cup itself, was gliding into the highest class of footballer, and Kendall made him captain. Then in only his third match, at home to Aston Villa, Lake suffered the first of the knee injuries which would wipe out his football future. In his sad, painfully soul-baring autobiography *I'm Not Really Here*, written with an unblinking eye for choice detail by his wife, Joanne, the carefree spirit and happy progress stop, and heartbreak begins, with a twist of the knee on page 200. His account of doomed efforts to recover, broken dreams and depression is a chronicle of City's lost years in the 1990s, our generation's fine young athlete lost like Colin Bell, but at the beginning, not in the maturity, of his career.

Lake's book concentrates on his battle with depression and to shape a new future after he was invalided out of playing the game he had always loved, but it is also an indictment of Swales's Manchester City. Lake accuses the club – as have other players, including Quinn – of being mean and miserly; indeed Lake believes his rehabilitation treatment was sub-standard partly because City were trying to save money. He describes being sent home from a crucial operation in Los Angeles, with the club having booked him only in economy class, so he was forced to fold his raw knee for a whole transatlantic flight. That experience was so traumatic, and he blamed the episode so centrally for his knee's terminal failure to recover, that his therapist told him later she thought being trapped in that confined space had triggered his clinical depression. Lake's account of Swales's attitude to him throughout this ordeal replicates from the inside the unsympathetic figure Swales presented to supporters.

'I believe Swales saw my injury as both an irritant and embarrassment,' Lake wrote, explaining that the club declined to pay him any appearance or bonus money, and that he finally lost his temper with Swales after two years' pain, telling him he seemed not to care. 'He gave the distinct impression that I was the failure and that my ongoing knee problem was somehow my fault, and nobody else's. He'd never shown any sympathy for what I was going through, hadn't picked up the phone to check how I was, and habitually swanned past me at Maine Road without saying a word. I grew to despise the man . . .'

Swales was himself walking towards his final reckoning with City supporters, over the games he played with managers and the club itself. Howard Kendall suddenly walked out on us, to try to make it work again with Everton, in November 1990. Faced with a decision about a manager, Swales actually made another good appointment, promoting Kendall's faithful grizzler, Reid. And although the football we watched was dull at times, too much of centre half Keith Curle swiping the ball up to Quinn, there were no elemental crises, no ripping it up and starting again, just the uneasy sense, in a full Maine Road, that we were making progress. City actually finished fifth in the First Division in 1991, just eighteen months after being bottom of the league when Kendall arrived in that drizzly winter. In 1992 Reid's new, muscular team finished fifth again, becoming founder members of the Premier League. It was hard to work out what the difference was from the First Division which had existed for the previous 104 years, except that you now had to buy a Sky TV subscription to watch a league game live on television, and Sky were telling you on their advertising billboards that it was suddenly 'A whole new ball game'.

After I passed the law exams, I went to do my two years' training with a clipped, upper-middle-class firm of solicitors in London, based on the Strand near the Royal Courts of Justice. It was useful, looking back on it, being initiated into the disciplines of work, learning the mechanics of what makes the world go round, but it was not the life of which I had dreamed, in an office in a baggy-arsed suit, conducting disputes, sometimes on behalf of clients whose cases were unworthy. As the early 1990s recession bit, and interest rates hit 15 per cent, the firm earned a steady living repossessing people from their homes on behalf of building societies. Nobody ever expressed a tremor of discomfort about that work; one of the partners told me he never felt sorry for the people evicted – the firm was interested only in the fees.

In that bracing, alienating life, football took on an enhanced quality of escape. To play the game at the weekend, on a Sunday with other Manchester emigrants who called their team South Mancunians, out in the air, studs in the grass, striking the ball, was a blessed release. Living in London, supporting Manchester City became a more solid connection still, a rooted part of my identity, helping to anchor who I really was and where I was from. The game embodied some core collective human values, too, out in the crowd where everybody is equal, compared with the commercial world which seemed to have none, except to make money.

With other Manc friends down there, I watched City whenever they were in London – spanked by Ian Wright at Arsenal, Quinn heading City a win at Spurs, beating Queens Park Rangers at Loftus Road, a goalless draw at Crystal Palace's gale-whacked Selhurst Park, which was the first time I saw Garry Flitcroft, a young midfield player who looked surprisingly good. Back in Manchester for the odd weekend, it was part of home, going to Maine Road, the smack of the Moss Side pavement, the bloody-minded, go on, impress me, mood of the crowd, the decent professionals in Peter Reid's team. It was a common thread of your life too, stretching back into childhood, supporting the blues at Maine Road, an important part of keeping your soul about you.

At that time, Nick Hornby published his book *Fever Pitch* about his life as an Arsenal supporter, which also rehabilitated in the media the idea of being a football fan. After Italia 90, *Fever Pitch* and the marketing hype around the launch of the Premier League, being a football supporter was no longer a hostile addiction to be contained, policed as the enemy within. It was now suddenly celebrated as an integral part of being a British male, and some males who had kept their love of the game quite secret when advocates were needed in the 1980s suddenly came out as fans. Tony Blair, who had been at boarding school in Edinburgh in his youth, claimed to be a Newcastle fan, and now David Cameron, upper-class stock from the Home Counties, a boarder at Eton and preparatory schools from the age of seven, wears being an Aston Villa fan as his badge of association with the common man. In a couple of years after Hillsborough, football support was transferred from being a pariah habit, to compulsory.

After I qualified as a solicitor in 1992, I decided I had to try for what I really wanted to do, be a writer, or face the unthinkable prospect that it might never happen. I started as a freelance journalist by cold-calling *The Times* with ideas for law articles, which were commissioned by the legal editor, Frances Gibb. I first wrote about football, for the great fan's magazine *When Saturday Comes*, just because I loved the game and thought it would be a pleasure to write about it. I never imagined that the two strands, an investigative instinct and knowledge, through being a lawyer, of the tools to do it, and my lifelong love of football, would combine into a journey of examination into the game's coming transformation by money. I still knew little of how football worked; I was fully involved only as a fan in the Manchester City soap opera, feeling, with a stronger bond than ever, that I was part of the club, living it as an integral drama in my own life, the unhappy endings always parked just around the corner.

Living in London, we were handily placed for a couple of matches in the landmark 1992–93 FA Cup run, when some people foolishly allowed themselves to believe that City's name was on the cup. Drawn away to Reading, we stood up along the side of the pitch in the old Elm Park, where City won 4–0 and Flitcroft was outstanding. On the train back, my friend David Michael said he just had 'a feeling' we were destined to win the cup. I told him never to say such things about City, never to say that anything is fated to work out well.

Promised work in Manchester, I moved back on 7 March 1993, the very day City played Spurs at Maine Road in the FA Cup quarter-final. We had our best team for years, we had waited fourteen years, since Allison's return, for City to be reclaimed as a truly top club, and many City fans did believe this was scripted to be the date of revival. Alan Hansen, beginning his long stint as a pundit on the BBC, had tipped us to win the cup. Swales unveiled at that game his new Platt Lane stand, a low, unsightly, sub-Subbuteo effort, far from the vision he had once unveiled to rival Old Trafford, and it seemed to stand completely apart from the rest of the ground, as if somehow it knew it was a disappointment.

It was all meant to be, of course. Mike Sheron, one of our own, scored early to make it 1–0 and we were all dreaming of a blue Wembley. Then Spurs danced around us and scored four. Terry Phelan snorted through for a second goal at the new Platt Lane end, which unleashed crowds of City fans from within it, tearing on to the pitch in wretched frustration. From the Kippax, you watched some of them being allowed to run too far across, making it all the way over to the North Stand opposite, where they started to make trouble with the Spurs fans. Police on horses galloped in to disperse them, and so the day which was fated to return Manchester City to the good times ended with a line of police horses just on the edge of the penalty area at the North Stand end of the ground, pissing on the pitch.

I produced my first words for the *Guardian* after that. I went back, called the paper, said I had been at the match and they asked for 500 words, although in the end it was squeezed and they used one of the observations, as a quote. The pitch invasion, I had written, was 'a spontaneous outburst of dejection'.

There were to be a few more of those. Spontaneous outbursts of 'Swales Out!' began just two weeks into the 1993–94 season.

Reid's team had finished ninth in the inaugural Premier League season. United had won it, their first championship since 1967 – although they had had plenty of FA Cup semi-finals, finals and victories, and the European Cup Winners' Cup, to keep them nourished in their years of supposed famine. City had signed nobody in the summer; the fans were booing the quality of the experience by half-time in the first home match against Leeds, and chanting 'Swales Out!' from the second, a 1–0 defeat at Everton.

Swales waited just thirteen days into the new season to defenestrate Reid, and the way it was done, with the bizarre appointment of John Maddock, a former journalist on the *Sunday People*, as the club's 'general manager', added fire to the fans' fury. Twenty years of resentment at Peter Swales, fourteen since he presided over the club's collapse, just as my generation grew into adolescence, boiled up and over.

Maddock famously promised that in place of Reid he would be appointing a manager 'of pedigree', a man of stature: 'A true professional who is going to help put Manchester City back on the football map.'

When this man of pedigree was announced, his name was Brian Horton, then the manager of Oxford United. That came as a heroic let-down, a managerial version of the new Platt Lane, to supporters who believed Reid's sacking was just another of Swales's vinegary games. The news of Horton's appointment slipped out during the first match after Reid's sacking, a 1–1 draw with Coventry City. The *Manchester Evening News* report the following day, clipped in Gary James's history of the club, *Manchester the Greatest City*, shows a crowd of fans (notably younger than fans today, who are probably many of the same people, twenty years older, because young adults have been largely priced out) piling up in protest to the gated entrance of the main stand. The headline states:

'City frenzy ends in riot.'

At the dawn of the multi-million-pound, satellite-TV, globe-conquering Premier League, the Manchester United team City had dissected 5–1, had been remoulded by Ferguson. They were heading to twenty years of winning football, twinned with a relentless zeal in the corporate offices – United floated on the Stock Market in 1991 – to make money from football's 'rebranding'. At City, there was no rebranding. We were having a frenzy, ending in a riot.

Manchester, the city centre, was on the up. The council's chief executive, Howard Bernstein, had eagerly grasped the new agenda of bidding for grant project funding from the Conservative government and the European Union. There were new trams in Manchester, running into town along the old railway lines from Bury in the north and Altrincham in the south, criss-crossing at St Peters Square and Piccadilly. The council attracted the money to build a £70m arena, for concerts, next to struggling Victoria Station, and Central Station, whose broken windows and stopped clock had marked time emblematically in the 1980s, had been refurbished into G-Mex. The country laughed – or rather, London did – at Manchester's impudent mounting of bids to host the 1996 and 2000 Olympic Games, but those losing efforts honed bidding expertise and brought consolation prizes, like the velodrome, in east Manchester and, ultimately, the 2002 Commonwealth Games. There were new restaurants and bars piping up amid the entertainments which had seemed to remain the same for ever, then the council began to zealously promote apartments to be built in the city centre for people to live in. Manchester was being talked of as a city in recovery, even a boom town.

I interviewed Bernstein for a business magazine, *North West Insider*, in the mid-1990s; he had to make it 8:30 a.m. because of his hectic schedule, and when I arrived at the huge room in the cavernous mock-Gothic Victorian town hall, he was already smoking a fat cigar. He told me then that Manchester's strategy was to make the city centre a busy, prosperous, attractive place to be. They were haunted by the desolation of former industrial cities in the US, like Detroit, whose centres had been abandoned by the professional and shopping classes. What was still needed, he said repeatedly, was 'quality retail'. When the IRA bombed the city centre in 1996, miraculously killing nobody as shards of reinforced glass flew like frisbees down Corporation Street, the council and developers took the opportunity to refashion the city centre, ushering in Harvey Nichols, Selfridge's and other swank, and sweeping a bedraggled bunch of Mancunian traders out from where they had grafted to make a living in the shell of the old Corn Exchange.

It was difficult to see, though, how widely Manchester was benefiting from all the improvements, or what, besides grants of public money for prestige projects, was driving the supposed economic boom. Manufacturing and industry continued to decline. The newspapers had long packed up their Manchester operations. The actual city wards of Manchester – not the wealthy suburbs, stretching into Cheshire, whose inhabitants now had choice shops to draw them in – remained mired in poverty, the general spending cuts biting into their schools, hospitals and quality of life. I began playing football again on the old park playing fields, which were in a sadder state, some approaching dereliction, than they had been when I had first stepped out on them, as a shivering ten-year-old, in the mid-1970s.

The first stories of the inflated wages being paid to footballers, from the Sky TV and commercial windfall, began to percolate, and the sight of United's starlets became a common one out in town. Young, well-dressed, successful, the embodiment of revival, the United players, including pin-ups Lee Sharpe and Ryan Giggs, would be surrounded by young girls, and lads wanting to buy them drinks. I remember seeing them out on Deansgate at this time, radiating success, while Keith Curle and a few other City players stood ignored in another area of the bar, looking awkward, with their smart-casual shirts tucked into their chinos.

Brian Horton proved himself to be enthusiastic, honest, likeable and capable, but even though he won his first match, 3–1 at Swindon, few City fans cared to notice. Furious cries of 'Swales Out!' began before or just after kick-off at Maine Road, filling the air up to the roof of the stands. The chairman, in his overcoat, seemed to sink lower in his lonely seat in the directors' box, giving the impression of a man digging in, not preparing to finally go. In an interview he gave the BBC shortly after it was all over, he told them he had wanted to get to twenty years as the chairman of a big club, and relished his time on the senior committees at the Football Association. To me, at the time, such internal football machinations were a mystery; I was just a fan. I could not see what he would want or stood to gain from such involvement, and could never fathom how he could cling on at City after all the howlers he had perpetrated.

It was into this poisonous climate of frustration, blame and hatred that our saviour first offered himself as a dream possibility. Francis Lee was a haloed figure from our glorious era whose passing Swales himself embodied. We all had pictures of Franny on our bedroom walls, and his team's achievements, and that image of him, arms outstretched in holy acclaim, having won the league for City at St James' Park, framed the faith the fans kept in City as inherently a top club.

Over the years we had always been told of Franny's progress, in newspaper articles, when you read them again now, of quite astounding sycophancy. Franny, we were told, had always been a self-starter, never happy with the modest wages of footballers in his era. He had spent his afternoons, beginning as a youngster at Bolton Wanderers, collecting waste paper for an early form of recycling. Franny, we were told solemnly, had made a great success of himself, in toilet roll. We read that, as we were meant to, with admiration and awe: he was one of our great players, and he had done well for himself, so good on him.

In our ecstasy at the emergence of Franny, hero of the golden years, we failed to read or chose to ignore some relevant detail in those same newspaper articles. There was a run of them after Franny sold his toilet roll company in 1984 for £8.25m. There were pictures and descriptions of his 'Tudor retreat in Cheshire', his racehorses and, always, his Mercedes with the personalised number plate, FHL 7.

Describing how well he had done to build his business during his time as a player, beginning at Bolton with 'salvaging waste paper', the *Sun* quoted Franny saying he had little interest in football.

'Horses are my love now,' he said. The modern game, the article said, 'leaves him cold'.

In the *News of the World* on 22 December 1985, an article quoted him saying:

'I haven't been for five years. I used to watch it on TV but of course that's been out of the question this season [due to his involvement with horse racing]. The game just isn't the spectacle it once was. It's been going downhill for six or seven years. And it's down to the Football League, the Football Association and the directors. They have done nothing to promote the game.'

We hadn't taken much notice of these reports. We read what we wanted to read, and saw what we had always seen: the image of our childhood golden time. He had returned with several less well known Manchester businessmen in a consortium, pulled together by another former City player from the 1950s, Colin Barlow. They coined a rallying slogan irresistible to fans: 'Forward with Franny'. They promised to deliver us from Swales, invest money in the club, and return City to the club's rightful station in the football firmament. In the elemental battle between darkness and light over the future of the football club, the great majority knew which side they were on.

Maine Road turned in on itself, a growling, howling cauldron of 'Swales Out!' There were reports that Swales had been visited at home by angry fans who wanted him out, that his wife had been spat at, that he had had eggs thrown at him at Maine Road. One report even said his old mother had been visited in hospital by two City fans. Somebody did actually try to get at him where he sat in the directors' box, and had to be jumped on by security men. Whatever the truth of the incidents, there is no doubt it was a relentless, vitriolic campaign, from supporters who were deeply hostile and had long had enough of Peter Swales. We put our faith in Franny. St Francis: the Second Coming, went one of the T-shirts.

I was swept up with it all, believing in it as a sort of fable, the equivalent, I suppose, of our name being on the cup. This was, finally, the redemption of a good and great club by one of the sky-blue icons of childhood. I did not read into Franny's history or intentions, knew nothing about the realities of the club and what a takeover would involve, and even by then I did not really think it was anything much to do with money. There were reports that a deal was being negotiated, it was on, it was off. I thought of it as our kind of Iron Curtain revolution: ousting the evil dictator at the football club who had long outstayed his popularity, and installing the people's champion.

Ultimately it happened on 5 February 1994: Swales was vanquished, Francis Lee 'flying in from his holiday in Barbados to complete the deal', as all the reports dutifully had it. Franny took over, and the match that day, against Ipswich Town, was a carnival of celebration. There was a banner, specially made for the occasion, welcoming the saviour, then a festoon of blue and white balloons was released to the Moss Side sky. Franny took Swales's seat in the directors' box and, with that familiar blonde hair and trademark dimpled smile, arms splayed in a blue-suited businessman's echo of his stance at St James' Park, he accepted the acclaim, the love and the yearning, of his old

Francis Lee, taking over as chairman of Manchester City, in February 1994

In the Main Stand, I was up with the standing ovation, as the banner was unfurled and balloons released. I really did believe, along with what seemed like the whole crowd, that this was deliverance. I always remember Paul Demby, older brother of my childhood friend Ric, an accountant with a senior corporate job and a lifelong City fan, turning round in the middle of it all, and questioning:

'But how do we know Francis Lee is the answer, that he really will turn it all round?'

I remember waving Paul away: what do you know? This was the fall of Ceauşescu for the Manchester City devotee, who had too long suffered under the dead hand of Swales. I still understand why I saw it that way; I knew nothing of what had really been happening at Manchester City, about the details of the club as an organisation and the motivations of those involved.

I had always supported football by following what happened on its surface, on the pitch, at its public face. I barely knew more about how the game was organised, what the clubs really were, how the league and FA fitted in, than I had at six years old when I had first fallen for City. But I was not a child any more. I was 29 years old, a Manchester City fan, yes, but also a lawyer, trained to interrogate the details of things, and a journalist, learning to employ those techniques in different ways across the varied canvas of life. I had never interrogated football, only sentimentalised it as a grand and involving narrative. So I understand why I was up on my feet, hands above my head, welcoming, with fervour, St Francis in his Second Coming.

But looking back, I still feel I should have known better.

CHAPTER 9

FORWARD WITH FRANNY

My education into how football really worked, what the clubs are in truth, and the new culture of greed the Premier League had ushered in, began in the chairman's office at Maine Road, in an interview with my childhood hero Francis Lee, shortly after he vanquished Peter Swales, in February 1994. When the appointed hour came, I walked up to the Main Stand entrance, where I had stood as a boy while my dad sorted tickets out with gruff-voiced muckers, and where the spirits lingered of lads yelling 'Swales Out!' and hurling their season-ticket books at the windows. I went inside Manchester City's offices for the first time and told the receptionist I had an appointment with the new Mr Chairman.

I do not think, as a journalist beginning to report wide-eyed on football's mutation into 'a business', I represented a challenge for Francis Lee to impress. I was coming to praise him. The new boss of Manchester City was then, and still remains, the only person whose image I have ever kissed on television. That is not the usual foundation for critical distance and professional scepticism in an interview. I had been in the same stand a few days earlier, feverishly applauding his arrival when the blue and white balloons went up. I believed that Franny must feel how we felt, shared our pain, and had come back to make it all right again. That was all he really needed to tell me.

When I walked in, there Franny was, still blonde, blue-eyed, if a little portlier than in his St James' Park pomp. He was sitting behind the chairman's desk, wearing, as I reported, a beige suit, pink shirt and yellow tie – a blinding clash. Colin Barlow was in a chair in front of the desk; they had been talking about their plans, and propped up on a chair next to Barlow was a huge, colour, artist's impression of the new, all-seater, cantilevered Kippax they intended to build.

'How long do you want: five minutes?' was Franny's opening welcome.

I said I thought I would need a little longer than that. We got into talking, and as I waited for Franny to articulate an affection for the club and inspire me with his intentions for it, it crept on me quite gradually that he was talking mostly about money, and the club's need for it.

Lee said Swales had left City financially stricken.

'This is a crisis, a desperate situation,' Lee said. 'Apart from the brilliant supporters and the fact that we've got some fair players here, everything is desperate.'

That was the point of the big new Kippax mock-up, they said. It would be no cut-price Swales effort; his meagre plans had been ripped up.

'It was being done on a shoestring with no facilities for supporters,' said Franny.

Their new Kippax would include several tiers of banqueting suites and restaurants, which would enable fans and sponsors to pay high prices for top-class food, and so make money for the club. That was to be the coming transformation.

There was evident history with Swales, from Franny's time as a player, which was still quite raw. Swales, with Tony Book, Lee's former colleague and skipper, as the manager, had sold him to Derby County in 1974, the first of the championship-winning stars to be cleared out. Lee had not wanted to leave, he said, because his business – described in all the profiles as a 'quality tissue paper company' – was in the north-west and he was a hero at City.

'They appointed Tony Book as manager, and he was told to sell me because I was too popular in the dressing room,' Franny complained. City were paid £110,000 by Derby for Lee, and it always rankled with Lee that Swales had bartered and negotiated Derby up from £100,000. In those days, players could be paid a signing-on fee from the club they joined, but it was usually diminished by the size of the transfer fee that club had to pay.

'They haggled for an extra £10,000,' Lee protested, twenty years later, sitting in Swales's old office, having finally seen him ripped out of the club after that bitter campaign. 'What sort of treatment was that, after my years of service to the club?'

In the 'Blue Room', a tatty, forlorn bar in the Main Stand, frequented in the days before a pre-match drink for the directors' clique was termed corporate entertaining, there had been a picture of Swales, shaking hands with an executive from City's sponsor, Brother. Somebody had cut out a colour picture of Lee from a newspaper, and stuck it over the head of Swales.

In the middle of all of this there was a knock at the office door and in wandered Brian Horton who, after all, was still the City manager they had inherited from Swales. Lee and Barlow looked up at Horton as if he was a kind of intruder, and waited silently for his reason for interrupting. Horton walked across to Franny, with a piece of paper in his hand, and slid it on to his desk, politely.

'That's the fax about the player I mentioned to you earlier,' he said.

Franny harrumphed, Barlow said nothing, and Horton turned and wandered out again, back to the manager's office adjoining that of the chairman in the old Main Stand.

As a fan amid the standing ovation, fancying this was our people's revolution, I had cheered Franny in, but as a journalist I had been commissioned to investigate the meat of the detail by which he had supplanted Peter Swales. I had trained as a lawyer to read and understand company and financial documents, and it turned out, to my surprise, that what Franny had done was a corporate deal. City's directors had produced an official announcement and a legal document had been issued by Franny as the club's new chairman, setting out how the deal had been done.

Franny had bought the required number of Manchester City shares from Swales and Swales's loyal co-director, Stephen Boler, a millionaire producer of kitchens, to give Franny 29.99 per cent ownership of the club. As I had learned, once a share-holder buys 30 per cent of a company, he has to make an offer to buy all the shares, so Franny had bought the biggest minority stake possible without having to find the money to buy the whole club.

He had bought 224,674 shares, the document set out; two equal portions of 112,337, one from the reluctant Swales, the other from Boler, who had sat defiantly shoulder to shoulder with Swales throughout the months of hostility. Franny had paid them £13.35 per share, so, if you got your calculator out, you could work out that 224,674 shares costing £13.35 each multiplied into £3m, £1.5m each to Swales and Boler. Swales had not, in fact, been extracted out of Maine Road; he still owned 10 per cent of Manchester City after the sale, the document said, and Boler owned 13 per cent.

The fans' campaign in support of Forward with Franny, and their implacable enmity to Swales, is always said to have left him a shattered man, his spirit broken by the ignominy of ending his long chairmanship in failure and ousting. He gave a long TV interview before he died, for a series the BBC was making on football's extraordinary history. Swales talked about his own career in business and in football; trading from a 'very small shop' in the 1950s, he and his partner, Noel White, bought the local semi-professional football club, Altrincham, which was going bust, for 'about £100'. They built up their TV and white goods business in the consumer boom for such modernities in the 1960s, then sold their company and made a bit of money.

Swales told the story of how he had been in a club in Hale Barns, the rich start of Manchester's Cheshire belt, in 1971, and saw a couple of City's directors discussing the boardroom battle they were having. That is the dismal detail which lies in the pre-history for fans of my generation: City had raised themselves from the Second Division in the mid-1960s, where they had meagre crowds at Maine Road, to the 1968–70 greatest period in the club's history, Allison an inspiration first time round, with Joe Mercer as senior counsel. And true to the club's character, instead of keeping calm and carrying on, laying stable foundations for future success, the directors had had to have a civil war. It was partly over Allison-worship, again, a younger group of directors wanting him to be appointed manager on his own, a wish Allison was granted in 1972. Swales said he approached them in the club, told them all the busy work he had done at Altrincham, in the non-league, and somehow persuaded the group he met that he was the man to sort things out for them. He said he 'could not remember' how he had helped them 'solve their problems' but he had done, and was 'rewarded' with a seat on the board in 1972. He was made the chairman in October 1973, and at that time he had had few shares.

'I really stayed too long,' he acknowledged of recent times. 'I'd got it at the back of my mind I wanted to be the first chairman of a major club to do twenty years. I really knew after eighteen and a half years that my time was up as far as the general support was concerned. I should have gone then but I wanted to do the twenty years and in the end that got me into trouble. But I did the twenty years, which they can't take away, can they?'

He said of his decision to bring Allison back in 1979 and make so many expensive signings, that it was because 'I wanted to be bigger than Manchester United, which was a bit silly really; I should have let them get on with their business and I get on with my business.'

Of the Steve Daley signing, representative of the recklessness which had sunk the club then and for so long, Swales was quite accepting, saying Allison had identified Daley as a player he wanted, but Swales had agreed the fee.

'In those days you could pay over any number of years, and that encouraged you to take ludicrous gambles. At Manchester City, we gambled on the future, we mortgaged our future, really heavily.'

He talked about how much he had loved it all, being at the centre of it, and his time on the FA's international committee, which meant, even as City sank, he was helping to select the managers of England, and was in the VIP seats for all the matches. He said he had become involved in football for 'the excitement' of it, that he would just have been 'a nine to five man' if he hadn't. He accepted, after doing his twenty years, including hanging on for the fourteen years since the 'ludicrous gamble' he had taken with City's future, that he had made mistakes:

'I don't think for a minute that during my football career everything I've done has been right. There have probably been more things wrong than right.'

Then the BBC interviewer asked him whether, over his twenty-two years as a director of Manchester City Football Club, he had made money for himself.

'In the end financially you did well out of it, didn't you?'

Swales acknowledged: 'Oh yes, sure, no complaints there at all.'

Although he did not specify how much, the £1.5m Lee gave him for that portion of his City shares was a great deal more than Swales had paid for them originally. He had a few hundred thousand pounds profit in his bank account, probably more than a million, to cushion the impact of his personal humiliation. Over the years, he had also charged Manchester City for his services, latterly invoicing the club on behalf of his company, PJ Swales Ltd, £50,000.

Lee, in turn, recouped around half the £3m he paid by selling on almost half those 224,674 shares he had bought, 109,341, to the Manchester businessmen in what had been called his 'consortium'. Barlow paid £250,000 for 18,723 shares, 2.2 per cent, and a long list of reasonably well-off men had put some money in for a slice of City. David Bernstein, a City-supporting plc businessman, managing director of Pentland, the leisure clothing group, was in the straggly list, paying £150,000 for 11,234 shares, 1.5 per cent of the club. Later, Bernstein would become City's chairman, then chairman of the Football Association itself.

Franny, principally, and his consortium, had also agreed to put £3.1m of new money into the club, as loans, earning interest for them at Lloyds Bank base rate, which they could later convert into more shares, rather than have the loans repaid. During the takeover battle, the journalist who had seemed to be first with stories from the Forward with Franny camp, Alec Johnson of the *Mirror*, had written an article which suggested that very considerable money would be made available for City if Franny and his consortium wrested control from Swales. Johnson quoted Barlow saying:

'Mr Lee and his partners have an aggregate worth in excess of £45m at their disposal.'

Looking at the list of Franny's backers, that certainly looked true, but they were never going to put anything like that, their whole worth, into City. Franny invested £1.5m, Barlow another £250,000, the associates mostly smaller amounts according to their agreement. David Bernstein paid £150,000 for this 'convertible loan stock'.

Before inspecting the implications of this for City – that after all the mayhem and enlisting of the fans' support, riding in on their childhood dreams and stored-up adult anger, Franny only bought 15 per cent of City; that £3m was never going to be enough to build the new Kippax and restore the club to glories, that Swales still owned, by agreement, just over 10 per cent of the club – the revelations of the deal's essentials rocked me several steps back.

I had supported Manchester City all my life and it had never, for a second, occurred to me that the club was in fact a company, with shares which could be bought and sold. I had thought of Swales as the chairman who had mismanaged the club, should have taken responsibility for that, yet could somehow not be forced out because nobody had the power. But I never realised that was because he owned shares, and that with the alliances he had built up, with Boler and others, he and his associates owned Manchester City. I had thought of the takeover as a battle between dark and light, the forces of negativity and sunshine in City's destiny, not as a corporate tangle between businessmen looking to make money for themselves out of owning the shares. If I thought of City as an entity, it was as a true club, something I belonged to with all the other supporters who had stayed loyal throughout the low years. I felt, and we had all been encouraged by the new marketing of football to consider, that it was a very important part of who I was, its story woven within my own evolving life. It was a quite shocking revelation, in itself, that the institution which called itself a club, and which is always referred to as such, as if it belongs to all of its supporter-members, was in fact something as mundane and businesslike as a limited company.

My training as a lawyer had taught me about all this: limited companies are formed by people who buy shares in them. Their personal financial responsibility for the company's debts and expenses is limited to them losing their shares; they would not be on the line personally, lose their house and all their money, if the company were unable to pay its debts. That was what 'limited liability' meant. An individual's liability for the company's debts, if the company was forced to go bust, was limited to the value of his shares.

As a company prospered and grew, its directors and shareholders hoped it would make a profit, and part of that profit could be paid to the shareholders, according to the proportions in which they held their shares: a dividend. And because a successful company offered that dividend income to shareholders, and because it had accumulated valuable property and other assets, the shares would become worth something to buy. The owners, the shareholders, could sell them to other people at a profit, for more than they paid for them. A standard way for the owners of shares in a prospering private company to make a profit from selling, was to float the company on the Stock Market, when it was making substantial money. That way a shareholder did not need to find another individual and come to an agreement to sell his shares, as he would have to if it were still a private limited company. The shares, when a company floated on the Stock Market, were then available to the wider public, given a value every day; anybody could buy them. The shareholders could sell them at a tidy profit on the market, however many they wanted, if it were successful and there was a demand to buy them. That is described as an 'exit', the final sale and cashing in by the owners of shares in a private company, at a personal profit.

I was quite stunned that all of this limited liability company, shares, owners and profit-making apparatus was the true nature of the football club I had supported as a badge of belonging since I was six. It had always described itself as a club, never a company, in anything which had ever crossed my consciousness; I had been ignorant of the fact that Peter Swales and men in the boardroom stood to make money out of it, from the fans' insistent loyalty.

Lee, Barlow and their consortium made no secret that their intention was to float Manchester City Football Club Ltd on the Stock Exchange, as Martin Edwards and his fellow directors had done with United in 1991. They made that clear in the official announcement which detailed the 29.99 per cent 'takeover' from Swales:

'It is intended that the club will in due course make an application for a listing on the London Stock Exchange.'

We had roared Franny in, our hearts full of the joys he had brought to our boyhoods, so that he and his associates could buy shares in Manchester City, then float it on the Stock Market and record a profit. Lee and Barlow had understood the way football was being transformed, in detail to which most fans, absorbed in their clubs' stories, had remained oblivious. On further investigation, I learned that there had been a key difference between the new competition for the twenty-two top clubs called the Premier League, and the former competition for the twenty-two top clubs called the First Division. Television money had always been shared around in the Football League, throughout the four divisions. The Premier League was formed by the top clubs breaking away from the Football League, so they no longer needed to share the TV money coming in. They did so on the threshold of unprecedented fortunes coming into the game, due to the emergence of Sky, satellite pay-TV, breaking up the old cartel of the BBC and ITV, who had kept down the price they paid to the clubs. The first five-year deal from 1992–7 with the Premier League clubs, forcing fans to buy a Sky dish and subscription if they wanted to watch a live league football match, which for years had been free on one of the terrestrial channels, brought in £305m. Sky stood to make a great deal more for themselves, by selling expensive subscriptions to supporters who could not view live league football any other way.

This great bonanza coming into the Premier League, ultimately from supporters and pubs forking out for Sky, was to be gobbled up by just those twenty-two clubs which had voted to break away from the Football League after 104 years of collective endeavour. Those sudden riches meant the shares in the club-companies, which had been bought cheaply in the 1970s and '80s, considered 'dead money', acquired as an expression of support, were suddenly worth a great deal more. The owners – they were never called owners, then, but chairmen – a new generation who had bought majority shareholdings in club-companies during that period, while football was heading to disaster and supporters to their deaths, were now, flush with the Premier League breakaway and Sky bonanza, widely considering floating the clubs on the Stock Market so they could cash in.

This was all explained to me by several advisers to Franny, accountants, merchant bankers, lawyers, who seemed to consider themselves extremely clever for helping to engineer it. Gerry Boon, a partner in the accountancy firm Deloitte and Touche, who latched on early to the 'quantum leap' of money pouring into football and involved his firm in many of the deals, described himself to me as 'a missionary' for this new era, in which the men who owned shares in the club-companies would rapidly become multi-millionaires.

One of Franny's advisers explained to me that the reason Swales left, ultimately, was not the fans' campaign – Swales had, as he himself emphasised during his resistance, faced down plenty of them before. It was all to do with money. Under him, City had finally run out. The Sky millions were coming in, but Swales had spent fortunes again, on Curle, £2.5m, and Phelan, remarkably, for the same fee. The accounts for 1993–94, the first of a football club-company I had read, showed City would lose £6m that year. Wages were increasing by £1.6m to £5.6m, and £7.3m was spent in transfer fees. Debts were £10m, including £1.4m borrowed for Swales's Platt Lane mini-stand, which had been christened by that pitch invasion in the Spurs cup defeat. I was told that some repayments of money owed were due to become critical in June, and that the banks were telling City they would have to sell their best players, the strong goalkeeper Tony Coton, Phelan, Quinn, possibly Garry Flitcroft. Added to this, Swales needed to find £2.4m to build even his scaled-down Kippax, an all-seated stand required by law following the Taylor Report into the Hillsborough disaster.

Many clubs at the start of the Premier League's financial battering ram were finding themselves in the same pincer: the pay-TV bonanza pouring in, but short of the money to build the stands necessary to see them into the modern era. Those were classic circumstances for takeovers by opportunist businessmen, as happened at similar clubs, Everton, Newcastle, Tottenham – the latter by Alan Sugar, whose Amstrad company was making the satellite dishes for Sky.

At City, the demand which finally did for Swales was, I was told, Brian Horton's signing from Middlesbrough of Alan Kernaghan, a steady enough defender but not one you'd think of as shaping a history. City had paid £850,000 up front to Middlesbrough, and as Swales and Boler were digging in to fend off Forward with Franny and the fans' fury, the other £750,000 payment for Kernaghan was due. City did not have it, they could not borrow it from a bank, and none of the directors were prepared to stump up. That simple shortage of cash for a centre half was what really forced Swales to vacate his chairman's seat after his twenty years, and brought Franny and his consortium in with his £3m paid to Swales and Boler, and £3.1m loaned into the club.

It is difficult now, knowing how Premier League football has since developed into a commercial leviathan bestriding the world, to recall and describe how wrong my discovery of these corporate machinations felt back then. It seemed to me instinctively not in keeping with football for my club to be a company with shares which could be traded amongst a few businessmen to make money. I had thought the directors, if I had thought of them at all, were there to serve the club rather than themselves. Yet it seemed we had all stood as one, cheering Franny in, driving Swales virulently out, so that Franny and his associates could buy the City shares, then float the club-company on the Stock Market, and register a major gain in two or three years' time.

In November 1994 came another profound revelation. Manchester City announced they would be raising a further £1.5m in loans to the club. It is instructive that that corporate offer, again issued in a legal document, fifty-four pages long, was itself intimately associated with eating. The Franny regime had gutted the interior of the Main Stand, demolishing the offices where I had interviewed him, replacing them with a large directors' dining room. City's offices were displaced out of Maine Road, in a new business park across the four-lane Princess Parkway, built on the disused grounds of the YMCA, where my club had played some rough amateur football against Moss Side teams in the 1980s.

When I talked to Barlow about the plans, he was quite scathing about the culture of Manchester City they had done away with, which had no place in the Premier League era, when money had to be made.

'We had people turning up drinking tea and eating toast on matchdays,' he said. 'The wife of one of the directors brings her own cake in.' I remember thinking that sounded quite nice, quite City.

'It was homely,' he said, 'but not businesslike.'

So they had knocked it all flat and created a 'boardroom dining suite' with thirty-six tables. The catering, he said, would be 'four-to-five star, and we don't use that phrase lightly'.

City fans with money to spend on that kind of experience were not only invited to buy a table but to cook their investment into the club's very corporate plan – the second Convertible Unsecured Loan Stock. Investors could pay for a table, for the 1994–95, 1995–96 and 1996–97 seasons, for £50,000. That would buy them lunch, or an evening meal at night matches for four, match tickets next to the directors' box and 'one blazer per table'.

In years two and three, the holder would pay £7,500 more for the food and tickets. The club would use the £1.5m it hoped to raise, from selling thirty of these tables, for rebuilding – 'I want to throw the profit straight at the Kippax,' Barlow told me.

When the time came for Manchester City Football Club Limited to be floated on the Stock Market, the holders of this corporate dining-loan stock would have the chance to convert the £50,000 into shares. Or they could have their £50,000 repaid by the club. At the same time as this offer was being made, the share structure of the club was being reorganised. The offer document explicitly stated, again, that this was being done in preparation for a Stock Market float.

'The capital reorganisation is a necessary precursor to enable the corporate restructuring to occur which is required to place the club in a position to be able potentially to obtain a listing on the London Stock Exchange,' it said.

One of the lawyers who worked on that offer sat down with me after the press conference when they launched it, to explain the reorganisation. They were forming a new company. It was called, straightforwardly, Manchester City plc (public limited company, one floated on the Stock Market). That plc company would in turn own the shares in Manchester City Football Club Limited, the company which would continue to employ the footballers, manager and take the fans' money. The shareholders of Manchester City Football Club Limited, Franny, Swales, Boler, the brewery Greenalls, would still own it in exactly the same proportions, but their holding would be in Manchester City plc.

If that seemed baffling and pointless, the reasons for it were explained explicitly on pages 40 and 41 of the document. The most important was that:

'Manchester City Football Club Limited [must] observe the requirements of the Football League and the Football Association from time to time in force in connection with the club's membership of either the league or the Football Association.'

Now, those rules, of the League and the FA, 'will not be applicable' to the new holding company, Manchester City plc.

The rules from which Manchester City were breaking free, by means of forming this new plc company ready to be floated on the Stock Market when its value was lucrative, were set out in the document. They were that if a club were to pay money out to a shareholder, an owner of the shares, or a director, the FA and league had to give their permission. Dividends, paid out to shareholders, had first to be approved by the FA. If a club wanted to pay a director a salary, it also needed the approval of the FA and league. There was a third FA and league rule which applied when a member club was wound up: if any money were left after its debts were paid and shareholders repaid the value of their shares, then any surplus could not be pocketed by the club's owners. The money would have to go to charity, such as the FA's benevolent fund.

It was explained to me that these Football Association and Football League requirements applied to all professional football clubs which were members, but would now not apply to Manchester City plc. My club would be free of the rules requiring approval for money paid out. Barlow told me that with all the work they were doing reorganising the club, getting investment in, building up the restaurants and the planned new Kippax, he hoped they might float on the Stock Market within a year and a half. He hoped, he said, to 'have a pattern obvious to be analysed by a broker', which meant rising profits giving the shares a profitable valuation for him, Franny and their consortium. David Bernstein, it was suggested, was brought aboard to help advise them on their drive to profitability and Stock Market flotation.

I found this reorganisation more than a little unsettling. It seemed from what I had been shown that the FA had rules which in effect protected football clubs from being treated as normal companies, there to make a profit for the people who owned and ran them. And that the FA tried to defend the clubs from being wound up and asset-stripped. That was how supporters felt about their clubs, of course, that they were to be cherished, not exploited. No fan gave a thought to making money out of it; you paid money in, for the privilege of watching your team represent your hopes and dreams, and you were encouraged to forge your very identity with it. Now many clubs were having new buyers, in our case Francis Lee, who we had imagined to be the most perfect possible new leader for Manchester City, a former playing icon of the club from its best of times.

Yet Franny had been quoted saying he had not watched football through the 1980s – we would have known if we had taken any notice – and had now come in at this time of financial opportunity for the buyers of shares in football clubs. To do so, he and his associates were eagerly bypassing the FA's rules, in order to float on the Stock Market. That did seem to be a 'whole new ball game'. And it seemed to me, instinctively, entirely wrong.

CHAPTER 10

THE MONEY GAME

The revelation that this new dawn for football, which had been sold to us as a joyous recovery from the 1980s with the safety of fans at its heart, was in fact a feeding frenzy for a group of opportunist businessmen, impelled me to look further into it. I was guided by the gut feeling that this was wrong, and so, on the journey, the detail of how football worked, what was eating it, pulled itself into focus.

Once you realised that the clubs were in fact companies and that some, like United, had floated on the Stock Market already, you could straightforwardly piece together some of the evolving story. Martin Edwards, whose father, Louis, had bought up a majority control of United shares for around £30,000, beginning after the Munich air disaster in the late 1950s, had personally made £6m by selling a small portion of the family stake when United floated in 1991.

Maurice Watkins, United's lawyer and a long-term adviser to Edwards, explained to me plainly that one of the primary reasons for United floating had been just this: 'To release cash to private shareholders.'

They were pioneers in this gold rush, as Manchester United

plc were of so much else in the Premier League era: corporate entertaining, merchandising, all the various ways, including seriously inflated ticket price rises, to make money from the loyalty of fans. Several other famous old football clubs were later floated on the Stock Market in a two-year flurry, 1996–7, making immediate paper profits (the value publicly ascribed to the shares compared to the small amounts they had cost) of tens of millions of pounds for their owners. These men had bought majority stakes and become the club-company chairmen before leading their clubs to break away from the Football League and form the Premier League, so keeping all the money about to flood in. Doug Ellis ultimately made £20m when he sold his stake in Aston Villa plc (which he had bought for £500,000) to the American MBNA credit card heir, Randy Lerner, in 2006. Sir John Hall, itching to realise his personal bonanza from Newcastle United plc for years, finally reaped £75m in total when he sold to Mike Ashley in 2007 (the shares had cost him £3m). Martin Edwards sold his long-held family stake in Manchester United plc in slices, to various buyers, over several years on the Stock Market, until in 2004, before the Glazer family bought United with £525m borrowed money, he was done. All the Edwards family shares had been disposed of, and Martin had made £93m for himself.

When you examined the flotation documents, the official prospectuses for the Stock Market, of United, Villa, Newcastle, Nottingham Forest and others, you found they had all done versions of what Franny did with Manchester City plc. They had formed holding companies so they could float on the Stock Market free of the FA's rules which restricted money-making from football clubs. All of the clubs listed the FA rules then in force; the restriction on the dividends which club-companies could pay to shareholders, the requirement that any paid football club director had to work full-time at the club, and the historic restriction against asset-stripping. All of the prospectuses stated that the great football clubs were no longer bound by these rules of the Football Association, the governing body of the game of football in England.

'These rules apply to the club [the FC Ltd],' they all said, 'not to the company [the plc].'

I wanted to understand these rules, what their purpose was, and why they had been introduced – there did seem to be some sense to them, some guardianship of the game's soul. I also wanted to discover how the FA had felt about the rules being bypassed in this way by football's biggest clubs. I discovered that the rules were set out in the FA's current handbook as Rule 34, and it seemed clear that the rules were intended by the FA to preserve football clubs as essentially non-profit-making entities – to keep them as clubs, by nature. I eventually went down to the FA's airless Georgian headquarters, at stuffy Lancaster Gate opposite Hyde Park, and went through all the rule books in long, fusty rows in the library, to find the origin of the rules. That in itself was an educational journey, into the beginnings and founding values of football itself, and so into those of my own club, Manchester City.

I found a minute of a meeting in 1892 that was the first record of the FA limiting dividends which could be paid out to shareholders in a football club. The FA had decided to impose this rule in response to Preston North End, England's first great professional power, requesting permission to form a limited company. From that detail, a great history opened up, and within it, the tension between football as a game to play, with a collective, sporting ethos, and the impulse of people involved with its clubs to make money out of them. The FA had regarded its role, as football's original governing body, to resolve that tension in favour of the preservation of sporting values. Yet now, as more money than ever before was flooding in, it appeared to be surrendering, allowing its rules to be bypassed and that ethos abandoned.

It had always seemed a mystery to me, the origins of football, the game which was there in all its dazzling wonder for us to grow into. But I learned that it is, in fact, well-documented. Kicking a ball is recorded as an ancient natural impulse, and there are records of games being played in China centuries ago. The origins of modern football, though, are accepted to be in the rough 'folk' games played in British villages, beginning with the festival of Mardi Gras, or Shrove Tuesday, introduced with the conquest of Britain by the Normans in 1066. Hugh Hornby, in his magnificent history of these mass, scrumming 'festival games', *Uppies and Downies*, quotes a celebrated description of a Shrove Tuesday in London by a Canterbury monk, William Fitzstephen, in 1174:

'The boys of every school bring fighting cocks to their masters, and all the afternoon is spent at school, to see the cocks fight together. After the midday meal the entire youth of the city goes to the fields for the famous game of ball. The students of the several branches of study have their ball; the followers of the several trades of the city have a ball in their hands.'

The passage describes the atmosphere among the players in this Shrovetide football festival as 'participation in the joys of unrestrained youth', and shows us not only that football has an exuberant thousand-year history as the people's game in Britain, but that playing it is an innate human thrill, serving as a reminder of how sad and joyless it is to see it being reduced today to a 'brand' or an 'entertainment product'.

The most renowned of these rough, rousing folk games to survive into our time is the Shrove Tuesday and Ash Wednesday contest at Ashbourne, in Derbyshire, first documented in 1683. Packs of plucky blokes form two teams, the Up'ards and Down'ards, have a mass skirmish to land the ball in goals which are three miles apart, across narrow alleyways in the town, car parks, the A515 road, fields, hedges, ditches and even a river. The game is a full-blooded contest of brute strength, with 'hugging' of the ball and pushing like rugby scrums, throwing once the ball is freed, and kicking, by faster lads seeking to make ground, all in the mud and wet. With hundreds involved, it can take seven hours for a goal finally to be scored.

As Hornby documents, these were the rough games that, over the centuries in England, royal decree, local laws and police sought to ban. There is a choice observation credited to a French visitor in 1831 at Derby – whose struggle between two local parishes, All Saints and St Peter's, gave the name 'derby' to all local rivalries between clubs in the same city. Seeing the 'broken shins, broken heads and torn coats' of this 'violent' contest, the Frenchman said:

'If Englishmen call this playing, it would be impossible to say what they call fighting.'

Others in authority, though, recognised football's joys and qualities. Hornby quotes Richard Mulcaster, headmaster of Merchant Taylors' School in London (still thriving today, fees £16,020 a year per pupil). Mulcaster bemoaned the roughness of it, including the 'bursting of shinnes and breaking of legges', but recognised:

'Footeball play . . . could not possibly have growne to this greatness . . . if it had not had great helpes, both to health and strength.'

He argued that football needed to be more civilised, to distil its fine elements and outlaw the thuggery, and in effect that is what happened. The public schools (which, by that historic quirk, are actually private, attended throughout the centuries by the fee-paying sons of the wealthy), refined football into a game of rules and skill. All over Britain, with a few stand-out exceptions like Ashbourne, the mass football games died out, partly under legal bans, but mostly laid waste by the industrial revolution. Work in the countryside and smaller towns dried up for many, wages were asphyxiatingly squeezed, and people migrated in their millions to the erupting, smoggy cities of Manchester, Liverpool, Birmingham. There, in the jerry-built slums with non-existent sewerage systems, which Engels would document in Manchester, there was no room or place to play, and life was too harsh anyway for much leisure.

While the working classes, including their children, were squashing into the unregulated hours and brutal working life of factories and mills, the public schools were reforming. Key headmasters, like Thomas Arnold at Rugby School from 1828–42, sought to shape these institutions as places of education as we now recognise them, rather than warehouses of bullying. Sport, or 'games', as many schools still call sport now, became integral to that project, appreciated and encouraged for its character-building and physical health benefits.

The public schools developed rules to change football, from shin-breaking wildness to a sport of designated boundaries and team numbers, requiring more skill, flair and co-operation than mere brute force. Famously, though, they all came up with different variants; some, like Rugby, developing a handling game, while most of the others outlawed hands. When young men left the public schools, they wanted to continue playing their games at universities or in the old boys' clubs they formed in London, but they found they were playing to different rules and so could not successfully play against other clubs.

That was the origin of the Football Association. A meeting was called in 1863 in Lincoln's Inn Fields, to agree on one set of rules, so all of these gentlemen could play each other. The eleven clubs which became the original members of the Football Association, the same organisation which today wrestles with governing the modern, multi-billion-pound game, at its £757m Wembley headquarters, were all southern and upper-class: Barnes, Surbiton, the War Office club, even two public schools were involved. It took a further six meetings to hammer out the differences, and the rules which emerged, for a kicking and dribbling game, with 'fouls' for handling and kicking opponents, became the template for the ostensibly simple but mesmerisingly skilful game which would captivate the world. Blackheath, old boys of the Blackheath Proprietary School, disagreed with the majority decision they considered not 'manly', to outlaw 'hacking', booting on the shins, from football, and they left, becoming a founder member in 1871 of the governing body for the rougher code, the Rugby Football Union.

The new game took time to spread out from the upper-class gentlemen with the money and leisure time to play, and into the rest of Britain's harassed population. The FA Cup was begun in 1871 with fifteen entries, and all the winners in the first eleven years were upper class. Old Etonians won the FA Cup in 1879 and 1882. They reached the final the following year, 1883, when their team included a baronet called Percy de Paravicini, and that was the momentous match, at the Kennington Oval, the cricket home of Surrey, when the dominance of English football by the upper classes was broken. Their opponents, Blackburn Olympic, were a team composed of weavers, a cotton machine operator, plumber, and other working men. Blackburn's 2–1 victory was hailed by one observer, according to the Football Association's official history, as 'a triumph for the democracy'.

Football had been taken into the industrial north, often by the returning sons of mill owners, or others who had done well up north out of the new manufacturing economy, and been sent to public schools. Blackburn Rovers was formed by ex-public schoolboys who wanted to play the great game where they lived and worked, and to make up the numbers, the clubs were opened up to able-bodied blokes in the towns. These ex-public school football envoys arrived in industrial cities whose harshest early conditions were easing a little. Workers, with a struggle, had begun to organise themselves and campaign in unions for better wages and more humane treatment. Manchester was a focus, with some radical distinction, in this political battle over the Victorian soul of the country, with the first Trades Union Congress held in the Mechanics Institute, David Street, from 2 to 6 June 1868. There was pressure in parliament too, from some liberals who campaigned against the exploitation of children and other of industry's human abuses, opposed by many upper-class Tories who asserted the right of factory employers to use child labour, otherwise their costs would rise and their businesses would become uncompetitive.

Throughout the nineteenth century a series of Factory Acts led to gradual humanising of work. In 1819, following an investigation into child labour, great progress was hailed by outlawing the employment of under-nines in cotton mills and limiting the working day of children aged between nine and sixteen to twelve hours. In 1878, the year Wanderers beat Royal Engineers 3–1 in the FA Cup final, another Factory Act prohibited children under ten being employed, and prescribed compulsory education for the first time in Britain for all children including the working class – up to the age of ten, when they could then be sent to the cotton mills and factories.

For adults, still working exhausting days in hard jobs, wages improved gradually, as did housing, and slowly most workers succeeded in pegging back the unrelenting six-day week, winning the right to half a day off on a Saturday. The combination of these civilising elements led to the birth of mass leisure – walking in the countryside, cycling, swimming, theatres, the music hall, eventually the growth of seaside resorts, and, most dramatically, football.

The recognised physical and morale-raising benefits of football led to the game being backed by many churches, who were seeking to attract worshippers, and also do some good for the poor, hard-pressed urban communities outside their doors. Fulham (St Andrews), Bolton Wanderers (Christ Church), Southampton (St Mary's), Aston Villa (Villa Cross Wesleyan Chapel), Everton (St Domingo's), Birmingham City (Trinity Church) and several other clubs formed at churches in the 1870s and 1880s grew to become the established professional names of today.

Manchester City, I learned, was one of them. The roots of the football club whose sky-blue stars of the 1970s I had grown up clipping out of *Shoot!* and Blu-tacking on my bedroom wall, were in the industrial grime and mud of Gorton, in east Manchester. There, a century earlier, Anna Connell, 25-year-old daughter of Arthur, the rector of St Mark's Church, had formed a working men's club, to provide people with some wholesome outlet from the grimness of life, the ever-presence of drink, and violence between rival gangs in the east Manchester streets.

St Mark's was round the corner from the Union Iron Works, the largest local employer, and beyond it, across stinking Thomas Street, was the Gorton Brook Chemical Works. Peter Lupson, a committed Christian, semi-retired languages teacher and football enthusiast, sought in his book *Thank God for Football!* to reclaim some of the forgotten history of how the church pioneered the origins of football in England's industrial cities. He placed Anna Connell's efforts in more detailed context, finding descriptions of Gorton at that time as a still hellish place, cramming in migrant workers from the countryside and Ireland, as fodder for the industrial works. The houses locally were described as thrown up by slum landlords: 'Cluttered together with more regard for the saving of ground-rent than for the comfort and health of their inhabitants.' Families lived in 'cold, cramped hovels' with two outside toilets for 250 people. The men did 'mind-numbing daily work' outside of which, for many, drink was the only escape. In the east Manchester streets were crowds of 'hungry and shoddily clad children'. There was a soup-kitchen near the church, serving 'poor, famished-looking creatures'.

Anna Connell went door-to-door to all 1,000 terraced and slum homes in the church's parish, and was helped in drumming up recruits by two men from the congregation, William Beastow and Thomas Goodbehere, who had senior jobs in the Union Iron Works. Slowly, people came for music, readings and drama. In 1879 they formed a cricket club. That did well enough, then, as at Sheffield Wednesday and several other clubs where cricket came first, they formed a football section so they could play sport all year round, including the winter, and not just in the cricket season.

It was 13 November 1880, when St Mark's (West Gorton) Football Club played their first reported match. This was the church club which grew in just a handful of years into Ardwick FC, and in 1892, by now professional, became a founder member of the Football League's Second Division, reforming in 1894 as Manchester City. St Mark's first game was against the Baptist Church, Macclesfield, twelve a side, which St Mark's lost 2–1. Gary James, in *Manchester the Greatest City*, says it is still unclear which scrap of terrain in Gorton the players found to play on.

'Wherever the pitch was,' James writes, 'it must be remembered that in 1880 it was nothing more than wasteland.'

Along with school old boys' clubs, and teams formed by churches, increasingly enlightened employers saw that they could have happier and more productive workers if they encouraged them in sport and constructive leisure activities. Arsenal was formed by workers at the Woolwich Arsenal, the club named Dial Square at first, after their workshop, in 1886. West Ham United was formed as the representative club of the shipbuilding company Thames Iron Works FC, in 1895. In the north and midlands, football came to the working classes earlier than that, and it was 1878 when men at the carriage and wagon works of the Lancashire and Yorkshire Railway Company, also in east Manchester, formed their club, Newton Heath. They played in shirts of green and gold, and also joined the Football League, as a professional club, in 1892, playing for another ten years before changing their name to Manchester United in 1902.

It was the fervour with which working men devoured the new thrilling, partisan and colourful spectacle of football – and not always in ways the church had in mind – which propelled the sport to such rapid popularity. Working men in cities had some time to play now, and, in their thousands, time to watch. So when the former public schoolboys in Blackburn and elsewhere formed clubs to play the game, they very rapidly, to their shock, attracted large crowds to watch the spectacle. The crowds brought with them some of the old spirit of the folk games, which had been bottled up through the harsh decades. There was drinking, betting, some fighting, and from the beginning, vitriolic abuse of referees for decisions which went against the fans' team. And while the upper-class ethos had been to promote the idea that what was important was not the winning, but the taking part, the local derbies and rivalries between the new football clubs developed a rawer intensity. That was why clubs began to pay players, so as to assemble teams which could defeat their opponents. That, as is well documented by the FA in its own records, was wholly opposed by the governing body, by whose rules the new game was played. Clubs which paid players were banned or disciplined.

A less understood part of this tension is that the FA's opposition to professionalism went deeper than moral disapproval of what they considered a debasing of their game's amateur ethos. It was also that the FA, from the beginning, was ambivalent about spectators, about the drawing in of large numbers of people to watch the game. Football had been developed for its qualities as a sport to play, for the exercise, team spirit and, as the monk had put it in 1174, for participating in the 'joys of unrestrained youth'. The clubs in the industrial cities were attracting crowds of regular supporters to stand and watch the game – and drink, gamble, swear at the referee and generally let off steam – and the clubs saw that they could charge them money for entry to the spectacle. That and other income provided the money to pay good players, as northern clubs began to do, against the rules and under the table, in the 1880s.

Eventually, after an FA Cup match in London in 1884, Upton Park accused Preston North End of having paid professionals in their team. Faced with an FA investigation which could have led to the club being banned, Major William Sudell, PNE's chairman, admitted it. He said he was driven by the ambition to compete with Blackburn Rovers – still North End's fiercest local rivals today – and could only do so by paying professional players. Sudell broke the issue into the open, and was supported by several other strong clubs for whom the importance of winning was more intense than it was for the gentlemen amateurs of the FA. It had been a tough fight for the clubs to be permitted even to pay their players for 'lost time', wages the men did not earn when they were off playing or training – a clear case of class-opposition from FA governors who had plenty of money for play time.

Manchester became a centre for the northern clubs' in-the-blood competitiveness, in opposition to the upper-class London FA. In late 1884 thirty-one clubs met in Manchester and were given a barrister's opinion that the FA was exceeding its powers by continuing to suppress professionalism. The *Official History of the Football Association* explains it this way:

'The FA was divided. Men such as Arthur Kinnaird and Charles Alcock [FA senior figures] were convinced that professionalism was inevitable and should be properly contained by legislation. Against them were men, a strong body, who were still in love with the notion of playing for health and fun.'

The clubs were not for budging, though, and formed a rival body, the British Football Association. They threatened a break-away, as happened in rugby, where the northern professional clubs formed their own code, known as rugby league. On 20 July 1885 the FA kept its game together, with itself as the governing body, by finally accepting that professionalism could not be resisted, and seeking instead to restrain it with a range of limiting rules. This set the pattern for what the FA, as the governing body, would seek to do, with results of varying effectiveness, throughout its great game's phenomenal development: try to embrace football's commercial growth, while seeking to preserve its sporting heart and underlying values.

There was inevitability to the next development, the formation of a professional Football League. The rationale for that came from the need for professional clubs to have regular fixtures, for which they would charge spectators entry, so giving a certain, known amount of income from which they could pay the players. Before that, clubs would have a series of friendlies, opponents frequently did not turn up, or fixtures were cancelled at the last minute. Forming a league was the idea of William McGregor, a Scottish draper and chairman of Aston Villa, and he invited twelve clubs (six from the north, six from the Midlands) to come together. There was already a baseball league in America, but McGregor's model was cricket's County Championship, started in 1873. The twelve clubs which have the distinction of being founder members of the Football League, the first in the world, are Accrington, Aston Villa, Blackburn Rovers, Bolton Wanderers, Burnley, Derby County, Everton, Notts County, Preston North End, Stoke City, West Bromwich Albion and Wolverhampton Wanderers. They agreed to form the league, with home and away fixtures between all clubs, on 22 March 1888, at the Royal Hotel, Manchester. Preston North End won the league in the first season, and the FA Cup, the first-ever Double.

The Football League itself had different priorities from the Football Association, and McGregor always said the two bodies could complement each other. The FA remained the governing body for the rules of the game, on and off the field. The league needed to develop a constitution to ensure its own survival and the clubs' financial health. At that first meeting, the clubs agreed to a principle which remains in place today, but bloodily fought over: the need for the big clubs to share money with the small. Today, the major clubs, like Liverpool (formed in 1892), argue over the fairest way for the Premier League to share out its £3.5bn television rights deals, secured for 2010–13. The original twelve clubs in the Football League recognised right at the beginning that without some financial equality, the big city clubs, which had the most heavily populated catchment areas and therefore would always attract larger crowds paying more money, could pay for the best players. Without sharing the money, there would be no meaningful competition. The principle was established at the birth of the Football League that it had to be an absorbing contest, with uncertainty about which team would win individual games, and the league overall. So, from the start, they decided that the home team, in the bigger ground, should not keep all the money from a game, but should share it with their opponents.

McGregor, the Football League's founding force, had argued for the money from each match to be split exactly equally, but he was voted down in favour of a flat £15 to the away team. In friendlies during the First World War, then preserved for league matches when the competition restarted in 1919, the split was changed to 20 per cent for the away team. That system remained in place for sixty-four years, throughout the great growth of the professional game, and underpinned its development. That level of sharing meant that the big city clubs did still dominate, but not completely. Competition was more even, and there was room for clubs from smaller cities and towns, well managed, to come through and succeed.

The FA's moral struggle over professionalism is well known and the rows were conducted very publicly, but the arguments over the nature of the new professionalised clubs, which led to the imposition of Rule 34, were barely documented. It turned out to have been the FA's means of trying to preserve the club ethos, to prevent sharp-eyed businessmen treating them like any other normal business opportunity.

With very few exceptions, the clubs were literally clubs. Like St Mark's, they were formed by people wanting to play the game, so they were membership organisations, involved collectively in football. No one member could be said to 'own' it. As those few stronger clubs began to pay players, the members became personally responsible for the club's financial commitments. Then as crowds grew, clubs needed to build more substantial grounds for supporters, and enclose the grounds so that spectators had to pay to watch. As early as 1892, when Everton moved out of Anfield after an argument about the rent with the landlord, John Houlding (who formed his own club, Liverpool), Everton went on to build a huge new purpose-built ground over on Goodison Park.

The members of the clubs, now mostly completely independent of the churches and original associations which had pioneered them, wanted to protect themselves financially from the personal liability of paying the players' wages and major construction projects. That was why they moved to form themselves into limited companies – so the members' liability would be limited, as in commercial companies, only to the value of the shares they held. It also meant that new shares could be issued to new subscribers, and the money paid for them could go to the club, frequently to help build the grounds.

Hence the first appearance of the rule in the FA handbook of 1892, agreeing to Preston North End's request to form a limited company, but limiting the dividends the company could pay its shareholders. By 1899 the body of rules was in the FA handbook which lasted until clubs began to bypass them and float on the Stock Market, almost a century later. Owner-shareholders could not reap large amounts of money from the clubs – legitimately, at least – because the dividends which could be paid out on their shares were limited to a nominal maximum. Directors could not be paid at all, at first, a rule which was later modified to require they work full-time at the club. That prevented 'owners' appointing themselves as directors while working in their other businesses, and leaking fortunes of the fans' money out to themselves in big salaries. The third element of the rules was almost identical to the one which remains in force, that a club could not be wound up, the ground flogged off, and the excess pocketed by the shareholder-owners. So there it was, as long ago as that, set down in orderly fashion in the FA rulebook of 1899–1900, the FA's edict that football clubs existed to play and progress the sport, not to make money for their 'owners'.

That was how I learned that my instinctive unease over Franny Lee's consortium's avoidance of these long-standing rules, so they could float Manchester City on the Stock Market, was a view of a football club which was established by the governing body itself. We all grew up believing in our clubs as clubs, not as companies with owners growing rich from them, and the FA had rules in place to preserve and maintain that collective nature. The major shareholders, who often histori-cally became involved in a financial crisis, putting money in to stabilise a club and pay its debts, and the directors, were supposed to serve the club and its supporters, not make money out of them. Over the years, they came to describe themselves as 'custodians' of the clubs.

You can read all of the FA's wrestles with the soul of foot-ball in two ways of intrinsic tension. You can admire the conviction of the game's early founders that the sport had values, and a purpose, and its clubs were not mere entertainments to be picked up, profited from, and discarded. Yet you can also recognise the class snobbery and hypocrisy, in rich, aristocratic men laying down rules about moral purpose to the masses who were having to do all the country's dirty work. Whichever view of the FA you favour, it has to be recognised that their insist-ence on some ethical values did endure, and provided football with ideals which survive today, even in the age of the break-away Premier League and takeovers with millions of pounds of debt by overseas buyers. The notions of fair play versus foul, of sportsmanship, the basis of the Respect campaign against racism and abuse of players and officials, have their roots in the standards preached at the beginning.

The effect of Rule 34 and the culture which it evolved was also mixed. The fact that the clubs were not normal businesses, owned and managed by full-time professional people who needed to record a profit, is recognised to have contributed to the fact that they were too often not well run. The amateur ethos, running the club and playing the game for the love of it, is admirable. However, amateurishness in being shabby, mean-spirited, part-time and semi-detached from the consequences of decisions can be disastrous. A different class snobbery also developed, between the merchant directors in their cushioned seats on the halfway line, the scotch and pies in their 'inner sanctum', and the supporters freezing, then occasionally and too frequently dying, on uncovered and unsafe terraces.

Yet the clubs did develop with a sense of themselves as collective institutions, representing their towns and cities, and the fans embraced them as homes of belonging for life. This was partly due to the culture that they were not simply there to make a profit. No other recreations, the local cinema, theatre, music hall, pub, which exist to entertain people and make money out of them as 'punters', ever claimed such loyalty. Fans grew up, for generations, thinking of the football companies to which they paid their money as their clubs. Although they were almost all limited companies, they continued to be known as clubs.

Many directors were, historically, true custodians; they paid out their own money to soak up their club's losses and keep it in business; they never took a penny out for themselves, in salary or dividend, and they did not make a profit if they sold their shares. It was also the case that the amounts of money these 'custodians' paid in, and the way they did it, was wholly different from the huge spending by owners in the Premier League era, first by Jack Walker at Blackburn, then Roman Abramovich at Chelsea, and now Sheikh Mansour at Manchester City. The big clubs, once they had been put on their feet by an initial injection of money, sometimes in the form of a loan, tended to be able to run themselves. Some clubs, particularly the smaller ones, relied on regular contributions from directors, which became effectively the cost of being on the board. But the amounts of money were very much smaller, and they were not to purchase dream teams of superstars, but to stay in business, and in the league at a reasonable level.

James Gibson, a businessman who lived in Hale, the same neighbourhood as Peter Swales years later, saved Manchester United from insolvency with a contribution of £2,000 just before Christmas 1931, paying to settle debts, the players' wages, and to buy all staff a turkey. In all his twenty years as the Manchester United majority 'owner' and chairman, 1931–51, in which he stabilised the finances, oversaw the establishment of a junior section for youth development, rebuilt Old Trafford, appointed Matt Busby and set the club on the route to greatness, he only gave money, and never sought to make it.

The relative evenness of the professional competition, with many different clubs winning the league and FA Cup, was also maintained to a repressive extent by the maximum wage – a crude salary cap. It was imposed on all professional footballers from 1904 so that clubs could keep costs down and level the playing field. According to the rule, which was broken habitually, clubs could not compete, as they do now, to outbid each other for the most talented players. England internationals played their whole careers for a single club, who paid them modestly for entertaining crowds of 60,000 people watching the nation's most popular sport. Under legal challenge from the Professional Footballers Association, the maximum wage was finally dropped, and the hated 'retain and transfer' system, which kept players shackled to clubs, was declared an illegal restraint of their trade.

Yet even after the maximum wage, only £20 a week at the time, was abolished, English football remained relatively even. Gate sharing remained in 1965, when the first television deal was done, £5,000 from the BBC for the *Match of the Day* highlights programme, and the money was shared out equally between clubs. They lived on their own resources, not with owners hugely backing them, and so, in the unfolding dramas we watched, the big clubs did have the financial advantage, when their grounds were full, but it was not so great. A well-managed smaller club could come through and make a genuine challenge, as, Ipswich Town, Derby County, Nottingham Forest and Norwich City all did in modern times. Liverpool, in the 1970s, had come through to dominate the Football League, first through the possessed commitment of the manager, Bill Shankly, then with assured succession planning. With that, came a full Anfield, and the financial strength did serve to reinforce the club's ability to replace players with record signings, Kenny Dalglish, Graeme Souness, later John Barnes. Yet the gap between the rich and their challengers was never as great as today, when hundreds of millions of pounds from an oligarch, or an oil sheikh, are needed if a club, even a big club, is to challenge at the top.

The concentration of wealth between a handful of clubs developed from the 1980s. With the maximum wage abolished, top club wage bills had steepled, and the game was suffering its decline from neglect, hooliganism, the fences, the stigma from the media and hatred by the government. The bigger clubs, led by Manchester United, Liverpool, Everton, Arsenal and Spurs, began to agitate throughout the decade for a greater share of the game's income.

The first breach of the decades-honoured structure of sharing money in the Football League was in 1983, when the big clubs succeeded in abolishing the rule of sharing gate receipts. So the principle that the league should regulate against the big city clubs inevitably dominating if they kept all the money from home matches was discarded.

The 'Big Five' clubs then levelled their sights at hoarding a greater share of the television money. Continually threatening that they would break away completely from the Football League if their demands were not met, they succeeded by the 1988–92 TV deal in securing 50 per cent of the total, £44m, for the First Division clubs, 25 per cent went to the Second, with the other 25 per cent shared between the Third and Fourth Division clubs. All the clubs in football knew the next deal, from 1992, would be hugely increased, because of the emergence of Sky TV, and the big five resolved to break away.

David Dein, Arsenal's vice-chairman, who had first bought shares in 1983, and Noel White, Swales's former business partner and now a director of Liverpool, were deputed to try to talk the FA into supporting the First Division clubs' breakaway. Fatefully, the FA betrayed its roots and historic ethos, believing, mistakenly, that it would become the undisputed governing body for those big clubs too, and it supported the breakaway. The deal the new Premier League then secured was for the live rights to be shown exclusively on Sky, for which golden licence to print money from football supporters, Rupert Murdoch's satellite broadcaster, together with the BBC for *Match of the Day*, paid £305m over five years.

That was the 'quantum leap' that Boon, of Deloitte and Touche, had enthused about, and it turned the Premier League clubs instantly from failing places emerging from the wreckage of the 1980s, to very lucrative businesses. That, I now understood, was what the fuss had been about over the formation of the Premier League. It was not just a renaming, 'rebranding', of the First Division, it was a genuine breakaway, to form a different competition, and its motivation was to make as much money as possible, and no longer have to share it.

Years later, I interviewed Graham Kelly, who had been the FA's chief executive at that time. Looking down at the table, thinking for a long time and speaking eventually, he acknowledged that the decision had been dreadfully misguided, the FA had been outmanoeuvred by the big clubs, and he did realise that some of those individual shareholder-owners and directors, including Dein, had gone on to make a great deal of money for themselves out of it.

'We were guilty of a tremendous collective lack of vision,' Kelly said.

With an unprecedentedly huge amount of money coming into football – paid, in reality, by supporters forking out for Sky TV and the dishes made by Alan Sugar's Amstrad – the big clubs soared away to keep it all. The Football League clubs watched a yawning financial chasm open up with the Premier League, and players' wages in the Premier League began their escalation to today's £200,000 per week, £10m per year, wage paid to Carlos Tevez by Sheikh Mansour's Manchester City.

The amateur grass roots of football, for the people who actually played the game for love, were deteriorating from years of public spending and local authority cuts under nineteen years of Conservative government, and saw none of the Sky TV bonanza. Malcolm Berry, chief executive of the English Schools Football Association, told me in 1996 the organisation had no funding at all except from sponsors. The branch in Manchester, formed in 1894, in whose U16 representative team a callow Ryan Giggs had recently played, had since 1923 been supported by Manchester City Council, along with other school sports and games, including chess. But in 1993, another victim of the government's squeeze on local authority finances, Manchester's council, which was at the time involved in a bid to host the Olympics, had scrapped the modest grants to sports bodies for the schoolchildren of Manchester.

Back home myself, I had found it difficult to play football to the level of commitment, and in the serious battles, required by the club of my youth. So, with some friends, we formed our own club. We joined the Manchester Publicity League, which had involved teams from the newspapers and printing presses until the whole industry decamped to London. The league still had three divisions, though, and we were told it was more affable than other Manchester Sunday morning leagues, in which brutality was still the defining experience.

We enjoyed the adventure, calling ourselves, for a bit of a joke, Dynamo Thursday, after the night of the week we all played eight a side on Astroturf. It was heartening to watch several guys, who had never played competitive football before and not been encouraged as kids, find their feet and improve into solid players. The league was decent enough, give or take one notorious head-butt of our winger, and the odd team riddled with thuggery. But the pitches, the facilities, in our city, renowned around the world for football, were disgraceful. The playing fields of Manchester had done nothing but decline in the twenty years since I had started playing on them, as a shivering ten-year-old. We were allocated a pitch at Fog Lane Park in Didsbury, south Manchester; for a while there were no changing rooms there, but they did open some sheds for us, next door to the children's small animal farm.

The main 'home' of most teams was Chorlton Park, two miles from booming Old Trafford, along Barlow Moor Road. There was an old, broken changing block there, splattered in graffiti, which the council had long ago closed down. We were men nudging thirty, all working, paying our tax and council tax, out playing football, getting healthy exercise, being upstanding participants in society. To do so, we had to get changed outside in the sleet and rain. We had to pee behind trees as young mums wheeled their kids in prams, or old folk walked their dogs. The pitches were overhung by conker trees, dog turds often lurked. Manchester had become adept at landing the pots of funding for special projects: £145m for Metrolink, £70m to build the arena; soon it would spend £127m building a brand-new stadium for the Commonwealth Games, then for Manchester City plc to occupy. Yet Manchester in the 1990s, with football coming home and booming, did not have the routine funds to drain and maintain playing fields for the children and residents to a standard above degrading. Dumped in the clagging mud by a tackle of some lad an unfair number of years younger than me, my thoughts would drift over to Martin Edwards, just along the road, en route to making £93m for himself, and wonder how the country, and its national sport, football, had come to this carve-up.

Contemplating the way in which football changed in the 1990s, you come back repeatedly to Hillsborough. That shattering disaster, in which ninety-six mostly young Liverpool supporters had been killed on the game's wretched landscape, was the end of the old era, when the men who ran football neglected the supporters' very safety. It laid the foundations for the years of boom, because the clubs were forced, by legislation after Lord Justice Taylor's final report, to make the grounds safe. Following his recommendation that the poor clubs be given financial help with the rebuilding – they had not mentioned to the judge the satellite TV windfall just over the horizon – £200m grants of public money were given to the professional clubs. After the 1990 World Cup, fans had already begun returning to football, and the ground improvements, rehabilitation of football's image and of the idea of being a fan and, soon, the overseas star players attracted to England by the riches on offer, would have crowds flooding back.

Taylor had recommended in his final report that all-seater stadiums become compulsory, and insisted they should not lead to higher ticket prices – he cited the cost of a seat at Glasgow Rangers' Ibrox, which was £6 at the time. In fact, in the Premier League era, despite the billions which supporters paid for TV subscriptions, clubs raised ticket prices tenfold. At Liverpool, the cost to stand on the Kop in 1989–90 was £4; in 2011–12, the twentieth season of the Premier League, the price of all tickets in the Kop to see top opponents was £45. A generation of young people, paying full price at sixteen or eighteen at all clubs, was priced out, excluded from the experience of supporting a football club, which my generation enjoyed so much and was so formed by. The grounds have filled, but mostly with fans my age and older, into their forties now, whose loyalty had been secured when it was cheap to go.

Nor did Taylor envisage that the owner-chairmen, whose game had produced the scandalous neglect which so shocked him, would, within a decade, be floating their clubs on the Stock Market and banking millions for their shares. He had condemned not only the complacent attitude of too many modern directors to the safety of supporters, but the generally self-serving culture which he found pervaded the boardrooms.

'As for the clubs,' he wrote in his final report, 'in some instances it is legitimate to wonder whether the directors are genuinely interested in the welfare of their grass-roots supporters. Boardroom struggles for power, wheeler-dealing in the buying and selling of shares and indeed of whole clubs, sometimes suggest that those involved are more interested in the personal financial benefits or social status of being a director than of directing the club in the interests of its supporter-customers.'

He called for the 'the fullest reassessment of policy for the game' – not for a Premier League breakaway, nor for Stock Market flotations. However, no rules were put in place to effect that wider change, and the FA, myopic, surrendered to the big clubs and their commercial ambitions. When those clubs' owners wanted to float on the Stock Market and realise their personal fortunes, they found the FA's Rule 34 was a block – as it was supposed to be. The very point of buying shares in a company on the Stock Market is as a financial investment, for the shareholder to be paid dividends out of the company's profits. The FA's rule limiting dividends was a barrier to a float. The requirement that directors work full-time was also inappropriate to a plc; non-executive directors, often extremely well paid for attending six or so board meetings a year, are required in public companies. Tottenham Hotspur, chaired then by Irving Scholar, were the first English club to float, in 1983. His advisers came across these old rules, relics of football's former ethos sitting unloved in the club's constitution, so they suggested simply bypassing them by forming a holding company, Tottenham Hotspur plc. Scholar told me that Spurs notified the FA but he did not believe they had ever had a reply. Certainly, the FA simply allowed it; they never protested, or sought to enforce or strengthen their rules, throughout the procession of clubs to the Stock Market.

The contrast of the FA's abdication in the 1990s, when the money was becoming so enormous and the need to protect the game's heart therefore more urgent, with the 1890s was stark. It was a great betrayal. The Hillsborough disaster, and the way the top clubs were allowed to rake in all the money flowing into football after that, would lead to more 'wheeler-dealing in the buying and selling of shares', and more 'personal financial benefits' and 'social status' for directors than ever before.

From learning the uncomfortable truths of Francis Lee's takeover at Manchester City, I was drawn down a trail into all of this: football's free-spirited origins, its founding values which chimed with how fans felt about it still, Britain's very social fabric, class divides and fights for dignity, and the struggle for football's soul with those who regard it as just a business to exploit. I became convinced that, dazzled by the game's dramas on the field and not educated in its underpinning philosophies, we had lost sight of the game's core values. We had forgotten that football was a sport with a social purpose and collective benefit, not just 'a business' in which fans' wide-eyed loyalty should now be considered a 'captive market', as some of the money men explicitly described it, from which 'owners' of 'clubs' could make fat personal profits. Supporters of other clubs, particularly United, were beginning to protest at the way English football was changing, at the soaring ticket prices and corporate mission of football's new direction, the plc and the drive for profits and dividends, share value, which is the core purpose of a Stock Market company. An old founding principle came to be rediscovered, in reaction to the nakedly commercial interpretation of football and sudden takeovers: that the clubs, in their true nature, belong to their supporters.

In July 1999 a conference was held at Birkbeck College, London, to discuss football's new commercialisation in the Premier League era, and explore alternative ideas of supporter ownership and wider sharing of the new fortunes. We are more familiar now, after years of unease at the English football plcs, overseas takeovers and 'owners' with agendas of their own, that Barcelona and Real Madrid, two of the greatest clubs in Europe, are owned by their supporters. They are mutual, collective, in form as well as idea, rather than companies which can be bought and sold. The president of Barcelona, Sandro Rossell, describes the club as 'a feeling, not a business'. We have learned that in the Bundesliga, the German premier division, all clubs, even the mighty like Bayern Munich and Borussia Dortmund, must be majority owned by their supporters.

At that time, though, the discoveries were fresh and the idea of supporter ownership came as a revelation. Andy Walsh, chair of the Independent Manchester United Supporters Association, which had been campaigning against high ticket prices (the cheapest price had increased from £3.50 in 1989–90 to £15; now the cheapest, of which there are only a few available, is £28), was there. So was Joan Laporta, leader of the Elefant Blau (Blue Elephant) fans movement calling for change to the incumbent regime at Barcelona. Because his club is a member-democracy, Laporta was able to gather support, stand as a candidate, and within five years had been elected president of Barcelona. Because United was a plc, Martin Edwards proceeded to make his fortune, then the Glazer family bought the club, with all that debt, and proceeded to drain from United, at the time of writing this book, £480m in interest, bank charges and fees to service their own takeover. When the Glazers won their hostile takeover battle in May 2005, Walsh, who had led the fight implacably against it, turned away with a group of fellow United travellers, to form their own club, FC United of Manchester, member-owned from the beginning. Brian Lomax, who had formed a supporters' trust, a mutual body of fans, at Northampton Town, which had then bought a stake in the club and elected him as a director, was a pioneer of supporter ownership. His argument was that fans could not achieve what they wanted, the enlightened running of their club, by ousting one single 'owner' for another; the problem was 'ownership', by a single businessman with his own agenda. Lomax would become the first chief executive of Supporters Direct, a body formed in 2000 with the backing of the new Labour government, to promote the idea of supporters owning their football clubs again, or at least having a collective say.

The journey into Britain's founding sporting history and ethos, and the evolution of its football clubs, including Manchester City's honourable story, begun as a force for good in Gorton's wretched streets, left me feeling I had been deeply naïve about Francis Lee's takeover. I had wielded no intelligent understanding of what Manchester City even was in reality, and what in practice Franny represented. We had ushered him in not because everybody believed, in an informed way and after due inquiry, that he was ideal for the club's future. We worshipped Franny, and excommunicated Swales because, when we were kids, whether literally or figuratively, we had all kissed his image on the telly. Now here he was having taken advantage of that iconic status, forming a holding company and bypassing Rule 34, as so many other clubs had done; planning, with the help of Barlow and David Bernstein, to float Manchester City, the original St Mark's (West Gorton) church club, on the Stock Market.

As it would turn out, though, Franny never did record a great increase in the value of the shares. Unlike United, Newcastle, Villa, Chelsea and others, City would not harvest the copious rewards of the Premier League breakaway. The reason they did not was due to a truly effective combination of ingredients: haplessness, cock-up and self-destruction – a stew becoming known as Typical City.

CHAPTER 11

THE CLUB WHICH ATE ITSELF

With his feet under the desk in the chairman's office at Maine Road, Francis Lee's plans to sweep away the mean-spirited follies of the Peter Swales era, beef up the club and make money seemed to start just as planned. They did not sack Brian Horton immediately, as we had all thought they might; they sacked him a season later, in May 1995. After that, Barlow told the press, they were looking to appoint 'a manager who can take us into Europe'.

Inside Maine Road, they had quickly gutted the old offices where the ghosts of former directors' wives were still tenderly unwrapping the tinfoil from their home-made cakes, and putting the kettle on. City's new future, of four- or five-star dining at tables in the Main Stand for £50,000 each, and one complimentary blazer, was being served up. The investment from this, and from Franny's consortium, paid for Horton to sign new players, including the pleasing talents of Paul Walsh and Peter Beagrie. The Kippax, the terrace running the length of the Maine Road pitch, whose rebuilding Swales had, critically for him, not been able to finance, was demolished after the final day of the 1993–94 season, as ordered by the Taylor Report deadline.

A fan, Phill Gatenby, had published a loving tribute to the Kippax, a nice booklet, which I bought on the way into the match which was a 2–2 draw with Chelsea.

I did not mourn the passing of the terraces as many other fans did. From my early teens when I had begun to stand on the Kippax, I had found it dark and the rake not steep enough to guarantee a good view in a large crowd. The floodlit European nights in the 1970s were marvels, but often as the 1980s soured, the Kippax could be sullen and miserable. It was there, or on the wide yard between the turnstiles and the steps, that you would see the occasional vicious fight, particularly on derby days. I was caught in one crush, up at the top, with everybody leaving and funnelling to the top of the steps, which became hairy before we were released and finally made it down.

Taylor's shocked description in his report of the 'dismal football scene' he had found in his appalled tour of the national game and the 'general malaise or blight' of the old grounds, one of which, Hillsborough, had just had ninety-six people die on it, did ring true with me about the Kippax:

> Football spectators are invited by the clubs for entertainment and enjoyment. Often, however, the facilities provided for them have been lamentable. The ordinary provisions to be expected at a place of entertainment are sometimes not merely basic but squalid . . . The terrace accommodation, in particular, is often uncovered [as one corner of the Kippax always was for home fans], and little has been done to improve the layout in accordance with modern expectations.

The overall picture of conditions and facilities to be expected by a standing spectator is depressing. It is in stark contrast to the different world, only yards away, in the Board Room and the lucrative executive boxes. I appreciate that they cater for an affluent clientele and bring in much-needed revenue. No one would expect or indeed want their plush carpeting or haute cuisine when visiting the terraces; but accommodation and facilities have often been below the basic decent standard necessary to give spectators dignity, let alone comfort.

One of the main thrusts of the Taylor Report was that hooliganism and general bad behaviour were encouraged, made almost acceptable, by the lamentable conditions around us in the grounds. I always felt that about the playing fields, too; that because they were so degrading, depressing and derelict, they encouraged thuggishness and a brutal expression in the game. The judge provided almost too much detail about toilets, going on at length about how because there were no decent ones, 'The practice of urinating against walls or even on the terraces [despite his constant reiteration of that as a feature of the 'bad old days', I never saw anyone pee on any terrace, ever] has become endemic and is followed by men who would not behave that way elsewhere. Thus crowd conduct becomes degraded and other misbehaviour seems less out of place.'

Taylor had noted that the fans in football generally were never treated as equals by the directors, or listened to: 'The football supporters' organisations complain that supporters have not hitherto been much consulted . . . about anything . . . affecting their well-being and enjoyment.'

But the judge then went on to not listen himself. The Football Supporters Association was formed after the Heysel Stadium disaster in 1985 to speak with a more enlightened fans' voice than the pervading and shameful images of hooliganism, and campaign against Margaret Thatcher's ID card scheme. The FSA had argued to Taylor against wiping away the terraces and the cherished, passionate culture which did survive amid the discomforts, ordering their compulsory replacement with seats. Their argument was that the clubs would use the mandatory seating as an opportunity to raise ticket prices beyond the reach of poorer, younger and older supporters, who had stayed loyal to football throughout its 'malaise'. Taylor, although he had observed and criticised the self-interest of directors – 'more interested in the personal financial benefits or social status of being a director than of directing the club in the interests of its supporter customers' – nevertheless had faith that the 'owners' and directors would not dramatically raise ticket prices. In that judgement, it turned out, the FSA, whose members had stood on those terraces all their lives, knew the football bosses rather better than he did.

Over the years since, as standing to watch football in the top two divisions ended and became actually illegal, the clubs have raised ticket prices with 1,000 per cent inflation, contrary to the recommendations in the Taylor Report. You almost never see crowds of young people at matches any more; they are mostly consigned to watching games on Sky in pubs. The average age, documented by the Premier League in its own fans survey, is always in the forties. Ron Gourlay, the Chelsea chief executive, talking in 2011 about the need for the club to expand Stamford Bridge or move elsewhere, said they had to get 'more youth' into the ageing Chelsea support. At City, they recognise two 'lost generations' of fans since the prices rose. You see very few teenagers in the crowd.

So I have come to understand why fans campaigned so hard to keep the terraces and to believe that they should, as the FSA argued, have been made safe and decent rather than obliterated. Many people who always supported their club standing up still feel, almost twenty years on, that a foundation of football's status as the people's game, where they could gather with mates and wholeheartedly support their club, was needlessly done away with.

The terraces themselves were not a cause of the disaster at Hillsborough – the fans died due to the mismanagement by the South Yorkshire Police, the appallingly unsafe state of the Leppings Lane end and ground itself, the dreadful 'pens' and the fences at the front. Standing at football is safe if the grounds and clubs make it so. It survives in the lower two divisions and non-leagues, in rugby, horse racing and other sports, and in the great new arenas of the Bundesliga, safe standing areas have been incorporated, specifically sanctioned by the German FA to allow young and poorer people access to the 'social inclusion' of watching football.

The accusation from football supporter groups in England has always been that the top clubs themselves encouraged Taylor into his all-seater recommendation because they wanted to gentrify the grounds. Seeing a future as part of the 'entertainment industry' and planning a breakaway to keep all the new pay-TV money, the clubs did not want teenagers and young men, including the poor working class, whom they often generalised as hooligans, to crowd affordably on to terraces. Supported with socio-demographic research carried out by the FA for its 1991 document, *Blueprint for the Future of Football*, the clubs foresaw a better class of supporter paying more money for a seat, dinner and trimmings. The *Blueprint*, produced with the assistance of Alex Fynn, who worked for the Conservatives' favoured advertising company, Saatchi and Saatchi, pointed to the increased spending power of British people, now more commonly referred to as 'consumers', emerging from industrial collapse into the new economy of financial and other services.

'The response of most sectors,' the *Blueprint* said, 'has been to move upmarket so as to follow the affluent middle-class consumer. We strongly suggest that there is a message in this for football.'

At City, Franny and his associates had got that message. The new Kippax, replacing the old groaning terrace and its two-decade-long yearning for better times, would have 'executive dining' pumped into its very stomach. There would be several levels of lounge, and a middle girth of corporate boxes where waitresses would serve expensive lunches and wine in glasses to corporations and fans-done-good who would pay plenty for the treat. Just like they had at United, all these years.

That would combine with the new directors' and loan-stock subscribers' dining in the Main Stand, and all the other restaurants the new regime was rolling in. Obviously other clubs were doing the same, and 'corporate entertaining' became a

defining feature of football's reinvention, but at City they did
seem to talk about it a great deal. It came upon me quite
stealthily, that the new era for the club envisaged by Francis
Lee and his consortium did seem to be rather a lot about eating.

We had believed that Franny, as a great and beaming former
player, would be the perfect saviour of the club, but he and his
regime seemed to struggle with accepting the extraordinary
wages the players in the breakaway Premier League could now
command. Niall Quinn's generation, to make ends meet, did
not need to spend their afternoons turning waste paper into
quality tissue. They bought racehorses while they were still
playing. In 1995 the striker Chris Sutton moved from Norwich
City to Blackburn Rovers, who were buying their way to the
championship with tax-exile Jack Walker's fortune. Sutton's
wage, £10,000 a week or half a million pounds a year, set a
new level for good English players. At City, players necessary
to keep the team in the Premier League could now demand
wages of £300,000 or more. Old-timers were beginning to resent
how they had missed out during their long and physically gru-
elling careers, and Lee and Barlow, ex-players themselves, were
in the position of having to actually pay these wages.

That sense around the club that the modern players had it
too easy was not eased by the arrival of the manager they finally
landed, six summer weeks after sacking Horton, to 'take us
into Europe'. When Alan Ball was appointed I remember
thinking that Franny really hadn't watched or noticed much
football in the years since he finished playing. Then, Ball was
still the 'flame-haired dynamo' of midfields, the inspirational,
tireless worker with whom Franny had played for England and

who had won the World Cup at Wembley in 1966. To us who had been watching the game throughout, it was clear that Ball's record as a manager, at Portsmouth, Stoke City (who were relegated to the Third Division in 1990), Exeter City and Southampton, was a scrappy endeavour pockmarked by failure, compared with the astonishing feats of his playing days.

The accounts of the City players from that time all report that Ball bounced into Maine Road declaring that he was a winner, presenting as evidence the World Cup he had won as a player nearly three decades earlier. During the 1995–96 season, City's financial difficulties, due to the debts and players' wages to which Swales had committed the club, began to bite, despite the new restaurants. Uwe Rösler, the East German striker, was acquitting himself well enough, and Lee's regime, Barlow told me at the time, had decided they could obtain 'better value' than highly paid English footballers by signing players from Europe. At Spurs, foreign signings were to mean the German striker Jürgen Klinsmann in 1994, a genuine World Cup star and landmark upgrade for the Premier League; United had Eric Cantona, strutting maître of the new red order, and at Arsenal, Dennis Bergkamp's grace was infusing a different vision for the art of football. At City, the European shopping was for cut-price, duty-free bargains. That would mean that sound Tony Coton was replaced in goal by German Eike Immel, who was 35 at the time. Terry Phelan, 'the scuttler', 5ft 6in of restless muscle, was sold to Chelsea, and City recruited instead the 31-year-old German Michael Frontzeck, who ran up the left wing looking like a wardrobe on wheels.

Georgiou Kinkladze was a footballer of twinkling gifts who

brightened City's autumn, but the other players complained he was pampered as the favourite while they were barely rated by Ball, and were never woven into a functioning team. Kinkladze's marvellous left-foot finish after a one-two with Quinn to beat Aston Villa 1–0 in November 1995 was City's first win of Alan Ball's first season in charge, in their twelfth game. Quinn himself, whose giant worth we had grown over years to appreciate, was dropped from favour. The crowd's grumbling impatience and anxiety for improvement was contagious for new and disparate players and the manager's method seemed tied to an old-fashioned line of defiant battling talk. That month, Ball signed Martin Phillips, a nineteen-year-old left-winger from one of his former clubs, Exeter, predicting publicly that Phillips was so extravagantly gifted he would become England's first ever £10m footballer. That promise went the way of Peter Swales's Old Trafford-quality redevelopment of the ground and the England caps for Malcolm Allison's tyros. It was the season United won the Double with their 'kids' – David Beckham, Gary and Phil Neville, Ryan Giggs, Paul Scholes and Nicky Butt, whose parents had seen them safely into Old Trafford, not Maine Road, during our years of crumble.

After the start of eight straight defeats and three draws, the team, which had so many strong players still within it, did wriggle up to the possibility of surviving in the Premier League. Then, with the battle against relegation just being joined, in March 1996, Francis Lee's City sold Garry Flitcroft, one of the outstanding young players who had chosen City over United, from out of the centre of midfield. City were paid £3.5m by Walker's Blackburn Rovers, and needed the money. I interviewed several players about the madness of that time, and they all said it was devastating to lose a player as centrally important as Flitcroft, at that late point in a season when City were struggling to stay up.

Barlow confirmed to me later what City would reveal in their accounts, that they had developed financial problems again because the new Kippax, with all its restaurants, had turned out more expensive than planned, swallowing up £11.5m. That was obviously a great deal more than the £3m Franny and his consortium had loaned in, together with the eager subscribers to the new generation of dining in the Main Stand. Just two years after our heartfelt battle to invoke St Francis's second coming, City were overspent, overborrowed and going down again. They had sold good English players who would have surely kept them up and replaced them with tired veterans of German campaigns. To encapsulate the era under Francis Lee, the former player and icon who we believed was the chairman best placed to understand our dreams and our football club's needs, I came to think of it like this: at Manchester City, we ended up selling our best footballers to pay for restaurants.

In 2002 Niall Quinn published his autobiography, a grand, lyrical account of his gallops in football, superbly ghost-written by the great Irish sports journalist Tom Humphries. It was sad, really, that Quinn's time at City, all those years of cushioned chest control and being more penetratingly effective than he looked, were sandwiched into just a few sorrowful pages, between his international dramas with Ireland and late-flowering love affair with Sunderland. Quinn wrote that he did love City, that the club was 'quintessential Manchester', its fans 'people who get rained on, all day, every day', so he had certainly soaked himself into the club. He told us that the club had great history, but it was too obsessed with its 1968–70 glories, whose pictures, the 'heroes of the revolution', were up on every wall, and that rather than being motivational, they stared down as a rebuke to the lesser talents of his time. Quinn said that when he joined, Maine Road was 'a crumbling pile', it was 'skinflint'; watching the money so tightly he could hardly get a pair of boots.

'But the club had heart. That's what I loved about it. It had heart and soul,' Quinn wrote, before a damning portrait of the Franny era. 'The sadness was that I was there long enough to see those things removed.'

The example he gave in most detail was about a small gymnasium, off to the left on the way down the players' tunnel from the main stand to the pitch. 'The beating heart and the living history of the club were in there,' he said. Players had trained in there and for generations had epic head-tennis sessions – in which, in Quinn's day, Book and the City physiotherapist, Roy Bailey, were the uncompromising masters. Kazimierz Deyna had been the head-tennis champion in his three years there, according to Quinn. Then he wrote that under Franny, looking for more space for an executive dining area, they ripped out that gym. So from Quinn, the sidelined stalwart of the club, came testimony that was not just financially but literally and physically true: the club had gutted a gym, chucked out the football, to build another restaurant.

Under Franny, Tony Book was sacked, and Colin Bell, Franny's former colleague, then working on the youth development side, was sacked too. Book, who had seen it all and done most jobs on the football side since his cruel demotion by Swales for Allison in 1979, said he accepted it. Bell was seriously upset, removed his international cap and medals from the displays at Maine Road, and took the club to an employment tribunal, where they reached a settlement. Bell wrote in his 2005 autobiography:

'I no longer have any contact with Francis Lee. Mike Summerbee has tried to act as a go-between and peacemaker . . . but I have decided that I will not attend any function at which Francis Lee is present.'

So it was not just that the hoped-for glittering future was receding; even the good years of the past, and memories of it, were soured after the return of the former playing hero we had all roared in.

The manner in which City, after all this, were relegated in May 1996 has a kind of pub quiz notoriety, a one-off cameo of comic-sadness to prompt the memory. Why was it, again, that Niall Quinn was running up the touchline in the final minutes of Manchester City's Premier League season, in that home game against Liverpool? The answer is that, to stay up, City needed a point more than Southampton or Coventry from that last game. Liverpool were playing United in the FA Cup final the following week, when they famously wore white suits and lost to a Cantona volley, and when they turned up at Maine Road, we could all see they were not thunderously interested. Yet still, our willing and earnest midfield worker, Steve Lomas, scored an own goal to put Liverpool ahead. It was, from 1993 to 1998, in that morning of the Premier League and of United's reawakening, all an own goal at City.

Quinn had been substituted for Phillips, who with 12 minutes left helped City equalise, to 2–2. Then the message was sent to Lomas that Coventry were losing, a draw would be enough, so Lomas took the ball into the corner to fritter time away. But Quinn heard differently, so he took his long legs running up the touchline, while he was off the pitch, to tell Lomas to stop time-wasting because they still needed to get on and win the game. City started panicking and trying again, but even against that jogging Liverpool team, they never did score. So City went down again, to the Second Division – by now called the First Division, the Football League trying its best to battle on as if the breakaway, gobbling all the money, had never happened – for the third time in my generation's supporting life.

Football people do recall the manner of downfall, but few outside City remember the eerie coincidence which preceded it. In the week of that final match, Peter Swales had died. Before the game the whole City crowd, who two years earlier had hounded Swales to his football passing, observed a minute's silence for his actual death. They say he died a broken man, shattered by his ousting, aged 62. He had haggled with Lee during the takeover battle, an ignoble squabble, to preserve three seats in the directors' box for him and guests, and a table for four in the dining room. They had argued him down to two directors' box seats, but with an agreement that he would not turn up for another game in that bitter 1993–94 season. He had never come back again. He told the historian Gary James, in an interview before he died: 'I can't go to Maine Road. How would the fans treat me?'

As the write-ups customarily summarise it, the minute's silence, of which football has many – just a minute to think and remember, then get on with the game – was 'immaculately observed'. As everybody hung their heads, I felt there was a touch of shame in it. It was not that 30,000 supporters were now reassessing Swales's record, or coming to a belief that he had in fact been more competent than we had allowed, not as bad as we thought. I did not feel that, and still think his position was untenable after the debacle of Malcolm Allison's return, and he should not have clung on after that, until prised out years later by all the bad feeling. Paul Lake's book about these years of loss and injury for him, published in 2010, seventeen years later, reinforced those fans' impressions, with a damning inside account.

There was, for me, a different kind of regret in that strange moral fable, orchestrated with such clarity by fate and the football fixture list. The shame, to me, was to be presented with the revelation that we had hounded Swales out, in an unforgiving public humiliation, without compassion, for a childhood hero we believed would magic us happy again. And now here we all were, gathered together at Maine Road, no better off after it all and on the brink of relegation. We had acted like a mob, reaching for a saviour from the past, and that had turned out to be no solution at all. Now, confronted by Swales's actual death, a tragic consequence of that ignorance, I felt a dawn of understanding. I realised that in placing our faith so feverishly in Franny, we had been childish and ill-informed about the realities of this institution, this football club, to which we all claimed we belonged. Then the whistle blew, the blue moon rose mournfully into the Manchester sky and, with that final farewell of own goal and farce, City went down.

Two years later, City were down again, to the Third Division (now called the Second Division by the Football League, still trying to ignore their beheading). In those two years of flapping, I struggle to remember a single match in much focus; my main memories are of a full but indignant, neurotic Maine Road, and a big man behind me shouting 'Absolute disgrace!' very loudly and very often. In the whole of their history, Manchester City had never sunk to the third level.

Alan Ball resigned in August 1996, after just three matches, later complaining in his autobiography, ever defiant, that he had had to sell City's best players to in-fill the financial black hole. Asa Hartford moved across as the caretaker manager, our distinguished midfield carrier from before the fall having to be in position when City lost 4–1 to Lincoln City in the League Cup. There seemed at City then a palpable sense of downward spiral, which nothing could halt, and the season stretched into October before another manager accepted the position. Steve Coppell, right-wing menace for United in their Tommy Docherty revival, and always a clever manager of Crystal Palace, famously lasted only six weeks, before appearing, ashen-faced, with implications that there were medical reasons why he could not stay. Coppell has still never said what it was which led him to make so rapid an exit, but he always looked to me like a man who had seen some vision of impending personal catastrophe. Phil Neal, another ex-playing stalwart of the 1970s, became the next unfortunate to be handed the caretaker misnomer, until in December steady, amiable Frank Clark became the fifth football man in four months to manage City.

Franny nearly had to make good on a promise he had rashly made at the Annual General Meeting in December 1996. More money was being raised for the club again, £10.8m, £5m of which was being invested for a 19 per cent stake by John Wardle and David Makin, partners in the retail chain J-D Sports, which the pair had just floated on the Stock Market and thereby become multi-millionaires. Stephen Boler, Swales's loyal colleague, was increasing his stake too, to 24 per cent, and with this increased shareholding for the new investment, Franny, whose club had run out of money, was reduced to 12 per cent.

Looking at the document for this rights issue, the meeting took place in the 'Level 6 restaurant' of Franny's new Kippax. It noted, right at the start, that the £11.5m cost of building the Kippax development had 'absorbed' all the money which came in from Franny and his associates. Coton, Phelan, Flitcroft and others had gone, Curle had been sold in the summer and Niall Quinn, after all his years of service, finally shuffled off without dignity to Sunderland, to play for Peter Reid, where he would be appreciated rather better. The club was promising the 'majority' of the £10.8m would be used to sign players who, 'together with the recent appointment of Frank Clark, will enhance the prospects for the club's return to the Premier League'.

Paul Stanley, an accountant and one of small shareholders, who were all fans in various states of dismay, asked Franny what the consequences would be 'if we go down' to the Third Division.

Franny quipped: 'I don't know, because if we go down,' pointing to his right, to the window of the Kippax banqueting room, which looked out on the pitch, 'I'll jump off the top of this stand.'

And people laughed. It was a jolt of reality, at the very thought that Manchester City could possibly end up in the Third Division. Clark spent his money on some smooth players like Kevin Horlock, in midfield, but the £3m signing of Lee Bradbury, from Portsmouth, stands out, a centre forward who floundered in the impatient glare of City's historic expectations. Meanwhile Quinn, in partnership with Kevin Phillips, at Sunderland's new Stadium of Light, was thriving again in the Premier League.

It was after a 1–0 home defeat to Bury, one of the worst results in City's history and a very miserable afternoon, that David Makin turned up on the BBC Radio Manchester phone-in, almost in tears. He was very Mancunian, sounding like one of the lads made good (he and Wardle had started J-D Sports with just one shop, in Bury, in 1981), and he was extremely upset and exasperated. He said the club was in another terrible mess:

'I will be devoting my energies over the next couple of weeks to getting the chairman out.'

Within weeks Franny, by now a minority shareholder, was indeed out. David Bernstein, who had remained as a director, was appointed chairman, a position with whose corporate responsibilities he was familiar, having been the chairman of several substantial retail companies.

So being removed as the chairman ultimately saved St Francis from having to throw himself off the new Kippax, that all-seater, unaffordable, executive dining monument to his second coming. On a sunny day in May 1998, Clark having been replaced by Joe Royle, the sixth manager, including caretakers, in two years, City did go down to the Third Division. It was the final match of the season, away at Stoke City's shiny new stadium, named after a building society, the Britannia, for which they had left the old Victoria Ground, their home since 1878. Stoke are one of England's and therefore the world's oldest football clubs, formed in 1868 by two old boys of Charterhouse public school, who were working as apprentices in the Potteries, at the local North Staffordshire Railway Company.

One hundred and thirty years later, Arsène Wenger's Arsenal were refashioning the modern sciences of English football winning the Premier League and FA Cup Double, whilst in the lopped-off 'First Division', Stoke City were already condemned to going down. Even if City beat them, points won by other clubs at the bottom of the division would still result in relegation for us, too. One of my friends did the driving to the match, and as we approached the stadium we began to see a huge industrial building, and chimney, looming directly ahead in the direction of the Britannia. As we drove closer, the signs for that chimney began to appear alongside those for the stadium and it became clear that the two buildings were next to each other. The signs said: Britannia Stadium, and to the other building: Incinerator. So there it was, we were heading not to salvation, but incineration. Inside the ground, City won 5–2, Kinkladze sparkled, the Stoke fans sang their equivalent of 'Blue Moon', 'Why, Why, Why, Delilah?' And City went down again.

CHAPTER 12

IN THE MONEY

Carrington, the training complex Manchester City opened in 2001 to cater for twenty-first-century Premier League football requirements, lies on green land to the south, away from the struggles of Manchester, the air easing into the well-appointed Cheshire suburbs. United went out there first when they became fabulously successful, to a purpose-built HQ down an interminable single-lane track, where a mucky industrial estate gives way to farmland. There the gilded first-team superstars can train to Sir Alex Ferguson's schedules, sealed off from onlookers and the young boys treasuring autograph books who used to be able to wander in off the rough streets of Lower Broughton, Salford, and see Best, Law and Charlton training at The Cliff.

In the 1990s, as the wages of footballers escalated into the millions with every quantum leap of Premier League TV deal, it became a cliché to note their unattainably flash motors, and recall the decades when the poorly paid stars of the people's game had travelled to their matches on the bus with fans. City's Carrington base is branded in blue and white, and wrapped around its functional buildings in a north-west English autumn are adverts to tempt tourists to the Gulf dynasty which bankrolls the club: Abu Dhabi – Travellers Welcome. There is the now standard sight, first seen at The Cliff in the early 1990s, of a young lad getting himself wet through, earning God knows how little, valeting one of those cars you see at footballers' places of work and seemingly nowhere else. I have never been much interested in cars, except that you need to have one big enough which works, but I make a note just for the record: it is a Porsche Panamera Turbo, black. Porsche, on their website, say the car does 0–100km/h (62 mph) in 4.2 seconds, and a basic one, before you customise it to your tastes, costs £103,807.

To see Brian Marwood, City's appointed head of football administration, in effect the director of football whose responsibility it is to coordinate the spending of Sheikh Mansour's millions on footballers, you go through and round reception to the workaday offices behind. On the way in is a poster for *Blue Moon Rising*, the film City had made following an amiable bunch of City-supporting mates in their clapped-out van through the 2009–10 season. City commissioned it thinking it could be a record of winning something, with all the money spent up to 2009, but during the season they ended up sacking Hughes, appointing Roberto Mancini as the manager, losing to United in the final seconds of the League Cup semi-final and being edged out of the Champions League-qualifying fourth place by Spurs. Instead of chronicling instantly acquired triumph, the film followed the lads to the Old Trafford defeat and a post-match despair with which their City-supporting lives were familiar. The film recalled 1968–70's ephemeral glories, Dennis Tueart's overhead kick and, with empathy and some grim laughs, all the sundry disappointments. So it became a medium for the Abu Dhabi billionaire owner to reassure the fans who had been really there in the Third Division, that in his stated aim to make City a 'global brand' in the 'entertainment product' of the Premier League, he appreciated and valued their loyalty.

Inside is the handsome gymnasium which the Abu Dhabi regime wholly rebuilt as soon as they took over, the first thing they did. Al Mubarak immediately authorised £300,000 to be spent on the specifications requested by Hughes and his coaching staff for his team to compete in the best condition. Wide and expansive, there are twenty exercise bikes, platoons of cardio-vascular machines, a showroom of weights, equipment for an elite way beyond anything Manchester City Council could serve up for the wellness of the general population. On the walls are motivational messages, one from Muhammad Ali, about the fight being won in the preparation, 'far away from the witnesses, behind the lines, in the gym', and pithier injunctions: Explode; What is your Limit?

There is a quote from Lance Armstrong, who overcame testicular cancer to reclaim the Tour de France:

'Pain is temporary,' that one says. 'It may last a minute, an hour, a day or a year, but eventually it will subside and something else will take its place. If I quit, it lasts for ever.'

Marwood, in his office, is small, neat, side-parting, smart-casual, firm handshake, just as you would expect him to be if you'd watched his tidy efforts on the wing for Sheffield Wednesday and Arsenal, which earned him one England cap, in the 1980s. After he retired, he became the chairman of the Professional Footballers Association, the union which took on the maximum wage back in the 1960s, and he helped set up their commercial department. From there, he went to Nike as head of football sports marketing, responsible for doing the kit deals with clubs including Arsenal and Celtic, and boot sponsorships with individual players.

After the Abu Dhabi takeover, Al Mubarak commissioned corporate consultant specialists Booz Allen and Co. to inspect from top to bottom the Thaksin Shinawatra-owned football company which Sheikh Mansour had bought. Along with the lack of a functioning human resources department, finance director and other key roles missing in the administration, the consultants saw how substantial and technical a Premier League football operation had become. With the youth academy, reserves and other teams to run, medical care to manage, the general well-being of superstars arriving in Manchester knowing nothing of the country or language, sports science, nutrition, performance analysis, facilities, scouting and identifying players, they were adamant it could not all be overseen by the manager.

'They came in from outside and said you can't have your first-team coach responsible for all that,' Marwood explained. 'It is a full-time job managing the first team. So they identified that role.'

At Nike, Marwood had worked with Garry Cook, whom Al Mubarak retained as the chief executive. Understanding the administrative abilities, football knowledge, reputation, contacts and ability to handle the spending of vast amounts of money required for the role, Cook suggested Marwood. He was appointed director of football, responsible for all the infrastructure necessary to support a manager and some of the world's best players, leaving the manager free to concentrate on coaching them. The new executives understood that directors of football had had an uncomfortable experience in England, because in Europe they tend to dictate what players to sign and what tactics to use, with managers restricted to coaching. City did not have that in mind, as they wanted support for the manager, but aware of the risk that it would be perceived as undermining the manager's authority, they avoided that title and called Marwood head of football administration.

'Nobody gets hung up on titles and I'm not hung up on it,' Marwood told me, 'but one of the reasons it was positioned like that was to take away the sensitivity around director of football. In Europe the director of football selects the players and is dictating tactics, but here that is not the case. We've tried to move it on. In the old days you had a small squad of players, a small backroom staff, it was manageable. Now you have so many different areas to attend to; the manager hasn't got time, and you want him to focus on the team and the results.'

Hughes's sacking, on 19 December 2009, was the most miserable mishap of the Abu Dhabi reign at Manchester City, the way it was done prompting widespread outrage in football. In 2008 they had decided to retain and support Hughes, whom they inherited from Thaksin, even though he had not managed City for a single game yet. In the introductory open letter to his 'fellow Manchester City fans', Sheikh Mansour had said:

'We consider Mark Hughes to be one of the prime assets of the club. We will back his judgement in what players to bring in and we look forward to working more closely with him in the future.'

When I had interviewed Al Mubarak in the Lowry Hotel just four months before they sacked Hughes, he had even made his pledge of loyalty to Hughes an emblem of the virtuous way they did business in Abu Dhabi.

'Mark is a great, honest, straight shooter and from day one there was an immediate chemistry there,' the chairman said. 'Here is this great manager, and believe me, Mark is going to be a great manager, and he just needed the opportunity. Last season [when the new City finished tenth] was very difficult, but we all faced it together. We don't leave our men behind, we stick with them.'

They had in truth harboured doubts about whether Hughes was indeed the right man for the journey and the multitudinous waves of money they were intending to pour in, during that first season. But as the team, transformed by the £220m spent on eleven new players, stuttered into a run of eight draws the following season, then capitulated to a 3–0 hammering on Wednesday 16 December at Spurs, they decided to sack Hughes and lined Mancini up. However, with four fixtures in a fortnight, Cook and Al Mubarak decided the best timing, from a football perspective, would be not to make the disruptive change in the few days before the coming Saturday home match against Sunderland. So they resolved to leave Hughes in charge for that one, then sack him and his staff immediately after. They would then appoint Mancini, who would have a full week to settle the players down and prepare for the Boxing Day home game against Stoke.

They laid all the plans for that, including who would break the news after the Sunderland match in three separate sessions to Hughes, his coaches and the players. They prepared a public statement, which would be issued immediately after the match, which said Hughes's performance was not 'in line with the targets set' at the beginning of the season, clearly to qualify for the Champions League. They tried to execute this plan, believing it would be difficult, practically and personally, but in the best interests of the club and team. However, their clinical strategy was scuppered when news of Mancini's appointment leaked, first from Italy. So as City's new, expensive and hesitant team scraped a scrappy 4–3 victory over Sunderland in the sleet of a freezing winter, the defence characteristically jumpy, everybody in the City of Manchester Stadium, including Mark Hughes, knew he would be sacked afterwards. He had been an awesome player for Manchester United and Chelsea, and a respected manager of Wales and Blackburn Rovers, and nobody deserves a public humiliation like that.

Management, in football, is an insecure occupation, and clubs do change – until the smart ones stick with the right person – but the episode showed three sides of City in precisely the light they were trying so hard to avoid. The Abu Dhabi owners looked ruthless and distant when all their efforts were to communicate understanding of the game and club, and not be seen as high-handed moneymen. Cook, with his statement, references to target-setting, and sacking meetings which backfired, seemed like a corporate maladroit. And the new City, seeking to transcend the failures of the past while doffing due credit to the club's history of endurance, looked like Typical City again.

In the outcry which followed, comparisons were even drawn between Al Mubarak and Swales, and the botched sacking of

Peter Reid sixteen years earlier. At the next home game, Stoke City again arriving for a landmark moment in City's modern history, there was tangible embarrassment and unease at the way Hughes's sacking had been handled. When Mancini was introduced, with his blue and white scarf tied just so above his overcoat, there was general restrained applause, with a small undertow of booing. But from the mostly middle-aged crowd at Eastlands, most of whom were there back in the day, there was nothing so energetic or impassioned as a frenzy turning to a riot.

There was also a hard streak in the fans I spoke to. Alan Galley, chairman of the supporters club, did say he felt it had brought City into 'disrepute'. Several shrugged, said they had not rated Hughes and it had to be done. Some said the performances had been poor and he was not the right man to 'take the club forward'. There seemed to be a ruthlessness in some of these fans themselves; they were intent on City being successful, they felt they had remained loyal through all the ignominious decline, while United were winning everything, and nothing now must stand in the way of an ascent to trophies. I found no one bemoaning the intrusion of a sheikh from far away into English football, or saying, as many columnists had, that a dictatorial and arrogant alien culture had victimised a great football man like Hughes.

Marwood, along with Cook, had been depicted in several accounts as the assassin, which fitted the stereotype of the director of football position, but he strongly rejected that characterisation.

'I believe the reporting was extremely unfair and inaccurate,' he said, explaining that his role was to support the manager, which he believed he had done. 'I only worked with Mark and his team for a short while but I would refute any suggestions that I undermined his work in any way. When you look at the players that we brought in last summer, the changes he wanted implementing in other areas of the club, whether medical, or academy, I think all of those things were done. Of course to lose your job is not a pleasant experience in any walk of life. But the role I played was not to undermine Mark and his team in any shape or form. It really wasn't.

'My job here is to facilitate the best possible practices in different areas of football excellence to get us into the position where we can achieve what we set out to achieve.'

It was a project which Mansour had demanded from the moment he first bought the club, and for which he was prepared to make an almost infinite amount of money available. It was all rather different from Francis Lee arriving with Colin Barlow and a dozen south Manchester business people bunging in what they were prepared to punt on City making it to the Stock Market. Booz Allen and Co., overseen by Simon Pearce, made their recommendations for the wholesale refurbishment of Manchester City both physically and structurally, and Marwood's role was to coordinate the new order. The business plan for the first team from the beginning had been to ensure two top-class players, preferably world-class, in each position.

Marwood said emphatically that the manager identified and agreed the players he wanted. Others would put names forward, from the scouts, or from his own knowledge, as he had with Adam Johnson, whom he had signed up for a Nike boot deal at the age of fifteen, and who he knew was coming to the end of his contract with Middlesbrough. City signed Johnson, for £7m, and the former Arsenal midfield invincible Patrick Vieira, on a free transfer, the only signings they made in the January after Mancini's arrival.

'People feed in suggestions and research is done,' Marwood explained, 'but in the end the manager makes the decision about players. We sat down with Roberto in February, March, and planned out what our summer programme would look like. And I think we pretty much got everyone.'

That summer the Abu Dhabi regime sanctioned and bankrolled Roberto Mancini's shopping with a vast financial outlay hugely beyond what the club could have afforded were it living on its own resources. City signed Jerome Boateng, from Hamburg, for £10.5m; David Silva, from Valencia, for £26m; Yaya Touré, attacking midfield force from the great Barcelona, for £24m; Aleksandar Kolarov from Lazio for £19m; Mario Balotelli, from Internazionale of Milan, for £24m, and James Milner, from Aston Villa, for £26m. Then in January 2011 they signed the striker Mancini had long coveted, Edin Džeko, from Wolfsburg, for £27m, who turned out rather more of a game-changer than Lee Bradbury had been for Frank Clark's £3m. This incredible series of international player purchases, unparalleled by any other club, totalled £156.5m. That brought the expenditure from Abu Dhabi, on player transfer fees alone, to £376.5m in just two seasons.

Many people in football take the view that this venture is repulsive and vulgar, contrary to the sporting heart and traditions of the game. The president of Uefa, Michel Platini, for example, wondered at a football culture which allowed a sheikh from Abu Dhabi with no connection to Manchester to buy up an institution as locally rooted as a football club, and pour money in without restraint. Uefa, from its base on the banks of Lake Geneva, surveys a landscape in which, during the greatest commercial boom football has ever experienced, 50 per cent of clubs in the top divisions across Europe were making a loss, with 20 per cent in serious financial difficulties. The Premier League always said there was nothing it could or even wanted to do: it welcomed all buyers and all forms of owner-ship, as long as they were not criminal and could prove their club had the money to fulfil fixtures and pay its tax. The FA, which surrendered the game to the Premier League in 1992, has nothing to say on ownership or distribution of money from the loaded top flight. The Glazers, who had borrowed £525m to buy United, £275m of it at very high rates of interest from hedge funds, were essentially welcomed as 'owners' of English football's greatest club by the Premier League, FA and the gov-ernment, when they arrived in 2005.

Uefa resolved to impose itself, and introduce some active regulation on the inherently corrosive relationship between top-class football and money. The European governing body took the view that debt in itself was not the destructive issue, because however appalled United fans were by the financial assault on their club, United could pay the interest and remain successful. So Uefa sought to attack loss-making, because that is what drives clubs into difficulties, whether caused by excessive wages or paying too much on their debts. Platini's organisation suc-ceeded in introducing a rule, to come into force in 2014–15, that clubs must move towards breaking even and living within their means. Beginning with 2011–12, then in 2012–13 too, clubs are permitted to make losses limited to €45m, which must be covered by the owner, the money put in not as loans but permanently. Clubs which fail to meet that figure, and make losses dramatically greater, will face a range of sanctions up to, most seriously, exclusion from participating in a European competition, the Champions or Europa League, in 2014–15. Andrea Traverso, Uefa's head of licensing, which is responsible for the 'Financial Fair Play' rule agreed by all the professional clubs affiliated to Uefa, consistently explained that it made sense for clubs to live according to their income, and this could help adjust football into an enterprise less defaced by obscene wages, financial scandal, and clubs in periodic states of collapse.

The misfortune for Sheikh Mansour's decision to buy an English Premier League club and fund it to the heights was that he did so just three years before this rule arrived. In November 2011 City released their financial accounts for the year to 31 May 2011, which showed that the club made the greatest loss ever in English football history, a staggering £197m. The wage bill was £174m, £21m more than the club's entire income. To finance this accumulation of players to claim trophies – City had won nothing since that League Cup in 1976 – Mansour had personally put a further £291m into the club. Previous financial statements by the club had revealed that Mansour had injected £500m in his first two years, and so this brought the total which he had spent on Manchester City, in three years, to £800m. That is the modern cost, in the multi-billion-pound, globally televised English Premier League, of constructing a squad, and the infrastructure to support it, which might have the means to compete at the level we watched Manchester City in the 1970s. All this conspicuously extravagant spending by the Abu Dhabi sheikh, and outlandish earning by the players, was happening at exactly the time Britain's debt-fuelled economy had been uncovered as a mirage, unemployment was climbing towards 3 million, and the poorest people, particularly in former industrial areas like east Manchester, were suffering spending cuts and a new age of 'austerity'.

Marwood, like Al Mubarak and all those shaping the new Manchester City with Sheikh Mansour's money, found it difficult to engage with the argument that this is, in principle, not what football is about. There is something alienating to the wider game and culture of football, the history of clubs rising on their own resources, in the idea that a club can be picked up by one rich man from far away, and so brazenly be funded to success. Marwood described it as 'a dream opportunity' for him to play so central a role in the Manchester City project, and he was keen to communicate that it was not so easily done, that a foundation of sophisticated and dedicated systems had to be constructed. City, he emphasised, were not throwing money around, in the flash way Sulaiman Al Fahim had indicated in those giddy first days, making golden-booted players offers they couldn't refuse. He explained that for the Abu Dhabi owners, schooled in huge corporate deals for oil and gas, billion-pound investments and long-term strategic development, everything was done according to worked-out plans.

'There is the accusation that it is wild and kamikaze spending,' Marwood grimaced, 'but there is a business case produced for each player we want to recruit. That is what our ownership is like, they do not do anything without a plan. It is not scrabbling around in the last couple of weeks of the transfer window, saying we need a left-back.

'The players on Roberto's list, it was like a spreadsheet. It is that detailed, not left to chance. It is worked through with the manager, and it is balanced. It is mostly young and developing players who will be with Manchester City for a long time, and a mix of English and non-English players. It is not the accumulation that people thought would happen under Abu Dhabi.'

He explained that for each major purchase of a player to be sanctioned by the board, they make a business proposition about how that player will be of benefit to the team and club. That involves compiling a detailed dossier. Players all over the world and from young ages are watched, scouted, then research is carried out into their attributes, character and personality. City are now scouting young players determinedly around the world, predominantly European junior teams and in Africa, like all the top English clubs now do, not just, as in the old days, hoping to unearth a rough diamond around Manchester. For the major signings, Marwood said, those £20m to £30m acquisitions, the dossiers would run to forty or even fifty pages. They are considered by Al Mubarak and the board, before the next wave of the Abu Dhabi cash reserves is released. He explained that to assess whether a player will fit with the requirements and targets the team-building had been set, they use a detailed SWOT method. This is a systematic matrix analysis developed by American management consultants, to analyse major projects or business acquisitions by collating, balancing and assessing their Strengths, Weaknesses, Opportunities and Threats. 'We go into player profiles, and SWOT. We note scout reports, how many times we've watched him, all relevant personal information,' Marwood explained. They want to be clear not only how effective the footballer is, but the issues he might have with settling in. 'We give red, amber and green for a player's adaptation, command of English, experience of transition, cultural fit, family. All their personal information, are they married, are they single, Mum, Dad, girlfriends, dogs. We take into account international factors and the calendar; if you are signing anybody from Africa you have the African Cup of Nations during our season. We include market conditions, media reports and cuttings, agent's information, and what the next steps are.

'We have a very good team of people here who understand these decisions now. And the chairman needs to see it, the owner needs to see it; we're investing a lot of money in these guys. Like any business decision, given the amount of investment, you can't just say: Brian thinks he's good, or Roberto's seen him play and thinks he's not bad; you can't do that now.'

Different qualities of players weigh differently; as the club may be looking for something in particular. Of Vieira, the tail-end-of-a-great-career signing whose rationale was widely questioned, and Yaya Touré, which many considered extravagant, at £24m and up to £200,000 weekly wage, Marwood explained it was about introducing Manchester City to the experience of winning:

'The feeling was that we needed players of presence, quality, with a winning mentality, who had been around environments and knew how to win; it was that type of culture we wanted to bring to the football club. Micah Richards, to take a prime example, he is an emerging young player, in that zone where he is still learning and developing. It is incredibly valuable to have him alongside Patrick, Yaya, every day, in the changing room, on the training pitch, going to away games. Yaya who has won the Champions League, he can play four different roles, he is a quality player, he really is. When we knew he was available, it was a no-brainer. 'This football club has gone from being tenth in the Premier League the season before last to just missing out on a Champions League place and now has Yaya Touré, David Silva, players of that quality. We've kind of crammed ten years' work into twelve to eighteen months.'

Marwood showed me the detailed, thirty-page, colour-coded analysis produced by this inter-departmental analytic system for just one fifteen-year-old they had been keeping an eye on. I thought about the fevered discarding of excellent players and signings of the overpriced eccentric collection, which was the vandalism of Malcolm Allison's second coming. Then I began to smile; I felt an involuntary laugh coming on, which I tried to smother. Marwood carried on, explaining SWOT analysis, what they weigh in the balance, the team of people whose job it now is to compile these reports, which will be sent for consideration to the chairman in Abu Dhabi once a player is identified to be bought. I was drifting perilously close to giggling.

'Sorry,' I said eventually when I thought he might notice, and told him I was remembering my first ever interview inside the doors of Manchester City, sixteen years ago, with Francis

Lee and Colin Barlow just after their takeover. I told Marwood about their mocked-up vision for the new Kippax propped up on a chair, and Brian Horton walking in and putting that fax about some player on Franny's desk.

He smiled tolerantly, and pressed on with his explanation that even eighteen months earlier, the club had no details whatsoever of any player on any system.

'It was in people's heads. Now we have a very comprehensive database of players from right around the world. We're building it, and that takes time and resources. We do succession planning. We look at every kid we have from the age of twelve, what we have in each age group, what we have coming through. So if we have five left-wingers, what is the point of signing another one? And we identify the holes, the gaps we need to fill.'

Up some stairs from his office is the players' canteen and lounge, with the team of performance analysts, in tracksuits but chained to computers, just off it. In another pair of offices is a department of five people responsible for 'player care'. Their job is to ensure the superstars arriving in Manchester from overseas are sorted with everything they need, in order that their minds are free and bodies conditioned to perform at their topmost pitch from the beginning. On the wall is a sort of in-house estate agency, suggesting homes of up to £2m and the different areas around Manchester they might consider buying. There is a little description of all of them: Alderley Edge, Hale, Didsbury, described as more 'edgy' and 'urban'. Lower Broughton, Cheetham Hill and Prestwich do not figure, and neither do Harpurhey, Miles Platting or Gorton.

'It's so important, especially with foreign players, that they settle very quickly,' Marwood explained. 'You're talking about house, bank account, child care, gardeners, nurseries, schools, so children and wives are settled, where they go to hospital. In my day, I had great support from Arsenal; there were other clubs where you got your contract and they didn't give a toss, it was sink or swim. It was unheard of to have someone in that position, player care.

'David Silva – he's in a house, he's got family over with him, he's having English lessons, it is about settling very quickly. We try to take it all away from them, so they can concentrate on their core accountability, which is football.'

Many in football were puzzled that the Abu Dhabi ownership retained Garry Cook, who had acquired the label 'gaffe-prone' for a series of clumsy public statements, talking as if he was constantly chewing on a Nike corporate-speak manual. His general image had never recovered from the first interview he gave, with the club still owned by Thaksin Shinawatra, in which he was asked about City's owner's human rights record and corruption charges in Thailand. In response he delivered the lines which always trailed him like a bad odour and depicted him as representing all that was off in modern football:

'Is he [Thaksin] a nice guy?' was Cook's rhetorical response. 'Yes. Is he a great guy to play golf with? Yes. Does he have plenty of money to run a football club? Yes. I really care only about those three things. Whether he is guilty of something over in Thailand, I can't worry. My role is to run a football club.'

In a subsequent interview I had with him, Cook said he felt

'dreadful' for having said that. He said he had meant to articulate that it was not his business, as an employee, to have a
view on Thaksin's political backstory. But he also admitted he
had 'failed to do due diligence' on Thaksin's record before he
took the job, which he described as his dream opportunity. As
he came to understand the financial and organisational quagmire into which City had sunk, Cook had grown to believe he
had made a huge mistake. He had left his rarefied and hand-
somely paid job at Nike headquarters in Portland, Oregon, for
a wretched and failing football club.

'I deeply regretted my failure to do proper research on
Thaksin,' he said.

All his other gaffes, including giving a speech in which he
welcomed Uwe Rösler into Manchester United's hall of fame,
were magnified by that dreadful early impression. Yet when Al
Mubarak and Pearce met him, they were taken with his enthusiasm and abilities, the job he was trying and wanted to do, and
they invested in him the responsibility to build the new Manchester City which would be an advertisement for the world-class
standards of Abu Dhabi. The financial accounts showed the
depth of that faith: Cook was paid a £1.4m salary in 2008–09,
£1.8m in 2009–10, and more than £2m in 2010–11, when one
serious error of judgement finally forced his resignation.

He had been transported as a chief executive from the night-
mare of a club under Thaksin which was struggling to pay the
wages, to the richest owner in the world making everything
possible. Cook was charged with doing the commercial sponsorship deals, which were within his Nike experience, and to
overhaul the structure, practices and morale of a club grown

accustomed to it all going wrong in the end. His brand of mid-Atlantic management-speak jarred at the typical Manchester club, but he saw to it that every area of the club's operation was reinvigorated. Corporate structures and systems, including that missing personnel department, were introduced where none had been before. There was attention to detail: the stadium's concrete bowl was humanised, the advance ticket office was moved in out of the rain, the customer relations department instituted a policy of calling people who had been to their first match to ask how it was for them.

I had known the club since I was six, but now City seemed to me to be applying professionalism to areas which had mostly been taken for granted before. They showed they did understand supporters; from that first open letter, to the making of the film and in all the language used, they knew it was important to say thank you for the loyalty. The stuff they sell in the City Store is almost unfair in the emotional buttons they know so cunningly how to press. Cook, for all his faults, was credited with all of this, and with the support given to the club's community work, so he was kept on as the man in charge of the Abu Dhabi project in Manchester, until he tried to cover up a thoughtless email mistakenly sent to the mother of one of the players, Nedum Onuoha, and in September 2011 was forced to resign. The club was in contract negotiations with Onuoha, one of City's most promising young players, who would eventually leave in January 2012 for Queens Park Rangers, where Hughes had fetched up as the manager. Onuoha's mother, Dr Anthonia Onuoha, had accused Marwood of deepening her stress while she was 'riddled with cancer'. Marwood had sent her email on to Cook, who had replied to Marwood with a joke which suggested she was using emotional blackmail by referring to her cancer in the negotiations. By accident ultimately terminal for his job, he copied her in on it. Then, when she protested, he compounded it; instead of admitting to his thoughtlessness and apologising, he told her that somebody had hacked into his email. The new Manchester City instituted a formal investigation using the very human resources and formal structures, up to board level, which Cook, as the chief executive, had introduced. It found, according to the subsequent statement:

'There is foundation to Dr Onuoha's allegations, and the chairman has written to apologise to Dr Onuoha for any distress caused.

'Following the findings of the review,' the statement continued, 'chief executive officer Garry Cook has offered his resignation.'

Al Mubarak, in the statement, thanked Cook for his 'remarkable contribution', his 'energy and tireless commitment'. That was genuine; they did believe that Cook, derided by many outside, had helped to heave Manchester City from its till-I-die pessimism to the threshold of top-club dynamism.

Mancini, sumptuous as a winning footballer with Sampdoria and an Italy international, and three times Italian Serie A winner as a manager with Internazionale, had glided into the heat following the sacking of Hughes, shrugging at the fact that one man lost the job before him. He arrived resolved to relish what was offered to him at the City of Manchester Stadium, with all the money piling so improbably in to Manchester City, one of the great opportunities in football. He identified that the first issue to address was a defence riven by disorganisation and panic, and he concentrated so absolutely on that, City became criticised for boring, unadventurous old-style Italian tactics. City won that first game against Stoke City 2–0, with the central defence, Kolo Touré and Vincent Kompany, immediately more assured and Carlos Tevez, then still the poster boy of the new Manchester City, scoring one and making the other for Martin Petrov. The players, particularly Craig Bellamy and Shay Given, had protested strongly against the clinical nature of Hughes's dispatch, but they all played convincingly straight away for the new boss.

Mancini emphasised to owners who, with all the money spent, did want to see good football, that he needed to fix the defence first, then they supported him, with that acquisition spreadsheet, to spend £156.5m on players in the summer of 2010, including the transformative, artistic Silva. His team, with Tevez a tireless, at times solitary striker, would coalesce the following season, Mancini's first full one, into a group which suddenly played with unified conviction. That was when the world was made to understand that for £800m spent, applied with the detailed, professional expertise which the sheikh's money had also bought and could insist upon, the new Manchester City, branded into a global advert for Abu Dhabi, was truly formidable, and not going to implode after all, into Typical City.

CHAPTER 13

THE COUNCIL HOUSE

In 1998–99 Alex Ferguson's Manchester United signalled the Premier League's coming dominance by sensationally winning the European Champions League with two injury-time goals against Bayern Munich, Ole Gunnar Solskjaer's poked-in winner becoming an iconic moment in English football's renaissance. At the time, Manchester City were trudging through the quagmire of the Third Division, playing weatherworn, potless clubs like Wrexham, York City and Chesterfield. United won the Premier League and FA Cup too, the unique treble, with the most starred group of 'kids' in generations, in a team entirely reinvented from the one which had lost 5–1 to City's bright, since fallen, young meteors ten messy years earlier. Joe Royle signed thick-necked enforcers like Andy Morrison to muscle City out of the depths, and City would count it as a historic victory to beat Gillingham on penalties in the Third Division play-off final, Paul Dickov having only scored the equaliser in the game in the 94th minute. United would come home from their victory at the Camp Nou in Barcelona on a fine day, beaming, waving football's greatest prizes from an open-top bus, and Alex Ferguson would be knighted. City had an open-top bus in Manchester to celebrate their promotion to the Second Division, but on their parade, it rained all day.

Yet looking at City's remarkable transformation since, that season in the Third Division was pivotal. The club went as low as it had ever been and, harried by Royle, stewarded with determined economy by the chairman, David Bernstein, began the long journey back. The fans stuck fast to the belief that Manchester City was, in its true nature, the great football club they'd grown up supporting, and this another aberration. They turned up to watch City play Bournemouth, Chesterfield and Colchester in crowds always nudging 30,000. That defining mass loyalty and guaranteed crowd was vital to Manchester City Council's decision, when preparing to build a brand-new £127m stadium for the 2002 Commonwealth Games, that City would be invited to occupy it afterwards. Those two factors, the new 48,000-seat stadium and the proven loyal fanbase,

Paul Dickov celebrates scoring the injury time equaliser for Manchester City in the League One play-off final against Gillingham, 1999

would underpin Sheikh Mansour's knowledge, when City was presented potless to him ten years later, that this was indeed one of the big English clubs, suited to the Premier League project for which he had been waiting.

As a City fan, that season was pivotal for me too. While everybody else was pledging their abiding and till-they-die faith all around me, I found myself, painfully and quite bewilderingly, losing mine. Investigating football as a journalist, sparked by the acquisitive nature of Francis Lee's takeover and by the abject inequality I discovered between 'owners' making multimillions from football plcs and the neglect of the game's grass roots, I had been awakened to the reality. While others dug deep, with a dream in their hearts, I began to feel semi-detached from emotional involvement in Manchester City's sagas. I felt that the fans' immovable loyalty to the idea of a club was being exploited by a very few people who had manoeuvred themselves into the position of owning the shares in the company. With this new, grown-up understanding, it was very difficult to maintain the innocent idea, absorbed in childhood, that this was a club to which I belonged. I found it instinctively difficult to support with all my heart 'the club' which, as an adult, I now knew to be an illusion. Sport is nothing without belief, somebody wrote – or, at least without suspending disbelief – and I found that my belief in City as a club had changed profoundly. I believed absolutely in the reawakening idea that football clubs should be owned by their supporters, collectively, because that reflects how supporters feel about them – and how the clubs, moreover, always talk about themselves. I began to feel that if I were to pay my money and stand and roar, as a grown-up, as if I belonged to a company owned by a handful of businessmen looking to make money out of me, I was being taken for a ride and was a mug. I found it was difficult to unlearn these lessons, believe in my old childhood captivation, and carry on as before.

So for me, the feeling of alienation and detachment from modern football as it was refashioned to new galaxies of prestige and success, was not simply a matter of rising prices, corporate entertainment and the cleansing of the atmosphere that fans were protesting about at Old Trafford and elsewhere in the Premier League. The questioning of the very nature of supporting a 'club' which felt strange and unwelcome arrived while my club were in the Premier League's earthy underside, with enjoyable trips to tumbledown grounds. But still, I could not embrace it as the collective experience I had believed in as a child. I found myself agonising and wrestling with this weakening of a lifelong loyalty to a football club, for that year and a long time afterwards. In England, the principle that you support the football club you grew up with all your life, was an accepted and unquestioned backbone of being a bloke. I had friends who made their compromises; they understood how it all worked, that the clubs were companies, the owners were there to screw them, but they held fast to the idea of the club which existed only in their own minds and memories. I wrestled with that, wanting to get back to an innocent and enjoyable support of my football club, which had been such a continuous theme during all the struggles and confusions of grown-up life. But I found that knowing what I knew now, about how the 'club' was privately owned and run with personal profit as the ultimate aim, I could not retreat back to the sentimental comfort of childhood. I found I grappled with the cataclysmic idea of not being a true believer any more, for longer and with a greater searching of the soul than I had when drifting away from my actual religion. Then I had moved on naturally from its rules and practices, to an accommodation with it as my tradition and upbringing, without regrets, for a life which was sweeter without it. Yet this mortal doubt of my football support, at a time when being a fan had become hyped, celebrated, indeed compulsory for all Englishmen, was a truer crisis of faith.

Ultimately, though, I saw John Wardle and David Makin, however decent they might be as people, as major shareholders who stood to make a fortune if City reclaimed Premier League status. The plan was still to float the club on the Stock Exchange, and David Bernstein, also self-evidently a dignified and competent professional man, was tasked with marshalling Manchester City plc to that position in which it could do so. This seemed to me a betrayal of the very heart and soul of what a football club is supposed to be.

City fans developed a detachment too, that season, but not to the idea of being fans,which they were absolutely reaffirming. It was to the reality that the club of Bell, Lee and Summerbee, Hartford, Watson and Tueart, really had landed in the Third Division. It was standing on Blackpool's Bloomfield Road, a sagging, patched-up old place then, parts of which under the old floodlights were condemned and taped off, where I first heard City fans sing that witty riff of disbelief at it all:

We are not, we're not really here,
We are not, we're not really here
Just like the fans, of the Invisible man,
We're not really here.

Surreal, funny, and also genuinely disbelieving. They sing it still, in the City of Manchester Stadium, but now it is at the unbelievable fact that Yaya Touré, Sergio Aguero, David Silva and Mario Balotelli are wearing sky-blue shirts and playing in the European Champions League. Then they sang it at York's Bootham Crescent and Macclesfield's Moss Rose. City played Macclesfield, a non-league club all our lives until just the year before, on 12 September 1998. The City fans all went down the A538 to the start of Derbyshire, and had to swarm on to the open terrace behind the goal of that tiny ground. The famous Manchester City, who should never have been there, struggled to get the better of Macclesfield Town, until with fully 86 minutes gone, Shaun Goater hustled a bobbler in.

I looked across to the touchline and saw Joe Royle and Willie Donachie, our elegant left-back of the 1970s, back as Royle's assistant, dancing about, beside themselves. They were running on the pitch, fists in the air, shaking and clenching, mini-versions of David Pleat's dance on the Maine Road pitch fifteen years earlier. At the time, I thought at first it was a little undignified, the manager of Manchester City being so unashamedly delighted with a late goal scored for a 1–0 win at Macclesfield Town. Then I realised it was admirable of Joe Royle, that he was still a socks-rolled-down football realist. He recognised the realities of the spiral City were in, and he fully understood the need to scrape a 1–0 win at Macclesfield. Good on him, I always think, for not considering himself above celebrating it deliriously.

For the first half of the season, City's players could not adjust to being down in previously unexplored battlegrounds, and Royle coined the phrase 'Cityitis' for the yips the team would suffer as the fans' exasperation pervaded their psyches. We played Mansfield Town in the LDV Vans Trophy on 8 December 1998, the only game City have ever played in the competition for Football League clubs in the Third and Fourth Divisions. There was a crowd of 3,007 at an echoing Maine Road, the plush restaurants of the new Kippax still open for business. Royle did not want the distractions of games for that trophy and City lost 2–1. Afterwards I chatted to a couple of City fans, a father in his sixties and son in his forties. They said they had always been City, and the current cocked-up management, the shambles which had brought the club so low, were not going to keep them away. It was faith in the idea of a better City, despite the people running it.

David Bernstein understood this, the bloody-minded determination of City fans to remain steadfast to the memory of what the club should be, and it gave him something to work on with investors (Makin and Wardle were persuaded to put more money in), advertisers and sponsors. And it was crucial to the credibility of the council's plan to build an expensive, permanent stadium in east Manchester, that City fans were demonstrating their club was big enough to occupy it. Asked if it was viable to hand a £127m stadium over to a club then in the Third Division, the leader of the council, Richard Leese, could smile and point to 28,000 people at Maine Road for every game.

The Commonwealth Games of 2002 were what Manchester ended up with when the International Olympic Committee and the government had to finally break the news that it was never going to have the Olympics and really might have to stop bidding. Howard Bernstein, the council chief executive, saw the Commonwealth Games as another means of attracting huge funding to Manchester, and all the necessary building of the stadium and facilities as a catalyst for the regeneration of the lost and forsaken tracts of east Manchester. Once, as the council described in a policy paper, 'the epicentre of the world's first industrial revolution', east Manchester and its old working-class livelihoods had been shattered by decline, culminating in the final demise of the Thatcher years.

Explaining the hopeful 'New East Manchester' project, to build new apartments and houses around the 'Sport City' site – and hope to inspire new permanent jobs and a sustainable future – the council noted of the area:

'In the last quarter of the 20th century much of the industrial base, and the employment that accompanied it, was decimated by successive economic recessions, and intensive competition from increasingly global markets.'

I had been to the site earmarked for the stadium in late 1998, and it was a sorry place. A vast, derelict scrubland, contaminated with geologies of now departed industrial muck. Ringed by some of the shabbiest housing, Philips Park was lying untended opposite, the gatehouse shattered and shorn of its roof slates. The whole area had an air of despair, of never having been visited since the industry packed up.

The answer, or the heart of it, was to build a huge sports stadium and have the Commonwealth Games in it, itself costing more than £200m to run. It was the most spectacular example yet of the skewed approach to collapsed industrial cities. There had been no real campaign to save the factories and the jobs they provided; they were all left to die in the face of the competition, almost triumphantly, to attest to the virtue of the free market. In a funding vice, and with the rates it could charge capped, the council did not have the money to keep the local park proud for the people who lived there, nor the pitches decent on which Manchester's council tax payers played their football. But it could bid for a two-week sporting event for elite athletes, and once it 'won' the bid to be the host city, east Manchester would be lavished with hundreds of millions of pounds from the National Lottery and the government. So they could build a £40m, Olympic-sized aquatic centre down by Manchester University off Oxford Road because a 50m pool was needed for the games, but they did not have the funds to keep open the little pool, which pensioners and the disabled could use, in Gorton. Manchester City were heading for a brand-new stadium built with £127m of public money on unbelievably favourable terms, but Gorton Tub, one of the few amenities in the clapped-out district where the club was founded, was closed down by the council.

Howard Bernstein wanted to build a permanent stadium, as a regeneration project and statement for Manchester, rather than a modest temporary structure which had been mooted by some who did not want to waste too much money. So that it would not stand empty afterwards, it needed an 'anchor tenant' after the games were over. Bernstein knew, unlike the organisers of the 2012 London Olympics who had no planned sustainable legacy for their stadium, it had to be a football club. In England, only a football club can attract a sufficient crowd to fill a large stadium regularly, and therefore keep it alive and paid for. United, at their rebuilt and till-ringing Theatre of Dreams, were sorted for a ground, so Manchester City, without a dream in their hearts for so many years, were approached to move in.

David Bernstein, despite City being in the Third Division, found that he was in a very good negotiating position, because the council desperately needed the club's agreement or the stadium would not be built in the first place. City were not as desperate for the move, because they had a serviceable ground at Maine Road. He told me at the time:

'I said from the beginning: we wanted to have a football stadium, not one with a track around it, and we had a stadium already, so we were not going to pay for it, up to the current Maine Road capacity.'

The council agreed with both of those propositions, so the remarkable deal they struck was as follows. The National Lottery, that ticket of hope, would, via the grant-giving body, Sport England, provide £78m to build the stadium. David Bernstein had refused to agree to City paying for any of the construction costs, including the conversion of the stadium for football when the Commonwealth Games were over. So ripping up the athletics track, building the new North Stand, digging down and installing seats right around the pitch so that it was converted into a 48,000-seat football stadium afterwards, was all done by the council and Sport England, at the public's expense. Lacking money for the very basics in the poor wards which, in reality, constitute Manchester, the council was able to find £49m to build this stadium and convert it afterwards for Manchester City.

City would pay nothing at all either to build or occupy this brand-new stadium, up to a 32,000 capacity. After that, there was a rent to pay on the seats sold above 32,000, which worked out at up to £2m a year when the stadium was filled. City could never have found £127m to build a new stadium without this windfall. Everton, a club with great similarities to City, is sinking into slow decline, as it can find no solution to expand or improve the sagging old Goodison Park, its much loved but outdated equivalent of Maine Road. City would be in the same position, not owned by one of the world's richest men, had the great gift of the stadium built with public and lottery money not landed in their lap, while they were still playing at some of football's backwaters.

The money City would have to spend when they moved into the new stadium was £20m, to build bars and restaurants, boxes and executive banqueting suites and the chairman's lounge, whose trappings would make Francis Lee and Colin Barlow's vision for the Kippax look like school canteens. The club would move and give Maine Road to the council, who would have the old ground demolished and new houses built in Moss Side.

It was a great deal for City and for the council, Howard Bernstein insisted, because it meant the stadium would not be a drain on public money after the games, and would bring back £2m a year which would be spent maintaining the other sports facilities around it. It meant the Commonwealth Games could be a great success and they, and the facilities built with public money for them, could be a catalyst for regeneration in that area abandoned for so long.

However, given what I knew about Manchester City plc and the aspirations of its 'owners', I wondered if the deal was a little too generous. I have always questioned how paying huge public money to host a fortnight's sporting event can really be considered cost-effective regeneration, although experts were saying it was so. If a stadium for Manchester City constituted regeneration – and clearly it was better to have something on that wasteland than just the ruins of its former industry – then why would it serve Moss Side well for Maine Road to be demolished? It was also being allowed to stand unchallenged as a policy for regeneration, as if that was the path to recovery for shattered cities. There are scores of similar areas across the north and Midlands, whose reason for existing was industry. And only one tiny corner of those areas could be uplifted by a Commonwealth Games, or, in 2012, an Olympic Games. I could not see how that could constitute any kind of convincing blueprint for the recovery of once-working swathes of the country where the jobs had been chased away.

So I felt keenly that while the regeneration benefits for the general area and the poor local residents were probably being exaggerated, the process would produce a personal bonanza of enrichment for the individuals who owned Manchester City plc. As I had learned, City was not simply some community football club, as it did and does like to portray itself, despite the community programme attached to it, which is constituted as a separate charity and does some excellent work. It was a company, owned principally by John Wardle and David Makin, Stephen Boler, Francis Lee with a minority stake, and even Rupert Murdoch's BSkyB, which bought a 9.9 per cent stake for £5.5m in 1999, the season after the fans proved what a loyal bunch of supporters, and consumers, they are.

These shareholders had made no secret of their desire to make money out of their shares by floating the club on the Stock Market, and this gift of a superb new stadium would help them dramatically. Lottery money, I discovered, has to be spent on 'good causes', the rationale for introducing the lottery in the first place, in 1995. The National Lottery Act stated that money should be distributed: 'For projects which promote the public good or charitable purposes, and which are not intended primarily for private gain.'

David Bernstein, when I talked to him, did accept the uncontestable fact that: 'Of course people could make a lot of money' from the gift of the new stadium. But he argued that did not mean they were 'exploiting the club'.

The council claimed that it was somehow protecting the deal from Manchester City's private 'owners' making money out of the stadium gift, but I could not see how. If the owners were to sell the club at a huge profit, its value greatly increased by being in the new, bigger, stadium, there was no clawback for the council tax payers, by which some of the money would come back to the council. The proceeds of any sale would all be pocketed by the owners.

The stadium deal was approved by all the necessary public authorities and it was cleared by independent auditors as good value for the council, responsibly negotiated. It is still the most remarkable accession to a new stadium by an English football club. At the time of writing, the development of Chelsea, Everton, Liverpool and Tottenham is stalled by their inability to find a solution to their need to expand. Of the top clubs, only Arsenal, which had the great blessing of being able to sell Highbury for a fortune in an inner London area of seriously high property prices, have managed to build a new stadium. A few other clubs have moved into new stadiums built by their councils, giving them all a huge boost: the largest were Swansea City, Hull City and Doncaster Rovers; but none was on such a majestic scale. City's luck in landing the new stadium, and the deal they struck with the council which spent £49m building it, is unique.

So City were heading to that new home, fit for a Premier League club, in 2003, as Joe Royle was manfully wrestling with a team to cope in the Third Division. He had Kevin Horlock, who expressed himself in midfield with some class, Terry Cooke, a former United youth player, on the wing, Dickov and the admirable Shaun Goater beginning to score the goals. But with Cityitis still flaring up from time to time, they struggled into December, and on Saturday 19 December 1998 they lost 2–1 at Bootham Crescent to York City, who scored the winner in the 86th minute. It was the new worst league result in the club's history. York was one of four clubs, along with Mansfield Town, Darlington and Wrexham, which Manchester City played that month who in 2012, with Sheikh Mansour's City top of the Premier League, were in the Blue Square Conference, having fallen out of the Football League completely.

The following week, on Boxing Day 1998, City went to Wrexham. At the cold and unpromising Racecourse Ground, Kevin Horlock scored in the 56th minute, and the team, which included Tony Vaughan, Gerard Wiekens and Jamie Pollock, worked hard to maintain the lead. That result, 1–0 at Wrexham, is recognised to have been the game which turned around City's season in the Third Division, and, arguably, their whole history since. Punctuated by defeats at home to Oldham Athletic and Wycombe Wanderers, City's momentum was enough to take them into the play-offs. They beat Wigan Athletic in a horribly anxious semi-final to reach the prize the club felt, really, too big to want so desperately, the 1999 play-off final, against Gillingham.

The friend with whom I went to that match at Wembley had been to the Wrexham game. He lived in London and supporting City was his connection to home, and an essence of himself, so he went to all the games. He said the Racecourse Ground had felt a mighty long way on public transport, had taken him an age to get there, and as it was Boxing Day it pulled apart his Christmas, but in the long odyssey back he had felt something important had improved in the attitude and purpose of Joe Royle's team. He believed they had laid the foundations there for more confident performances. The run to the play-offs included a 6–0 victory on 9 March at Burnley. When we came out of the away end at Turf Moor, there was a very tense separation between the two sets of supporters, largely because

Burnley's were more depressed than City fans at where their great club had found itself.

So City made it to Wembley the year United won the treble, and it was still exciting, walking up Wembley Way, seeing the twin towers, but the place looked shabby up close, ringed by burger vans, overpriced chips and litter. Approaching it for the Third Division play-off final was a ghost of the thrill from 1981. Inside, the seats which had been put on the old curved terraces were hard benches, we had pillars in the way, and it all looked its age, the peeling sometime-grandeur of the Empire Stadium.

City did not play well, and Gillingham, more purposeful, went 2–0 up in the 81st and 86th minutes. There was no time to come back from that, so after Gillingham scored that second goal, many City fans heaved sighs, stood up in disgust at another epochal let-down, and left. They say some were taking the years of decline and disappointment out on innocent Gillingham fans outside, on their happy way home. We stayed; I always have, hating it if I went as a kid with anybody to the glories of a match and they wanted to leave early, 'to beat the traffic'. When Gillingham's second goal went in, a City fan behind us, wearing a faded denim jacket buttoned up to the top and a green woolly hat, started to shout:

'Scunny! Fucking Scunny!' he roared. 'Scunthorpe fucking United. That's who you're fucking playing next year, stuck in this division. Fucking Scunny.'

And everybody else was quiet, watching Manchester City come so abject, in a faded Wembley.

When Kevin Horlock then scored, right at the end, nobody

really reacted because it was still too late to make a difference. Then Paul Dickov found himself in Gillingham's penalty area, with the ball at his feet, deep into the injury time of Manchester City's history. He showed great confidence, grace under pressure which he must have had innately to make him an Arsenal young player in the first place. He put his head over the ball as if it was the most natural and easy thing to be doing, as if he did not know what pressure was, and thumped the ball high into the net.

There was that pause of disbelief, that City had just come back, that the worst hadn't happened, just once, and City had actually equalised. Then everybody was up, even the fucking Scunny man, roaring and celebrating. John, next to me, who had been on all those solitary journeys from London, was jumping up and down on the spot, like a little boy. He was looking at me, it was this extraordinary moment, and I was on my feet too, of course I was, stunned by the drama, of football's natural capacity to create stories, by what was clearly, apparent even then, a landmark in the trajectory of the club: the moment of revival.

And yet even in that moment I had to realise that something was missing; I was not quite feeling it. I was not beside myself; I was not the boy who kissed Franny Lee on the telly, nor the young man who had struggled for breath when I heard that our young City had beaten United 5–1. Right then, as City fans released some of the twenty-year resentment since the return of Malcolm Allison, and hailed a bouncing back at Wembley, I felt a detachment which actually shocked me. It really had made a fundamental difference to me, to understand what

Manchester City really was. I found even in those minutes of recovery, I was not cheering in my heart.

Everybody knew City would win the penalties because the momentum of the story was with them, the last-minute salvation of a big club finally not prepared to take it any more and grasping its destiny. City's goalkeeper, Nicky Weaver, stoked himself up for an occasion he clearly felt he had been born to star in – a penalty shoot-out at Wembley – and City went up, a remarkable victory.

Amid the celebrations, the startled delight, I looked down and saw David Bernstein, in his suit, practically skipping around the pitch with Chris Bird, the club's head of press. They were punching the air, Bernstein and Bird, smiling and waving at the City fans; they were both City fans themselves, and clearly genuinely delighted. But still, it seemed to me to strike a wrong note. I saw Bernstein, whatever his virtues as a man and administrator, as the plc-director whose job was to orchestrate financial success from the morass Franny's return had got City into. He had been charged, ultimately, with making money for those who 'owned' City, mainly Wardle and Makin now. Even as all the fans around me shook their heads in disbelief, knowing this would always be a game they would talk about having been at, when Typical City clambered out of the Third Division in the 94th minute, I felt: this isn't my club any more.

I thought right then, inescapably, in the very midst of the first good thing that had happened in years to the club I had supported since I was a boy, that somebody who really did not deserve it was going to make a great deal of money out of all this.

CHAPTER 14

THERE'S ONLY ONE FRANK SINATRA

Thaksin Shinawatra, who had been accused of human rights abuses, ousted as Prime Minister of Thailand in a military coup, charged with three counts of corruption and had his financial assets in Thailand frozen, bought Manchester City in June 2007. City's directors, chaired by John Wardle, who with David Makin would receive £7m from Thaksin for his shares, recommended all City's shareholders sell to Thaksin, on the very day that the Thai was charged with corruption in his home country. Before Thaksin was welcomed into English football by City's directors and owners, by the Premier League and the original guardian of the game's sporting values, the Football Association, Brad Adams, executive director of Human Rights Watch in Asia, wrote to protest. Thaksin, Adams argued, should be barred from buying and owning the top football club because Thaksin was 'a human rights abuser of the worst kind'.

The three major human rights abuses of which Thaksin was accused when he had been Prime Minister of Thailand, by both Human Rights Watch and Amnesty International, included the killing of political protesters and the murders of 2,500 people by security forces. In October 2005, after Thaksin had 'told the

Thai military to use any means' to suppress an insurgency in the south of Thailand, 1,300 Muslims demonstrating against police were arrested and taken to an army base 'where many were beaten', Amnesty said. They were crammed into airless army trucks, according to reports, and 'at least 78 died, reportedly as a result of overcrowding during the journey and ill-treatment'. Thaksin's government did appoint a commission to investigate, but the findings were never made public and, according to Amnesty: 'No one was known to have been brought to justice for the killings.'

In January 2003 Thaksin had declared a 'war on drugs', and Human Rights Watch quoted from his speech, in which he said: 'There is nothing under the sun which the Thai Police cannot do. It may be necessary to have casualties. If there are deaths among traders, it's normal.'

In the following three months, 2,500 people were shot dead, including a nine-year-old boy and a baby of sixteen months who was in her mother's arms when she was killed. In December 2003 Thaksin declared 'victory' in the 'war on drugs'. He always denied these people killed by the security forces were, in effect, executions. Human Rights Watch claimed that the deaths were 'not properly investigated', there had been no trials so no proof any of the victims were in fact drug dealers, and nobody had been convicted of any of the killings, 'reinforcing a climate of impunity among the security forces'.

Human Rights Watch also alleged that Thaksin had suppressed the Thai media.

The corruption allegations followed an investigation the military authorities had launched into the circumstances by which

Thaksin had become a billionaire while he was Prime Minister of the country. All of this was absolutely public and known, available at the click of a mouse, at the time Manchester City's directors were solemnly recommending the great old football club be sold to him. In its 2006 report on Thailand, the anti-corruption organisation Transparency International said of the country under Thaksin:

'Corrupt activities have become highly sophisticated, including conflicts of interest and policy-based corruption. Despite some successes, Thaksin was alleged of [sic] having absolute power, corruption, conflicts of interest, violation of human rights and using inappropriate populist policies to win the rural poor.'

In January 2006 Thaksin's government had passed a law removing a previous restriction, which had required that 75 per cent of any Thai telecommunications company had to be owned within the country. Just days later, Thaksin himself sold 100 per cent of his own company, Shin Corp, which owned Thailand's largest mobile phone company, to the Temasek Corporation, owned in Singapore. He received $1.9bn for the sale. He and his family structured the sale, according to reports, so that they would pay no tax, which further infuriated opinion in Bangkok. The massive demonstrations which followed that sale paralysed Bangkok and the ensuing political crisis gave the army their reason for removing him from power.

They set up what they called an Assets Examination Committee to investigate how Thaksin had made his money. After a long inquisition, it came up with three charges, including that he had abused his power by helping his wife, Potjaman, to buy a piece of government-owned land in Bangkok, at under its market value. In June the AEC froze most of Thaksin's proceeds from the sale of Shin Corp. Potjaman had already been charged with tax evasion and perjury relating to a transfer of shares in Shin Corp in 1997. Besides the corruption charges and freezing of assets eventually brought against Thaksin, his children, Panthongtae and Pintongta, were hit with a $789m tax bill the authorities claimed should have been paid out of the Shin Corp sale. In June 2007, the Thai authorities would freeze all his bank accounts and assets in the country, after prosecutors alleged he 'earned unusual wealth from a conflict of interest'.

Thaksin denied all the charges, and said they were politically motivated against him by the Thai establishment, who felt threatened by him after he won two elections with the support of poor voters. After Adams wrote his letter outlining Thaksin's alleged human rights abuses, the Premier League replied that it had a specific 'fit and proper person' test to determine who could take over a football club, which did bar convicted criminals. However, as Thaksin was only charged with corruption offences, not convicted, and had never been found guilty of anything in relation to alleged human rights abuses, he was a fit and proper person to take over Manchester City.

Wardle issued a statement in support of selling his shares to Thaksin, saying:

'This offer provides an exciting opportunity to take Manchester City to the next stage of our development and deliver the on-field success we have all been striving for.'

*

Work as a journalist for the *Independent* newspaper and then for the *Guardian*, exploring the new culture, finances and takeovers in English football, had led me into investigating sundry 'owners' of football clubs. Many were personally profiting from their involvement in the Premier and Football Leagues, while dozens of Football League clubs had fallen into financial crises since the 1992 First Division breakaway. I had discovered that in the lower divisions, some owners and directors made money in less straightforward ways, and that had been an education in the history of and fans' pride in some of those clubs City had played in 1998–99.

Chesterfield, formed in 1866, is the fourth-oldest football club in England, and therefore the world. In the summer of 2000 the club had been taken over by a 29-year-old of no obvious business pedigree, Darren Brown. As it turned out, in the grimmest episode in the club's long and, to the fans, cherished history, Brown had proceeded to take £800,000 out of the club for his own purposes, including paying his own debts, living large, and putting a deposit down on a smart new house. Desperately concerned supporters were campaigning for their club's very survival, and to go there and meet them was to discover steadfast loyalty to a club which would never come close to the Premier League. Chesterfield miners had been solidly out on strike during the bitter dispute of 1984–85, and the club had been a haven for them, cutting the price of tickets for miners and rattling collection buckets for them. When in 1997 the team had reached the FA Cup semi-final against Middlesbrough, in which only the referee's failure to recognise a ball over the line denied them a goal which would surely have taken Chesterfield to Wembley, it was their finest hour. There was even a song composed for the cup run, 'We Can Build our Dreams'.

I was shown internal accounts which documented £400,000 going out of the club, and reported the nefarious Brown regime in my column in the *Independent*. Brown ultimately was charged with nineteen different criminal offences, pleaded guilty to two counts of fraudulent trading, and was sentenced to four years in prison. The good people of the town still had a struggle to keep their football club alive; the supporters' trust, hastily formed at a meeting of 1,000 people at the Winding Wheel theatre which felt like a revivalist gathering, bought their sinking club, then had to put it into administration. They were eventually forced by financial difficulties to hand the club over to local businessmen who supported Chesterfield, but the democratic trust still retained an elected supporter representative on the club's board.

At York City, the chairman, Douglas Craig, was demanding a huge personal profit for selling the club and ground or, he promised, he would expel the club from Bootham Crescent which would be demolished for housing. A trust formed at York too, supporters giving up large amounts of their own time to organise against Craig and fight for the future of a proud lower-division football club. At Wrexham, two south Manchester businessmen, Mark Guterman and Alex Hamilton, had come together and actually made a written contract agreeing that they were buying Wrexham with the sole intention of making the most money they could for themselves from the land on which the Racecourse Ground stood, the football club's beloved home since 1872. After a furious campaign by the supporters' trust, Hamilton and Guterman were ultimately defeated, and banned from being company directors for seven years.

All over the country supporters were forming trusts, mutual bodies, to campaign in crises or against owners exploiting them, and to seek an involvement in their own clubs. United fans were prominently involved in campaigns against Rupert Murdoch's BSkyB bid to buy their own club, and for a better, more equitable way to run football. However, the clubs were so expensive to buy, even the small ones like Chesterfield, Wrexham and York, that the fans' trusts struggled to hold on to their ownership of them, and in almost every case, except that of Exeter, had in the end to find trustworthy-seeming businessmen to take them over.

City had gone up, promoted to the Premier League, but they only stayed up two seasons before being relegated yet again, in 2001 at Maine Road. Joe Royle departed, apparently following a man-to-man chat with David Bernstein over a biryani on Manchester's 'curry mile' in Rusholme, and City appointed Kevin Keegan. He had a charismatic, catalytic effect on the mood, and returned City to the Premier League, with Eyal Berkovic and Ali Bernabia in midfield, playing some of the freest-flowing football since the good times. City moved into the new stadium in 2003, the £78m from Sport England and £49m from Manchester City Council having built it as the centrepiece of the successful Commonwealth Games, then paying for the track to be ripped up and the stadium converted for City to occupy.

Typical City, though, ended up limping in to their new stadium, loaded with debts and losses, having overspent during Keegan's time in charge. In 2002–03 Bernstein had sanctioned losing £14m for players to establish the club in the Premier League, then they spent another £21.5m on signings. Bernstein grew uneasy about the continued spending, though, and eventually fell out with Keegan and Wardle over the £6m signing of Robbie Fowler from Leeds. Bernstein left City before it took possession of the new ground whose favourable terms he had negotiated with the council. City kept spending, and alongside high-quality French internationals Nicolas Anelka and Sylvain Distin, came a gaggle of players who never made it: Mikkel Bischoff, Tyrone Loran, Karim Kerkar and Vicente Vuoso, a twenty-year-old signed for £3.5m from Argentinian club Independiente, who never played a game. City's accounts to the end of May 2003 show they lost £15.4m, following the £14m the previous year, and had total debts and liabilities of £104m.

Despite the Premier League's continued TV boom, a £1.6bn deal secured for 2001–04, and the gift of the new stadium, City were in money trouble again and seriously struggling. Alastair Mackintosh, the chief executive, staved off potentially serious financial difficulties by selling Shaun Wright-Phillips, to Chelsea, for £21m in July 2005. Keegan left and was replaced by Stuart Pearce, who complained that he had no money to spend, and in 2006 and 2007 a grim City side finished fifteenth and sixteenth in the Premier League.

So in June 2007, somewhat desperate after looking for new investors and having the club up for sale for a year, they agreed to sell to Thaksin. City's directors and major shareholders wrote in the official document recommending all shareholders sell too, that they had given 'irrevocable undertakings' to sell to Thaksin: Wardle and Makin, who owned 29.95 per cent of

Manchester City plc, Mark Boler, son of Stephen, who died in 1998, 18.75 per cent; Francis Lee, now down to 7.13 per cent. Overspent and overborrowed, City stood out as the only Premier League club to be sold to an overseas investor as others were, but not for a fat profit to the shareholders. Thaksin was paying £21.6m for the whole plc, so Wardle and Makin were to receive around £7m in total. Francis Lee would be paid around £1.5m for selling, bringing a final end to his Second Coming. Wardle and Makin had loaned around £20m to cover shortfalls over the years, and Thaksin agreed to pay them £17.5m back, so they had to take a hit on their loans as well. The other City directors had all agreed to sell too: Bryan Bodek, a Manchester solicitor, and Mackintosh, the chief executive. Dennis Tueart, overhead-kick hero of all our bedroom walls, was a director – his corporate entertainment company, Premier Events, being paid £30,000 a year for his part-time services – and he too had agreed to sell to Thaksin.

The document issued by Thaksin's company described him as 'a self-made billionaire' and 'a passionate follower of English football'. It said he had promised to put money into the club. In Appendix 3 on page 56 it did set out some details of the trouble he was in:

'In June 2007, the Assets Examination Committee in Thailand, set up under the authority of the current military administration, issued a freezing order against bank accounts and assets in Thailand of Dr Thaksin Shinawatra and his immediate family, in relation to alleged conflicts of interest, corruption and related offences in Thailand.'

However, it said: 'All the allegations made by the Assets Examinations Committee and other Thai prosecutory agencies are entirely refuted by Dr Thaksin Shinawatra and his family, and he will be vigorously defending all of such allegations. Formal court hearings in relation to such allegations have yet to be heard. The first formal court hearing is scheduled for around 10 July 2007.'

The City board, chaired by Wardle, stated: 'The board of Manchester City believes [Thaksin's] ownership of Manchester City will help provide the club with the financial strength necessary to improve its performance in both the Premier League and, in time, enable the club to qualify for European competition on a regular basis.'

I talked to Wardle about the decision to sell the club to Thaksin. He said that he and Makin had become involved in the club after they had 'a couple of quid in our pockets' from floating J-D Sports in 1996, and: 'It emptied our pockets over the next ten years. We put money in to basically keep the club going. It reached the point when we could not put any more in.

'Towards the end of Stuart Pearce's last season in charge [2006–07], fans were getting very restless, and that is why we decided to take the Thaksin Shinawatra bid.'

Wardle explained that when Thaksin's bid came in, the fact that the lawyers certified that the money was there to pay the £21.6m to Wardle and Makin and the other shareholders was all they could take into account. He said as a plc, the directors had only to consider the money being paid, and whether it represented fair value, not human rights or corruption allegations.

'We made sure the lawyers said everything was correct. We had to make sure he was the right and proper person to take the club; all boxes were ticked, and the money was there. It was clean as a whistle. I didn't have any concerns; everybody signed it off.'

At that time I spoke to the secretary-general of the Thai office of Transparency International, Dr Juree Vichit-Vadakan, who said that although the country now had a non-democratic government imposed by the military, many people supported the overthrow of Thaksin because there had been 'widely reported allegations of corruption, nepotism and cronyism'. She argued that those involved with selling him Manchester City should consider if they wanted all this at their doors:

'British people should think harder whether they want somebody to buy a football club who is surrounded by moral uncertainty. Is money always the most important thing in life?'

I had met football supporters battling to save their clubs, and calling for the FA to rise to its mission to govern the game in the interests of the sport, not the money men. United fans had fought implacably BSkyB's proposed takeover in 1999, and bitterly opposed the Glazers. When the Americans took over in 2005 with their debt-laden buyout, Andy Walsh and a large group of other supporters had turned away, to form their own club, supporter-owned FC United of Manchester. The Manchester United Supporters Trust, with 32,000 fans signing up online, had stayed, but maintained profound opposition to the new owners' financial assault on the club. In 2010, after the Glazers refinanced with a £500m borrowing by Manchester United, exposing all the money which had poured out of Old

Trafford, the fans came up with that symbolic protest: wearing the original green and gold colours of Newton Heath. It was their way of stating allegiance to the collective Manchester values of the club founded by the workers on the Lancashire and Yorkshire Railway in 1878, not the leveraged buyout merchants of Florida.

I had assumed, given this rising tradition of protest and awareness by supporters who owned their 'clubs', that City fans would rise up in revulsion at the sale of theirs, in the new stadium Manchester's council built for it, to an ex-Thai Prime Minister carrying so much trouble and scandal in his baggage.

Many City fans were appalled. Mike Barnett, a lifelong fan and former editor of the club's magazine, resolved not to go to a City game again while they were under the ownership of Thaksin. There were others who felt disquieted, who stopped going, and as the season went on some energetic supporters formed a trust and tried hard to raise concerns about the new owner. Yet the overwhelming majority of supporters did not express any objection at all to their club being owned by a man accused of being 'a human rights abuser of the worst kind'. Mostly they welcomed him as a man who had money and could bring success. Some argued that he was a decent man because he had won elections, and all the allegations against him were worthless because they had been brought under the unelected military regime. A club spokesman quoted in the *Manchester Evening News* appeared to take Thaksin's side in the tumultuous politics of Thailand, and said that City fans had 'warmly embraced' him.

To acclimatise the fans to his ownership, Thaksin offered

free noodles and Thai entertainment in Albert Square before the season started. That was said by experienced Thai commentators to be similar to events laid on in rural Thailand by Thaksin's political party when it was seeking votes from the poor. Around eight thousand City fans turned up to help themselves to Thaksin's free scoff in front of Manchester Town Hall, and listen to Thai singers. Then Thaksin went down in City lore by trying to sing 'Blue Moon'. At the time, if you looked for Thaksin Shinawatra on YouTube, you found pro-democracy demonstrations against him in the main square of Bangkok, and City fans eating his noodles in Albert Square. Soon, City fans came up with a fond nickname for him, a play on his name. Thaksin Shinawatra – Frank Sinatra. They called him Frank, and embraced him as one of their own.

He appointed Sven-Göran Eriksson as the manager and provided the wherewithal to immediately sign exciting new players including Martin Petrov, Vedran Corluka and Elano, a real, live Brazilian international. Under Eriksson, City played liberated football, to crowds exceeding 40,000 yearning for the old status finally to return. They won the first three matches, including a 1–0 home win in the derby against United on 19 August 2007, and sat in the autumn sunshine atop the Premier League.

Thaksin used the club nakedly for political grandstanding back home, where Premier League football is watched by millions of Thais. Crowds of Thai politicians and dignitaries were entertained at the stadium, and Manchester City's scoreboard beamed birthday greetings to the king of Thailand. The team and individual players had to go on pre-season tours to Thailand, to gladhand and reflect well on Thaksin. Manchester City were an adornment to the manifesto of a politician in exile from his own country, facing corruption charges, but in Manchester – and English football generally – few seemed to care.

City lost to Arsenal and Blackburn but beat Aston Villa, Norwich, Newcastle, Middlesbrough and Birmingham City before playing the champions, Chelsea, at Stamford Bridge on 27 October and losing 6–0. After that, the team was a little inconsistent but still produced excellent results including 2–0 wins at Spurs and Newcastle. Then, however, with Elano injured, in the new year they skidded into a few weeks of deteriorating form, leading up to the derby match with United, at Old Trafford, on 10 February 2008.

It was, the fixture software had determined, a scheduled visit by Manchester City and their supporters to Old Trafford, in the week that United were commemorating the fiftieth anniversary of the day eight of their players died in the Munich air disaster. For years, some City fans had sung a vile song purporting to rejoice in those deaths, and there were huge worries from both clubs that they would do so again, disgracing themselves and City. Both Manchester clubs conducted the preparations for the game with respect and dignity, and City mounted information campaigns and pleas for the supporters to honour the Munich memorials.

United held a series of events for the families of those who died, twenty-three in all, including United officials, journalists who had been covering the European Cup quarter-final in Belgrade, the plane's co-pilot Captain Kenneth Rayment, and other travellers. United arranged a series of interviews with the surviving players who had been on the plane, Sir Bobby Charlton,

Bill Foulkes, Kenny Morgans and Albert Scanlon (Harry Gregg was too ill to travel to Manchester). I went to listen, and write about it for the *Guardian*. Old men now, these former United survivors spoke very movingly about the disaster which had devastated their youth and killed their friends, young footballers blessed with all the talents. Charlton said that he thought about the dead players, his mates, every day, and he felt a mission, still, to tell the world how good they had been. Sir Alex Ferguson had asked Charlton to talk to the current team, including several young foreign players who knew little of the crash, and they also watched a documentary about the disaster which Ferguson said had moved them. It was a disaster which inspired worldwide sympathy for Manchester United and, as the current chief executive David Gill said, that support was the foundation of the club's growth.

Matt Busby's recovery from his own awful injuries, and his obsession with driving an Old Trafford haunted by dead players to the European Cup victory ten years later, remains English football's greatest story. But over the years we had learned of the human tragedies which playing football cannot salve, of young fathers dead, and of the club doing too little for the families of those who died and the survivors. Grieving families were given little compensation and barely ever contacted for years. Johnny Berry and Jackie Blanchflower, fine players who survived, but whose injuries left them unable to play football again, lived in club houses, and they were asked to leave them. Blanchflower's wife had said the club was 'very cold' after Munich. Neil Berry, Johnny's son, who became a head teacher and wrote a deeply moving book about the effect of the crash on his father and family, described it as 'a time of indescribable pain and grief'. Of the way the family was dropped by United, he wrote:

'On reflection it would have been nice to have had some kind of ongoing support from the officials of Manchester United, not necessarily financial. But as Dad always said: "You're only as good as your last game." He had played his and the regime at the time did not want to know of his circumstances and preferred that he just vanished.'

Fifty years on was a time for United to make sure they conducted themselves properly, and the modern Manchester United demonstrated a determination to do so. After a week of memorial events held with due dignity, the families of those affected, including Neil Berry, were invited to the match against City, which would commemorate Munich profoundly. United would wear shirts in the style of 1958 with no sponsor, the names of those who died would be displayed on the hoardings around the Old Trafford pitch, City would also wear a vintage-style shirt, and there would be a minute's silence.

Both clubs were terrified that some City fans, however few, would bring shame on themselves, the club and English football by violating the minute's silence and singing that Munich song. Ken Ramsden, who had joined a still-shattered and grief-stricken United as a tea boy two years after the crash and rose to become the club's long-serving secretary, said that that sour and disgraceful song had started with hooliganism in the late 1960s and 1970s. At the time of the crash, he said, the whole of Manchester had come together in shock and grief, City's officials and medical staff had provided help to United, and the fans demonstrated sympathy and solidarity.

'It was a shame,' he said of the nasty Munich ditty. 'Because that is when football became tribal. Then we had to have segregation of crowds. Before that, supporters of opposing clubs used to walk to matches together and the rivalry was a lot friendlier.'

It was strange, after a week of calls for City fans to behave, that down Sir Matt Busby Way on the approach to Old Trafford, United fans were singing songs about fighting, kicking City fans' heads in, and the nick nack paddywack one which ends with: 'Why don't City fuck off home?' Inside the ground, a lone piper led the teams out in those 1950s-style kits, the sun shone, the names of the dead were displayed on the billboards, and then, when the minute's silence was called, the loudest sound was of City's fans shushing each other. They had arrived with a determination not to make the following day's headlines for disgrace, and the minute's silence was totally observed by every single one of them, with commemorative, plain blue and white scarves held proudly above their heads. The relief around a hushed Old Trafford was so palpable you could almost physically embrace it.

And so Manchester, including City's fans, did itself and the victims of its most tragic sporting story proud. Then the game kicked off and United seemed almost muted. Ryan Giggs spoke later about the team having been too affected by all the memorials. I interviewed Rio Ferdinand subsequently, and he said the same:

'I think the emotions of the day got over us and we looked into it all a lot more than we did into the game itself. On the day we didn't play well and City did. There is a real genuine feeling for the history at United; it is drummed into you, about Matt Busby and the Busby babes.'

It was an insight for me, that the Manchester United which had become so dominant in the Premier League era, commercially relentless in exploiting its 'brand', and owned now by the financial invaders, the Glazers, was still a club in a heartfelt part of its culture. That the current millionaire players were genuinely moved by the respects paid to their predecessors from the 1950s, when the Busby babes were cut off as they were moving football from black and white into colour.

After 25 minutes, with United playing a halting, awkward game, Darius Vassell scored for City and the 3,000 City fans who had kept proudly silent for that pre-match minute filled their corner with glee. Then just before half-time, the Zimbabwean striker Benjani Mwaruwari glanced a header into the far corner of United's net, City were two up at Old Trafford and their fans were hugging themselves again. United could not rouse themselves all afternoon; they resorted to booting the ball up to Carlos Tevez, playing as a lone striker for United, and when Michael Carrick did score, it was the 90th minute and too late.

City had claimed a famous victory at Old Trafford on the day Munich was remembered, the fans had behaved well, and so they celebrated endlessly afterwards. Kept in the ground, due to the segregation Ramsden had lamented, they ran through a symphony of songs. After some time, all the United fans, and the occupants of the directors' box, had gone, except for a contingent of Thais connected to Thaksin (although not the owner himself). They were taking pictures of Old Trafford and the City fans on their smartphones and cameras, looking like tourists charmed by the novel experience of an English football match, rather than people who actually owned one of its great clubs. Then somebody in the City away corner saw them, and a chant went up which soon they were all uniting in joining in:

'One Frank Sinatra! There's only one Frank Sinatra!'

Following that derby day defeat, when United's squad looked threadbare, as if finally stripped too far by the Glazers' financial drain, Ferguson's team, of course, went and won the Premier League and Champions League on a rainy night in Moscow, beating Chelsea on penalties. It was City who unravelled completely, as the consequences of Wardle, Makin and the Manchester directors selling to Thaksin were finally, predictably, brought home.

City's form after the derby victory declined; they won only three games out of twelve and at a game which Thaksin himself attended, in the blue-cushioned seats of the directors' box, City lost 3–2 to Fulham, after having been 2–0 up, Fulham's winner conceded in the 90th minute. Losing feebly to a bout of Cityitis was not what Thaksin was used to witnessing from the ventures he commanded, and days later, Thaksin was reported to have told Eriksson that he was to be sacked at the end of the season.

It was the football sacking that made the supporters upset with Thaksin for the first time. The man under whose rule 2,500 people are alleged to have been slaughtered in the 'war on drugs', with impunity for those who did the killing, was accused of being ruthless for paying off Sven Göran-Eriksson at Manchester City. For their part, the players in effect demonstrated to the owner that they did not consider his dismissal of Eriksson hugely well thought out. After a 1–0 defeat to Liverpool at Anfield, they went to Middlesbrough for the final game of the season and capitulated 8–1. That was the last Manchester City result before Sheikh Mansour took over Manchester City.

Thaksin returned to his personal and political nightmares. On 31 July 2008, his wife Potjaman was found guilty in Bangkok of violating the land sale laws and sentenced to three years in prison. Both she and Thaksin violated their bail conditions by flying to Beijing for the opening ceremony of the Olympic Games in August 2008, then they fled from there to England. At that point the owner of Manchester City became officially a fugitive from justice in his home country, still facing corruption charges. His assets were frozen and it was clear that he had no money for Manchester City.

The accounts from Thaksin's single season owning Manchester City, 2007–08, show that he did put some money into the club, but not as much as it had appeared from the numbers of players signed. In fact he had loaned City £21.3m, also taking over Wardle and Makin's £20m loans. It was obviously true, then, what many had suspected, that Elano, Petrov and the several other signings from overseas were signed in instalments, not as the result of massive investment from Thaksin.

He had charged City interest on the loans of up to 11.83 per cent, and it seemed as if most of it was at that highest rate, because the interest owed to him after just one year was £5m.

A company owned by his son, Panthongtae, had been paid £47,912 by the club for, the accounts said, 'the provision of promotional media services as part of the team's tour to Thailand'.

Manchester City, with Thaksin on the run, fell into a financial plummet. They made an enormous loss, £33m, and had to take out more loans, as well as mortgage the following season's Premier League TV payments to Standard Bank, to get the cash in early. Yet at the same time they kept spending, signing on 2 July 2008, for £19m, a gangly Brazilian striker from CSKA Moscow, Jo. Garry Cook, who arrived at City in the summer from Nike, told me that he soon realised there was no money, and that players were being signed on deposit. 'The fabric of the football club had been taken away,' he said.

Vincent Kompany, the then 22-year-old Belgian centre half who had joined from Hamburg for £6m, said later: 'At the time I signed, I was supposed to meet the owner, but then I was told he had to cancel it go to into hiding somewhere. It was a bit of a funny situation.'

A year after John Wardle had sold the club to Thaksin Shinawatra and said in official statements that it was the deal to bring City the money and European success the fans craved, the club did not have the money to pay its staff and was in danger of falling into insolvency.

'We got into a position where we couldn't pay the players,' Cook recalled, 'and John Wardle was asked to lend the club £2m.'

Wardle said he had ceased official involvement with the club when Eriksson was sacked; he believed Eriksson 'did a tremendous job' and the way Thaksin sacked him was 'so unethical'. When City came back and asked him for a loan to pay the wages, Wardle told me:

'I wasn't happy; I felt I had done my part. But they asked me to put the money back in, and I was assured it would come back, which it did – eventually.'

Staff who worked there at the time have said the club was in turmoil, and they did not know when they came to work at the City of Manchester Stadium whether their jobs would still be waiting for them. Wardle was ultimately asked three times to lend his £2m to tide them over, which he did.

That was the state of Manchester City when Sulaiman Al Fahim had his audience with Sheikh Mansour bin Zayed Al Nahyan of Abu Dhabi. The club brought to him had by now been in the Premier League for six successive seasons, and had just finished ninth. It had a new stadium, built by its local council, which could seat 48,000 fans; that, Khaldoon Al Mubarak has always affirmed absolutely, was a crucial factor in Sheikh Mansour's decision to buy Manchester City. Its fans had proved over forty years that they were unshakeably, bloody-mindedly loyal, addicted to the hope of seeing Manchester City successful, apparently whatever it took. And so Sheikh Mansour agreed that this would be the club to transform with his unthinkable wealth.

Abu Dhabi United did not say at the time exactly how much they had paid for Manchester City, in the deal concluded in the Emirates Palace Hotel in Abu Dhabi, the exhibition of gold and marble, where the country's family-run parliament meets.

Then, in March 2011, a curious court case was reported to have opened in Dubai. Thaksin Shinawatra was suing his former lawyer, an emirati named as KMA, for embezzling £60m of the money Thaksin was paid for selling Manchester City. The reports from Dubai said Thaksin had allegedly been convinced to deposit the money in the name of the lawyer, who had then bought a private jet with part of the money, which the lawyer denied. The details, which emerged in the court, were that Sheikh Mansour had paid Thaksin £150m for City.

Thaksin's own costs from the City venture were the £21.6m he had paid to Wardle, Makin, Mark Boler, Francis Lee and the other former City shareholders, his loans of £21.5m, and the £17.5m he had given Wardle and Makin for theirs, £39m. In round figures, Thaksin had spent just over £60m on Manchester City. One year later, by now convicted in his absence in Thailand of the corruption offences, and with Manchester City on the brink of ruin, Thaksin was paid £150m for his shares.

Sheikh Mansour, with a club and a new stadium, could sign Robinho for £32.5m immediately as his statement of intent, appoint Al Mubarak to ensure the project was carried out expertly, and prepare to spend whatever it would take to fund a club to the top of the football podium. For Manchester City Council, which had spent £49m of council tax payers' money providing that stadium for City, the deal included no clawback of any profit a Manchester City owner would make when selling the club with the benefit of it. Thaksin Shinawatra was on the run, determined to fight his political battles in Thailand, but he had done pretty well out of his time as the owner of Manchester City. 'Frank' had cleared a personal profit of £90m, in one year, from the shares John Wardle, David Makin and Manchester City's other 'custodians' had sold him, and from the £127m home the council had built for the football company, in the poorest part of town.

CHAPTER 15

WELCOME TO MANCHESTER

It was still in the dawn of Manchester City's Abu Dhabi ownership and swingeing Conservative–Liberal Democrat
government cuts to public services when Sheikh Mansour signed
Carlos Tevez for £45m and City proclaimed this triumphant
coup with that billboard at the beginning of Deansgate: Welcome to Manchester. Tevez, arms outstretched, was in sky blue,
as was the whole poster – the point impudently made being
that the previous two seasons he had been playing at United.
There, with Tevez not always a first-choice striker because Sir
Alex Ferguson could also select from the galactic talents of
Wayne Rooney, Cristiano Ronaldo and Dimitar Berbatov,
United had won the Premier League twice, in 2008 and 2009,
the Champions League in 2008 and then been runners-up in
2009 when United were hypnotically outpassed by a mesmeric
Barcelona. Sir Alex Ferguson had said he did want to sign Tevez,
although later United's manager said Tevez had not been worth
the option price United had of paying £25.5m to his 'owners'.
When Tevez's adviser, the Iranian Kia Joorabchian, surfaced
after the cross-Manchester negotiations that summer, Tevez was
being paraded as a Manchester City player, the front man for

sheikh-owned City's new statement. With this enormous outlay of money, to buy Tevez and pay him the £10m a year necessary, Mansour's City were declaring their true intention to challenge United's thirty-year dominance.

Enough was known at the time Tevez arrived to understand that the poster, standing in front of a 1970s precinct derelict since it opened, opposite the glitter of Harvey Nichols, heralded a more complex message than City's new marketing people intended. Tevez's rampage into the English Premier League had always trailed clouds of murk. Tevez and Javier Mascherano, both of whom Joorabchian had brought to West Ham United immediately after they starred for Argentina in the 2006 World Cup, had been our introduction to the 'third-party ownership' of footballers. Common, we learned, in South America and increasingly Portugal, this was where businessmen, not clubs, 'owned' the 'economic rights' to players. That meant that when the players moved, the businessmen-investors, rather than the clubs selling the players, received the transfer fee – often these days, in the multi-millions – from the buying club. West Ham had been fined £5.5m close to the end of Tevez's first season for having failed to inform the Premier League that this was how Tevez and Mascherano were 'owned'. It was revealed that the 'economic rights' in the players were owned by companies with unnamed investors registered in tax havens; Tevez by companies called MSI and Just Sports Inc., Mascherano by Mystere Services and Global Soccer Agencies. The independent disciplinary panel which considered West Ham's breach of Premier League rules had decided not to deduct points because, they argued, one player could not make the difference between winning and losing. They might have been forced to revise that view had they seen Tevez score the only goal against United, who were already champions, in the Old Trafford drizzle of the 2006–07 season's final game. That goal kept West Ham in the moneyed Premier League and Tevez's uncontainable display that day must have sealed Ferguson's resolve to sign him. Sheffield United, who were relegated instead of West Ham, subsequently sued for their financial loss and an arbitration panel determined that West Ham should pay £20m in compensation.

Acting partly on distaste for the idea that individual businessmen 'owners', could make money on the buying and selling of footballers, the Premier League then banned 'third-party ownership', in January 2008. In its statement, the league referred to the principle, time-honoured since football clubs began paying each other for the registrations of players, that transfer fees keep money circulating among clubs and so act as some kind of redistribution down the football pyramid. The Premier League also made reference to the state of South American football, where the world's greatest players have been incubated for generations, but where most clubs constantly stagger on the edge of financial ruination.

'The clubs decided that third party ownership was something they did not want to see,' the statement said. 'It raises too many issues over the integrity of competition, the development of young players and the potential impact on the football pyramid – it was felt the Premier League was in a position to take a stand on this. No one wants to see what has happened to club football in South America repeated over here.'

When Tevez moved from West Ham to Manchester United

in the summer of 2007, it was on a two-year loan deal from his 'owners'. Joorabchian has never revealed who those 'owners' were, and all the companies which have ever turned up in the tangled Tevez story were registered in tax havens. At the time he signed for City, the company which 'owned' Tevez's rights turned out to have been called Harlem Springs, registered in the British Virgin Islands. In such tax havens, many of them former or present British protectorates, no capital gains tax – on the profit, or gain, an owner makes when selling an asset – is payable, whereas in the UK 18 per cent tax is currently payable. My education into how British people become 'tax exiles' to avoid paying capital gains tax had been Jack Walker, who moved to Jersey in 1974 and so had no tax to pay when he sold the shares in his Blackburn-based business to British Steel for £330m fifteen years later. He indulged some of the proceeds on buying Blackburn Rovers and paying for the players to win the 1995 Premier League, and they put up a statue of him at the ground.

The other use of tax havens is for secrecy; in such places the owners of companies can hide their identities, unlike in the UK, where the shareholders of a company are published and available for inspection at the Companies House registry. Joorabchian has never said who owned Harlem Springs, or how much City paid them to buy Tevez's 'economic rights' outright, as required by the new Premier League rules outlawing third-party ownership. But sources close to the deal said authoritatively that the price City had paid to gazump United, as Ferguson came close to exchanging contracts with Harlem Springs, was £45m. So the sign which went up at the opening

of Deansgate, just over the Irwell and the Salford border, opposite Manchester Cathedral, was proclaiming a deal whereby a
sheikh based in Abu Dhabi had paid £45m to a company registered in a tax haven, to beat a company (Manchester United)
registered by the Glazer family in the low-tax US state of
Delaware, for the services of an Argentinian footballer. Welcome to Manchester.

It was a little different from the signing of the centre forward who last stormed City to a League championship, another
small but game and determined lad, signed for £60,000 from
Bolton Wanderers in only City's second season back in the First
Division. Carlos Tevez would have no need to become involved
in toilet roll to supplement his footballer's wage in the long
Manchester afternoons. His weekly pay was a basic £198,000
per week, just under £10m a year, with an agreement approved
by Sheikh Mansour that Tevez would always be the highest-
paid footballer at Manchester City.

The City fans, of course, were delighted. Here was a genuinely world-class player, who had won all those topmost prizes,
snatched from the grasp of United. When they saw him in
action, they were also excited by Tevez, in the way he plays,
legs pumping, chest out, never stopping, as if to embody in
human movement the favoured phrase and required commitment of the English football fan: he gives a hundred and ten
per cent. Tevez seemed to be able to keep his mind on his football while some in the first wave of expensive Sheikh Mansour
signings were squabbling on the training ground and becoming
extravagant disappointments. Manchester City began increasingly to rely on Tevez. Of the other strikers, Roque Santa Cruz,

signed for £17.5m from Blackburn, where he had given ster-
ling service for Mark Hughes, spent almost all his time at City
injured. Emmanuel Adebayor, £25m from Arsenal, never
seemed to settle after he ran the length of the pitch to celebrate a goal against his old club, and was periodically
photographed losing his rag at Carrington. Craig Bellamy was
more outraged than anyone at the sacking of Mark Hughes,
his old manager with Wales, and he was soon gone from
Mancini's club, loaned out to Cardiff. With Mancini concen-
trating on shoring up the defence anyway, Tevez often played
as the only striker, scampering across the broad acres of the
City of Manchester Stadium, harrying opposing defences, at
times beating teams, as he had for West Ham against United
that fateful day, almost on his own.

Mancini had taken over on Boxing Day 2009 with City facing
not only a flurry of fixtures in the league, but, a mark of City's
progress so far, a League Cup semi-final, to be played home
and away, against United. The fixture brought back memories
of the match now thirty-five years earlier, to which I had half-
run hand in hand with my dad, to see City win 4–0 and Colin
Bell carried off in agony under the floodlights. This time, the
approach to the match seemed to become dominated more by
the personal dramas of Carlos Tevez than the contest itself
between the tangled histories of the two great Manchester clubs.
Ferguson, although he had agreed to sign Tevez for United, then
said he had thought Tevez overpriced at £25.5m, which United
had had the option of paying Harlem Springs at the end of the
two-year loan. Then Gary Neville chipped in, saying he could
not argue with that assessment and United did not miss Tevez.

Outside the stadium the night of the home leg, City were handing out free commemorative flags – in the Abu Dhabi era, such mementoes no longer have to be bought outside from swag men, like we all did outside Wembley in 1981. Although I was reporting on the game for the *Guardian*, I thought I would take a couple home, for old time's sake, and for my daughters, although they know nothing of City. To them Manchester City is some obscure part of their dad's upbringing, from 'the olden days' in Manchester, when things were done differently. Like the old friends who turn up once in a while and laugh about stuff which you had to be there, back in the day, to find funny.

The match reports in the following morning's newspapers would mostly say the atmosphere for the derby semi-final at the City of Manchester Stadium crackled, that it was fiery. True, a flare was lit in United's end, but I found it quiet, really, for a match of such claustrophobic rivalry. It was the first time City did their Blue Moon Rising thing; they turned the lights off in the stadium, then projected the image of a moon into the seats, and had the phrase Blue Moon Rising circulating round the advertising hoardings. It was excellent staging, perhaps by the same new marketing and design recruits who had come up with the Tevez billboard, but it left me a little cold. Football matches such as these never used to require such staged melodrama. The fans always worked up the expectation themselves, and City fans had claimed the song 'Blue Moon' themselves – only the miserable part of it, not the golden resolution. It is a feature of modern football stadiums, as the raucous young people have been priced out and the atmosphere generally sedated, that the clubs take their fans' anthems and culture, and sell it back to them.

From kick-off, Tevez went on an immediate mad run into United territory. His knees were scurrying higher than usual, his head bobbing from the neck with the obvious effort he was putting in. He looked to be making a statement of his own at the very beginning: that he had arrived determined for the script to be about him, and the challenge to his status and quality laid down by Ferguson and Neville. And so it turned out in the end, and he deserved it to be, having dragged City back from 1–0 down against a more fluent United by the force of his own will and the unignorable way he plays, in which he seems almost ostentatiously to be emphasising how hard he is trying. At times, on the field, he comes close to caricature, as if he is acting a vision of what maximum commitment should look like, but he is very effective indeed. City won a penalty towards the end of the first half against a much smoother United team which passed the ball with a practised understanding still lacking in Mancini's City, and Tevez grabbed the ball with the eagerness of a street urchin determined to show no bigger bully could get one over on him. This whole night was an important step in the Abu Dhabi project to be associated with a top football club, not one which crumpled in nerves or mismanagement in the moments of truth. Tevez put the ball down and sprinted up and there was no hesitation or hint of Cityitis in the way he thrashed it straight past Edwin van der Sar into the roof of United's net. It reminded me of what Joorabchian had said of Tevez's qualities: that he is a winner, that he has won every league he has ever played in.

It was after that goal that Tevez did the hand gesture to Gary Neville, which fans could remember from the old hooligan days, to accuse someone of mouthing off. Neville, on the touchline among the substitutes, replied by giving Tevez the finger, and here they were, these multi-million-pound modern superstars, demonstrating that the simplicities of football, if you are not careful, are just for kids. In the second half, Tevez scored City's winner with his head and willpower, scrappy but inevitable. This time he loosed himself from City colleagues trying to share in the celebrations, went over to the touchline, and held his hands to his ears, as if to ask Ferguson and the United directors: what were you saying about me not being worth it? That was how the game ended, 2–1 to City, and, sure enough, the post-match noise was all about Carlos Tevez.

But it was still only the first leg played, and City's was only a narrow, single-goal advantage. To me, even in this zenith of his Manchester City popularity, Carlos Tevez had seemed to be playing more to shape the personal story of Carlos Tevez than that of Manchester City, although the way he had throttled a big game was a sporting feat of wonder. In the week of the return leg, Tevez gave a radio interview to ESPN Argentina, in which he referred to Neville as a 'moron' and a 'sock-sucker' (meaning arse-licker in Mancunian), for supporting Ferguson's remarks, and said he had got his 'revenge' although he did acknowledge there was another game to be played. In the same interview, he talked about how unhappy he was living in England, where he had been for three and a half years, and that in all that time he had learned no English – 'I just can't get it into my head,' he said.

'The truth is that it's very, very hard for me to live here, so far away from my loved ones,' Tevez cried to Argentina.

In the second leg at Old Trafford, United scored twice, so putting themselves 3–2 ahead, then Tevez barged City back in the game again. Finally, though, United won with that ingrained capability, which City would have to overcome if they were to move above their rivals eventually, to score in the very final moments. Wayne Rooney headed in a cross from Ryan Giggs in injury time and the noise was now about Manchester's football story, of United's continuing superiority over City, and no longer about Carlos Tevez.

At the end of the 2008–09 season Carlos Tevez was voted City's player of the year both by the fans and his fellow players. Recognising all his qualities, City made him captain. The contrast of this era with the heyday of Tony Book, gnarled captain in City's last trophy-winning era, a bricklayer and part-time player at Bath City before he played first for Malcolm Allison at Plymouth Argyle, then joined Allison at City aged 29, barely needs pointing out. Forever called Skip as he stayed with the club, he careered down every possible job from that pinnacle of sitting on his team-mates' shoulders carrying the FA Cup around Wembley, finishing up as the kit manager when he was sacked during Francis Lee's second coming. Carlos Tevez, in twenty years' time, will not be sorting out the dirty kit in Manchester City's laundry room.

In December 2010 the first public line was drawn in the saga of Carlos Tevez wanting to leave Manchester City. Unnamed sources told the *News of the World* that Tevez could no longer face life at City. Saying he missed his daughters, who had returned to Argentina, and that his relationship with senior executives at City had broken down, there was even a suggestion that Tevez might retire from football altogether rather than be forced into continuing to play for City, who were paying him the £200,000 a week.

City responded with a written statement which was unusually forthright, and named Joorabchian explicitly. Having been the representative of whoever the offshore investors were who 'owned' Tevez's economic rights, he was now described as the player's own representative.

'The Club remains disappointed by this situation and particularly with the actions of Carlos' representative,' City's statement read. It confirmed that he had put in a written transfer request, and made it very clear that the request had been rejected. 'Carlos' current five-year contract has three-and-a-half years to run and he is the highest paid player at Manchester City Football Club. This is both an unfortunate and unwelcome distraction, and the Club will remain focused on the games ahead in what is turning out to be a very promising season.'

That stance, the refusal to pander to the desires of Tevez against the commitment of five years to which he had signed up, marked the start of a greater confidence at Sheikh Mansour's Manchester City. The stories in newspapers about Tevez's torment at the club, that he did not enjoy Mancini's training, that he wanted away from Manchester, finally snapped the new ownership's indulgence. There was a sense that for two years in the Premier League, they had been somewhat star-struck, emerging from the relatively obscure, if overpoweringly rich,

Abu Dhabi, into the global spotlight of football. Now, by saying no to Tevez, by insisting that he honour the contract he had signed for so vast a paycheque, Manchester City drew themselves together and insisted on their authority as an institution. It was clear, too, that Tevez had made the strange mistake, by putting a transfer request in, of writing himself out of huge loyalty bonuses modern footballers get themselves entitled to, just for not asking for transfers.

So there was a sense that the balance of power was shifting, and following a week of discussions, City emerged on top with a clarification statement:

'Manchester City can confirm to its fans that "clear the air" talks have been held with Carlos Tevez. During the meeting Carlos expressed his absolute commitment to the Club and formally withdrew his transfer request. Carlos' contract remains unchanged and both Carlos and the Football Club are keen to focus on the opportunities that lie ahead.'

Gradually, as some of the old Mark Hughes signings, including Adebayor and Bellamy, were loaned out to other clubs or put up for sale, and with Tevez quietened for a while, the stories of training-ground scraps and defiance of the manager in Mancini's squad became less prevalent. City's defence adhered to Mancini's emphasis, with Vincent Kompany formidable and Joe Hart – with Micah Richards, the two City youngsters surviving into the new era of multi-million-pound signings – preferred in goal to Shay Given. Their performances became more the convincing product required of almost £400m spent on players, with Yaya Touré leaner and astonishingly effective, and David Silva threading inventive skill into the muscular momentum. Manchester City were now achieving their target set for them in the Abu Dhabi business plan, headed comfortably to finish third in the Premier League, and qualify for the Champions League for the first time ever.

The FA Cup run came upon the supporters stealthily, with early-round victories over Leicester City after a replay, 5–0 against Notts County (another replay) and a 3–0 win against a limp Aston Villa team suddenly propelling City into the quarter-final against Reading, whom they beat 1–0. That put the club through to an FA Cup semi-final against Manchester United at Wembley, another history-making contest.

Manchester United are simply not defined, and do not think of their position in football, according to their relationship with City, except that they feel it is rightfully for them to be superior. United's club history, the book or the film, is the most dramatic epic in English football, Matt Busby arriving as a new manager at an Old Trafford bombed during the war, and transforming United into football's greatest name. There are the babes, their unbearably poignant final league game, an adventurous and virtuoso 5–4 victory at Arsenal, retained in posterity by a famous black and white picture of Tommy Taylor, one of the eight who died in the crash, airborne in a crowded penalty area. There is Munich, the loss, and Busby's odyssey to the European Cup in 1968, that football resurrection, even if real life is more cruel and complicated and closure could be not as simple as that. Then there was what passed for United's decline in the 1970s and 1980s, although United-supporting mates always seemed to be going to one FA Cup semi-final or final after another. That was followed by Manchester United plc claiming the Premier League era as theirs, Sir Alex, Cantona, Ryan Giggs, the kids and too much silverware to mention. City might figure once or twice in United's story, perhaps noting that United shared Maine Road after 1945 while Old Trafford was being repaired, perhaps, at a pinch, they have to acknowledge Denis Law's 1974 backheel. Otherwise it is all Best, Law and Charlton and photographs of silver cups. City, because so much time since the war has been spent beneath United, are forced, unavoidably, to measure their progress and experience against the reds. For a time after Peter Swales's 'ludicrous gamble' with City's future – which City clearly lost – when the club was penniless up to the early 1990s, the VHS official history seemed to cobble together any old derby shown on telly where City had not been beaten. Ian Brightwell scoring the equaliser in a 1–1 draw, good goal as it was – 'I just wellied it,' he'd said, memorably, in the post-match interview – actually made it into the very history of the club itself. Only when City made it for those brief 1970s years to the sunlit uplands above United could the club's history be about the greater challenges in football than derbies they could not be expected to win. So because United, even laden with the Glazers' debts and disgorging millions to service them, remained the Premier League's top club, City would have to overcome them directly, in order to achieve the success craved by the supporters all these lost years, and now demanded by the money of the owner in Abu Dhabi.

During the dominant Manchester United years the label stuck that while United were supported by day trippers and glory-hunters from the south and abroad, City were the 'real

Manchester' club. However much City fans liked to comfort themselves with this idea, growing up alongside crowing United fans meant they knew it was nonsense to suggest that more people in Manchester support City. Dr Adam Brown, a sociology academic at Manchester Metropolitan University, even did some proper research on the postcodes of the season ticket holders at the two Manchester clubs, and found that within Manchester, support was about even.

But it is true that in some ways City, before Abu Dhabi, felt like the true Manchester club, and I came to think of it like this. United is the club for the headlines of Manchester, for the landmarks, the way it likes to see itself in history, as a city where the council swaggeringly produces a list of firsts, industrial pioneers and world-changing inventions. United, I thought, became after the war the football club representing the Manchester in which things actually worked and money was made. I came to think of it as the club embodying south Manchester, Sale, Hale, the Cheshire set in places like Alderley Edge and other green belts where I have never been. There the bosses and manager classes of industrial Manchester found an agreeable country life in stately mansions, far from the stinks their enterprises were creating, and the people who make proper money in Manchester live there still, away from the city itself. United was the club representing a Manchester which knew what success felt like.

Yet even the other side of Manchester history which has made its mark, the radical, left-wing, campaigning tradition of the trades unions, suffragettes, Peterloo, seemed to find its football expression at United rather than City. At Old Trafford, socialist political activists like Andy Walsh teamed up with the renowned journalist Michael Crick and other campaigners to lead the sophisticated fight against Rupert Murdoch's planned BSkyB takeover. Then United fans implacably fought the Glazers, their defeat followed by the breakaway FC United of Manchester which Walsh led, and the mass, two-fingered defiance of the green and gold by the mass of fans who stayed at Old Trafford. At City, I had been briefly involved in an attempt to form a trust in the mid-1990s, but there were no political driving forces among the fans as there were at United, and no coherent protests ever formed about the structure of the club or football at large, only demonstrations against whichever chairman was in charge when the club was on the slide.

I came to think of City as the emblematic club for the real Manchester, not the one made in the headlines of its history, but the one lived day by day. For the city which had actually had its heyday by 1850 and was struggling to keep up ever since, which showed the rest of the world how to do industry then had to watch as other cities did it with more coherence, more planning and less cruelty. City is the Manchester club for the people who just had to get on with it, who filed in and out, clocked on and off and, as Niall Quinn put it, were rained on every day. Personally I stopped feeling, in the late 1980s, that supporting Manchester City was about wanting to win things. I enjoyed watching Paul Lake, Andy Hinchcliffe and our kids at Maine Road, and came to feel it was just about belonging, a connection with yourself and your roots, accentuating the positives, and trying to have a laugh in the face of adversity. Until City grew stronger, reached that FA Cup quarter-final against Spurs in 1993 and we all realised we really did want to be successful again, very much. City was the club where there was no grand epic, no plane crash and odyssey back to the summit, no colonising of the football prizes and commercial rewards of the Premier League and even its ideological opposition, but endurance of whatever life bloody threw at you. It was the true Manchester club in the sense that there were no songs about glory, glory, or marching on, on, on, but about standing alone, without a dream in your heart, about things being so awful you had to joke about not really even being there, about being steadfast and loyal, for its own sake – till you die. All of which provides one rounded explanation for why the takeover by Sheikh Mansour, and Abu Dhabi's money suddenly acquiring a squad of superstars, feels out of character for the club.

When City won through to play United at Wembley in the semi-final of the FA Cup in 2011, it was another necessary confrontation in the determination of Abu Dhabi to overcome United and attain success in football. City fans made the journey to their first FA Cup semi-final for exactly thirty years, since Paul Power had curled the club to Wembley against Ipswich Town in 1981, with inflatables and fancy dress and all the apparel for a football party. United fans, grown used to endless semi-finals and finals and the long trip and expense of a ticket at the new £757m Wembley, filed dutifully down with their minds on the higher challenges of the Premier and Champions Leagues. When Yaya Touré vindicated Brian Marwood's explanation of the winning qualities he brought to Manchester City by scoring the only goal, that was a historic moment, a genuine crossing of the two clubs' destinies.

So Manchester City reached the FA Cup final and went on to win their first trophy since Dennis Tueart had scored the overhead kick in 1976, when none of us would have believed such a decline was waiting to be engineered for us afterwards. The man sitting behind my friend David Michael in the new, plush Wembley, as soon as the band struck up 'Abide with Me', burst into tears. Then he cried all the way through the game, as Yaya Touré scored the goal against Stoke City which took the players up to the Royal Box to be handed the cup. The chairman of Wembley had been our own David Bernstein, overseeing the need for the stadium to host as many events as possible, charge whatever fans would pay, £90 a ticket, £10 the programme (I've still got mine from 1981; it was 80p – that is 1100 per cent inflation) and lay on endless levels of banqueting, to repay the huge borrowings taken on by the Football Association to rebuild the ground. And the Manchester City captain leading the blue team up the steps to lift the cup in ecstasy, his grinning face forever associated with the return to success of a club whose fans proved their loyalty in the Third Division, which culminated in their last trip to the old Wembley, was Carlos Tevez.

In the summer, Sheikh Mansour and Khaldoon Al Mubarak sanctioned a further £75m to be spent buying footballers to come to east Manchester. Stefan Savic, for £6m from Partizan Belgrade, was barely noticed. They acquired two more of the young players Arsène Wenger had been polishing at Arsenal, Gaël Clichy for £7m, and £24m for the midfield craft of Samir Nasri. Wenger complained loudly about the brutal force of excessive money, although the Emirates Stadium, with 60,000 seats and some of the highest prices in the world, is far from a monument to financial equality in football. The player Mancini really wanted was Sergio Aguero, Carlos Tevez's colleague in the Argentina national team, and £38m of the Abu Dhabi oil fortunes was released to pay Atletico Madrid for him.

Tevez, back home in Argentina, rather betrayed the boosterish branding of Manchester which his signing had promoted on that billboard two years earlier. Cutting through the hype about Manchester's renaissance, its supposed accession to the status of a major European cultural city which the council likes to promote, Tevez described a grey and grumbly place, and was a little unfair about the number of places to eat.

'There's nothing to do in Manchester,' he moaned. 'There's two restaurants and everything's small. It rains all the time. You can't go anywhere. There comes a moment where you say, "Where am I going to go with my family?" and you begin to feel bad.'

He made it clear, so soon after being the face of Manchester City's tectonic revival, that he still wanted to leave: 'Of course, one trains, plays, does things, and when the family or friends come one feels bad and you can't take them to the movies because they don't understand anything. I will not return to Manchester, not for a vacation, not anything.'

A bid came in from Corinthians of Brazil, for whom Tevez had played and become 'owned' by the offshore companies, before he was first brought to West Ham with Mascherano. But City, more confident now , insisted there would be no cut-price sale of the player who had cost them so much, and the deal did not happen. Mancini now had an array of world-class attacking talents much more substantial than Ferguson's at the Glazers' United: Aguero (£38m), Džeko (£27m), Balotelli (£24m) and Silva (£26m) as well as Carlos Tevez (£45m). So Tevez, having been the sole star and prime boast of the new Manchester City, for his continual wanting away and self-absorption, found himself in the blue-cushioned seats of the substitutes, reduced to ten minutes of darting cameos when Mancini deigned to bring him on.

That is how Carlos Tevez came to travel so quickly from the player you could always guarantee would give 100 per cent for your side, to embodying the shocking opposite of commitment. Called to warm up to try to save the day with City 2–0 down to Bayern Munich at the mammoth Allianz Arena in the Champions League group from which they ended up not qualifying, Tevez refused. He was seen on television waving Mancini dismissively away, and sitting chatting to Pablo Zabaleta, who looks ashen next to him. Mancini's post-match fury, and his statement that Tevez had refused to come on and would never play for the club again, was not substantiated by the disciplinary investigation which followed, according to the corporate human resources procedures which Garry Cook had introduced and ended up being hoist on himself. Tevez was fined four weeks' wages, £800,000, for failing to obey the manager's instruction to warm up. Tevez had insisted that he was already warmed up, and would have been willing to go on and play – and his representatives also let it be known that he was frustrated by being reduced, after his manful efforts, to a subsidiary role below all the others. The fine was reduced to two weeks' wages after an intervention by the PFA, which judged that was the maximum fine which could be levied for that offence.

On the evening that Tevez waved away the instruction from his manager to warm up as his team struggled in the biggest European match arguably in its entire history, Graeme Souness, shin-scarred veteran of European campaigns for Liverpool, said on television:

'The man in the street thinks a lot is wrong with modern footballers. He [Carlos Tevez] epitomises what the man in the street thinks is wrong with modern footballers.'

It takes years of the hardest work to clatter through as a professional footballer, and the journey to the very top from the grimmest slums is the toughest fight of all. Carlos Tevez was a boy from a notorious Buenos Aires slum, nicknamed Fuerte Apache, with a scar down his face and neck from a childhood accident, who is said to have first played football by kicking stones around in bare feet. He had found his way to his beloved Boca Juniors in Argentina, then he was signed by Corinthians in Brazil, where his registration ended up owned not by the club itself, but the businessmen represented by Joorabchian. They were looking for a multi-million-pound profit for themselves, tax-free, by moving Tevez to England in 2006 and three deals later, Sheikh Mansour provided £45m of Abu Dhabi's money for the final buyout. Tevez had made it from Fuerte Apache to become the highest-earning player at the richest club in the world's richest league. But then his journey back down from the summit was rapid indeed, from poster boy of the new Manchester City, to its pariah. After three clubs, three dressing rooms, hundreds of Premier League football matches and five years living in London and Manchester, the poor kid from Buenos Aires could still speak very little English. He had not even been able to understand what it said on that billboard, which was put up to announce his signing, parading his image as a welcome to Manchester itself.

CHAPTER 16

MANCHESTER THANKS YOU, SHEIKH MANSOUR

In September 2011 Sheikh Mansour's Manchester City announced their intention to build what they were calling a training 'campus', which would be the world's very best, on an 80-acre site opposite the new stadium, sitting largely derelict after the industry on it finally died. The team responsible for designing the complex which Manchester City would need to be a top European football club in the twenty-first century, as required by Abu Dhabi, had travelled the world for ideas. The club's head of infrastructure, Jon Stemp, another professional handed a dream project backed by effectively limitless money, said they had been to four continents. City's construction team and football experts, headed by Brian Marwood, had visited the surprisingly basic La Masia, Barcelona's hothouse for incubating wonderful footballers, and Arsenal, where Arsène Wenger also believed training should be stripped down and functional. They had borrowed ideas from the Miami Dolphins NFL team, who draped their training complex in trophy-winning heritage, and the New York Knicks basketball team, which was next to the head office, so that everybody stopped working to watch training every day and, Stemp said, 'have the pulse of the team' in their working habits.

The resulting plans had the football world staggered at the ambition, another confirmation of Abu Dhabi's seriousness about the Manchester City project. Rather than continue signing ready-made footballers for £38m and £45m and £27m a time, the vision was to attract the world's best young players as teenagers by offering the most lavish of opportunities. The new 'campus' is to have seventeen training pitches, a 7,000-capacity stadium for the reserve team so they can become used to playing in front of a crowd, the most refined medical and exercise regimes that money can buy. Across from tired old Philips Park and the Miles Platting swimming pool, which was threatened with closure again after the council was being forced by the government to make £170m cuts over two years, Manchester City's 'campus' will feature several pitches laid with turf identical to that of their opponents. Down to such sods of detail, the seeds of the future are being sown.

Manchester City did not say publicly how much the 'campus' would cost, but estimates put it well above £100m. The sheikh was to spend on this part of his football project almost as much as the council has to cut from schools, care for the elderly, libraries, sport and leisure, in two years, with the loss of 2,000 jobs. Major cuts were having to be made to their services for the children of Manchester. So the council was delighted with this latest investment from the gushing oil wells of Abu Dhabi, and planning permission was granted in

December 2011. Of the local people who visited the exhibition of the plans in the stadium, which portrayed the whole Premier League project as a continuation of the Christian ethos of Anna Connell, 93 per cent said it looked beneficial for the area. Sir Richard Leese, the leader of the council, glowed that the stadium and campus were: 'At the heart of the regeneration of the wider East Manchester area' and 'excellent news for the local community'.

The release of the plans followed City's announcement in the summer that they had entered into a ten-year 'partnership' with Etihad, the Abu Dhabi airline. Etihad was going to have its name on City's shirts, which would become global televised adverts for the airline, and also sponsor the stadium itself, which the council built. It was immediately renamed the Etihad

The City of Manchester Stadium, built with £127m from the National Lottery and Manchester City Council, now renamed the Etihad Stadium

Stadium. The airline will also have its name on the 'campus' across those acres of former industrial land in east Manchester. The price Etihad had agreed to pay was quoted as £400m, although suggestions from the club were that £350m over ten years would be more accurate. As Etihad is the state airline in Abu Dhabi, ultimately owned by the Al Nahyan family as all state enterprises are, the deal was widely seen as another way for Abu Dhabi to subsidise Manchester City. Uefa's financial fair play rules, requiring clubs to live within their means, of which Sheikh Mansour's City is by definition the absolute opposite, allow sponsorship money as income, so the £350m coming from Etihad helps City towards the target. Uefa's rules, however, require sponsorships to be for 'fair value', not just another means for an owner to throw lavish and inflationary sums at his club, and European football's governing body must test the Ehihad deal against this measure in 2014.

The land which is to become Manchester City's Etihad training campus is around half a mile from the stadium, in a patch of east Manchester called Openshaw West. Manchester has been very good at projecting its prestige assets, the rebuilding of its city centre with 'quality retail' and its Premier League football clubs, as evidence of an astonishing revival, and they have tried manfully to improve the city since the hangdog days of industrial decline in the 1980s. Yet the facts on the ground present a grim contrast to that sunny and aspirational picture. A 'strategic overview' published by the council about east Manchester talks up how the city has revived itself:

'Into the 21st century Manchester has [undergone] and still is undergoing a remarkable economic transformation, moving inexorably towards becoming the UK's first post industrial city, where the new economic base will be geared almost exclusively around a service and knowledge-based economy,' it says.

However it has always been difficult to ascertain how substantially the transformation has improved the lot of the general population, whose jobs disappeared, and how real the new 'service and knowledge-based' economy is. At times it is hard to know what civic leaders mean by 'knowledge-based', as if when Manchester made things, no knowledge went into the process.

In 2010 the government published its annual *English Indices of Deprivation 2010*, the official statistical detail about poverty, unemployment and other measures of misfortune, broken down into neighbourhoods, 'super-output areas', of 2,000 people. An excellent and honest analysis of these figures was produced by the office of Manchester City Council's chief executive, Sir Howard Bernstein, and it had to find, as its topmost, glum headline:

'Manchester is still ranked the fourth most deprived local authority in England.'

The only three local authority areas more deprived than Manchester were the stubbornly run-down areas of London, which constantly cope with waves of poor immigrant populations: Hackney, Newham and Tower Hamlets. Of the former industrial cities, Manchester, which has seemed to make the most strides with its eyecatching civic ventures, is more deprived overall even than Liverpool, where boarded-up homes pockmark the very approach to the city. Birmingham, Nottingham, Newcastle, Sheffield and Leeds, none of which has two top Premier League clubs broadcasting their names around the world, are all more balanced overall and less deprived than Manchester.

Partly this is because their more comfortable suburbs fall within the city's local authority ward boundaries, whereas Manchester's map is a patchwork of almost relentless poverty and post-industrial deprivation. In these neighbourhoods, particularly in the east where industry was and the stadium now is, there is no remarkable economic transformation to a service and knowledge-based economy.

'Manchester is still ranked second most deprived local authority in terms of income deprivation,' Bernstein's report notes miserably, 'third in terms of employment deprivation and fifth in terms of the extent of deprivation.'

Eddie Smith, the chief executive of New East Manchester, the regeneration company tasked with trying to dredge recovery from the terminal slump of these old industrial areas, was alongside Sheikh Mansour's representatives at the 'campus' presentation. Smith's predecessor, Tom Russell, had taken me on a tour of the area some years earlier, pointing out Sport City, the new houses and apartment blocks, the business park with Fujitsu on it, where he sighed that the jobs were not really for the locals. Russell said they had tried for years to drag the area out of its slump but before the Commonwealth Games nobody was interested. He said the games and sports facilities, the success of the event and attention on east Manchester had been a catalyst; they had then been able to attract Asda, more public money for transport and community projects, the new houses and some new jobs. But Russell had acknowledged that hosting a sporting event, and spending hundreds of millions of pounds on it, is no blueprint for regeneration; it was playing the strange funding games into which the government forces local authorities. If the council had been allowed access to similarly huge amounts of money to shape its own regeneration plans, he said, they would almost certainly not have decided the best and most cost-effective thing to do for an area like east Manchester was to build a massive football stadium and attendant concrete facilities for elite athletes.

At the unveiling of Manchester City's 'campus' plans, Smith explained that when industry died, 100,000 jobs were lost in east Manchester. Just twelve days earlier, Smith had issued a report to the council setting out the need to revise down the hoped-for regeneration targets in east Manchester. Over ten years they had tried ceaselessly to pull east Manchester up around the stadium and Sport City, yet the progress had been very much slower than hoped for, because so many jobs have perished and because creating new ones is desperately difficult. Now the recession was forcing Manchester's council to face another slowdown in the revival of the area. Smith's report states that in east Manchester, 32 per cent of the population is in receipt of at least one welfare benefit, double the national average. In Manchester as a whole the figure is 22 per cent.

Smith's analysis was that after the depths of east Manchester's collapse in the 1980s, followed by the regeneration efforts which have included public money to improve local schools, Beswick library and other services, the area 'stabilised', with 'economic and population decline reversed, and employment and people returning to the area'. Its challenge now, he said, was actually to find a new future, try to attract businesses into the area, to become 'A recognised employment and residential location, based on successful companies choosing to locate at the heart of a thriving conurbation.'

Yet since 2008, when the onset of recession caused by the banks' negligence happened to coincide with Sheikh Mansour's purchase of Manchester City, the fortunes of east Manchester declined while City itself were rising up.

'East Manchester, like other parts of the country,' a council report stated, 'is experiencing rising unemployment, a downturn in commercial development and a significant fall in new residential development. During 2009–10, this translated into an increase of some 60 per cent in the numbers of east Manchester residents claiming job seekers allowance.'

Throughout New East Manchester's document, hope is expressed that new jobs will come if the area improves, that new businesses will be created, as a result of the stadium, training 'campus' and a new Metrolink station. The revised-down target is for 5,500 new jobs to be created by 2018, and that these will be principally driven by 'sports/leisure related employment'.

You can see why the council is so thrilled to have Sheikh Mansour, and the unimagined wealth he is wielding in a desperately poor place where few businesses have chosen to invest in the nine years since the Commonwealth Games. Manchester City appears throughout the document as some business to cling to; the hope is that 'working closely with MCFC', and having a 'formal partnership' with MCFC, there will be a 'transformational plan for east Manchester, focusing initially on the 200 acres of land around the Etihad Stadium'.

So on Manchester City now, where Abu Dhabi has since 2008 spent £800m largely on transfer fees and footballers' wages – £65m on Carlos Tevez alone, if you add up his transfer fee and two years' wages – hopes to transform the very future of east Manchester, the one-time cradle of the industrial revolution, are pinned. Just three years previously, the project which was going to transform east Manchester, and be built on exactly the same site on which the Etihad Campus is now planned, was a 'supercasino', for which the Labour government had invited competing bids from local authorities. Manchester, having become so practised at winning such bids for special projects against other towns and cities, inspected the criteria, calmly put its plans and partnerships together, submitted its application and was granted the licence to open the 'regional casino', beating the long-time favourite, Blackpool. East Manchester, one of the most grimly deprived areas of Britain with more than 30 per cent of people on at least one benefit, was, as the answer to its existential challenge caused by the death of industry, going to have a 5,000-square-metre casino, with, the specification noted, 1,250 unlimited-jackpot gaming machines.

The supercasino, and eight large casinos which were also sanctioned as part of a new Gambling Act, were explicitly stated to be a regeneration project, providing jobs for local people. In fact the Casino Advisory Panel, which recommended Manchester for the supercasino, pointed out that Manchester was poorer than all the other places which had applied for it: Blackpool, Cardiff, Glasgow, Greenwich, Newcastle and Sheffield: 'Manchester has the greatest need in terms of multiple deprivation of all the proposals that were before us,' the panel's chair, Professor Stephen Crow, said.

Manchester's bid had said a huge casino would bring in other investment, create that 'leisure destination' on which the ambition for a reinvented east Manchester is based, and generate 2,700 jobs. Sir Richard Leese said at the time: 'This is fantastic news for Manchester, and the region. Manchester has an unrivalled track record in the delivery of major regeneration schemes so we are confident we have the expertise to deliver a world-class venue, creating thousands of new jobs for local people.'

The supercasino to revive the area would be built in close association with Thaksin Shinawatra's Manchester City. The government seemed utterly oblivious to the widespread astonishment that a Labour government had become sold on a massive casino in the poorest parts of the country as an answer to their economic problems. The lobbyists for the gambling industry had been repeating relentlessly the statistic that a very small proportion of gamblers are addicts, or develop a problem with it which affects their lives, and it appeared that the lobbyists had won over the government.

Only in February 2008, when Gordon Brown took over as the Prime Minister, was the 'supercasino' plan scrapped, the Labour government then saying it recognised the 'potentially negative impact' a casino could have. They said they would now try to work up proposals for regeneration which did not rely on a supercasino – and, he might have added, which did not look quite so desperate for proud formerly industrial cities. Sir Richard Leese pronounced himself disappointed at the loss of so much potential benefit and new jobs, in the supercasino, in Manchester.

When Sheikh Mansour bought Manchester City and the council entered into negotiations and a partnership with them, it was reported locally at first that Abu Dhabi was going to wholly transform east Manchester, building houses, hotels, restaurants, shops and offices, the whole historic decline reversed with a wave of the Sheikh's magic wallet. That turned out not to be the case at all. Abu Dhabi has stated its intention to be a decent neighbour where it invests, but its principal interest is in investing for its own gain, whether financial or in terms of its image. Their interest was in a training ground for Sheikh Mansour's football club, which he, the board, Brian Marwood and Mancini believed they needed.

It is an almost unbelievable investment in east Manchester, after so many years of abandonment, to clean up and transform that huge derelict site. City said that the project would create 160 jobs for its construction, and 90 when it was completed. In 'The Temple', the heart of the 'campus', up to 400 young footballers can be in training at any one time, with seven pitches dedicated to the academy. There are 40 rooms to accommodate some of the boys who will arrive from Africa or Europe, and live on-site in east Manchester while pursuing the chase to be a professional footballer and get to drive one of the Porsche Panameras in the well-guarded car park.

Having seen the fly-throughs, computer graphics and other visions of City's new training empire, I asked if I could go to the site itself. One of the project managers, Howard Metcalfe, took me, a short drive across from the stadium, round a single row of old terraced houses, which have been staring at a contaminated dump for years. Turn in to the muddy car park and you see bulldozers already busily tilling over tons of filthy earth, the stadium's bowl lurking grey in the background.

Up some metal steps into the site office, and on a wall in the corridor is a large, colour, aerial photograph of what the 80-acre site looked like just before they started to dig it up. You can make out very clearly the outlines of the buildings which have gone, still marked in adjoining rectangles of different colours. It looks like what you see of areas where there has been a fire, hurricane, tsunami or other act of complete devastation. The place is a cemetery of Manchester's industrial past. As a Mancunian, I felt a deep sadness in seeing this so starkly. Now it is to be replaced by the hope that football and 'leisure' and undefined 'knowledge', begun by the investment from a sheikh in a country which has wealth in its earth, can dig Manchester out of its hole.

The main factory which was left on the site some years earlier was known as the Clayton Road Aniline Works, part of the dyeing process. There should be no great nostalgia for it; it was a stinking enterprise. Lately the company was owned from America and, in the end, they just moved it elsewhere. Metcalfe told me that in the industrial archaeology beneath the surface, they had found fourteen shafts from a colliery which had mined a coal seam beneath. After that had come heavy industry of different kinds, mainly engineering, he said, possibly mills, too, and thousands of people must have been employed. One by one the factories closed, everybody lost their jobs here, and about five years ago, he said, it was all finally knocked down. They had even found the remains of one-up, one-down houses, and a cobbled street, buried for years beneath the surface.

There are old maps of east Manchester which show how the place was laid out, the tight rows of terraced streets built to house workers, around the factories, chemical and engineering works close by. Then the factories closed. But the houses remain, staring at nothing and what used to be. The Conservative–Liberal Democrat coalition government, contemplating the ruins of the new economy, which was to be based on knowledge and financial services, talks about 'rebalancing' it back in favour of manufacturing. But having seen it laid waste last time the Conservatives were in, with little effort to save it, or invest in improving its techniques, only brutal suppression of the protesting workers in trades unions, it is difficult to see what their plan is for exhuming it now.

So Manchester has had to search for another future, which it perceives as striving to make itself attractive so that businesses will be tempted in and create jobs. There is talk that Etihad will site their new European call centre in Manchester, employing local people. The council has bid manfully and often successfully for what grants it can get. It can be seen as some vindication of spending so many millions on the Commonwealth Games, and handing the stadium to Manchester City plc, that Sheikh Mansour then bought City, and Abu Dhabi money is falling in, like the jackpot tumbling out of a casino one-armed bandit. The council always tries to reap the best community benefits from the major projects, and it has struck a deal with Manchester City on the 'campus'. Of the 80-acre site, 5.5 acres, in the far corner, are to be cleaned – remediated, as the technical term has it – by City. That in itself could cost around £8m, I was told, given the degree of contamination left by the old works. It is possible that the council will look to introduce a school on there, maybe a sixth form college, because there is no sixth form, currently, in the whole of east Manchester. For that, the council will need to persuade national government, which has slashed the education budget, to put the money in. Opposite, on the other side of the road, there are plans for a sports centre and swimming pool, to which City say they are committed in principle to contributing £3m as part of their developer's statutory responsibility to improve a neighbourhood where they are being granted permission for a major project.

Manchester City are at least doing that, but it is not philanthropy, nor is Sheikh Mansour acting as the munificent benefactor for the whole area as the initial gleeful reports naïvely depicted him. This is business: the 'campus' will house the requirements identified by Abu Dhabi's Manchester City as necessary if it is to have a chance of making itself sustainably successful, by attracting tomorrow's brightest talents in football. Whether this financial sustainability, living within their means, is possible for a club which lost £197m in the year it announced the plan, remains to be seen. Looking at the scheme in its totality, it seems, among other things, a startling monument to inequality. So many millions spent from the inheritance of a young oil sheikh, for the training of a few elite footballers, the best of whom will be paid £10m a year. In the far corner, a small piece of land, one-sixteenth of it, could possibly become a school for the people who actually live in the area, if the government, which is cutting funding more deeply than any in history, ever puts the money in.

There had also been talk of Abu Dhabi buying the stadium, of which it is the sole occupant, but they declined to do so. Instead they negotiated a new rental agreement from the one the two Bernsteins, David and Sir Howard, had agreed back when City were in the Third Division. The deal by which City paid a proportion of their income above 32,000, the old Maine Road capacity, earned the council around £2m a year, from City's overall gate receipts, in 2009–10, of £18m. They were entering a new arrangement because, under the original deal, the council had control of the naming rights to the stadium. Manchester City wanted to do their deal with Etihad, so the council had to agree for the stadium to be named after the airline, and for that they would be paid more money. City proceeded to seal the £350m over ten years from Etihad for the stadium, shirt and 'campus', and in return the council, Sir Howard Bernstein said, were to be paid an extra £2m a year. That money, £4m a year, will be invested in maintaining the other facilities on the Sport City site. Both the club and the council said the extra £2m paid for the council releasing the naming rights is fair value; neither side felt the other was holding it to ransom. Like all the projects, including the original stadium deal with City, independent financial consultants verified that it complied with all the relevant law and represented a fair deal for the use of public money.

Sir Howard Bernstein told me at the time that he was 'delighted' with the planned 'campus' and deal the council had struck, saying that it should provide a 'platform for regeneration'.

And so it possibly might, in a city that lost most of its industry and ended up the most deprived in the country outside London's problem districts, while attracting the most prestigious projects on offer to the regions. The great football clubs were produced from the industrial muck – City, scampering out of the deprivation in Gorton 130 years ago, United formed by workers in a railway depot. Remarkably, the football clubs which were the outlet of industrial workers, their local places of belonging and letting off steam, are in danger of looking like a large part of all we have left. For 2010–13, the Premier League landed £1.4bn from television companies overseas to show the matches. So the football clubs, which began as places of recreation in areas which were sending engineered goods around the world, have become islands of exports themselves. Looked at that way, from outside the Etihad Stadium, if Sheikh Mansour bin Zayed Al Nahyan decides that he wants to sink so much money into Manchester City, we should indeed be grateful. In Manchester, all the sheikh's money spent on players' wages means City do, at least, pay a very large PAYE tax bill, so the wider public does benefit from the Abu Dhabi investment.

In the contaminated land of Openshaw West, his family's fortuitous winning of the global economy jackpot, discovering oil to last a hundred years, meets the death of Manchester's industry. Building a 'campus' on that land for elite millionaire footballers could turn east Manchester into a 'destination', as the council fervently hopes, with crowds coming to gawp at the state-of-the-art facilities and fine figures of footballers, and hotels, bars and restaurants might spring up to cater for them. And perhaps, that, as with the City of Manchester Stadium, it will be years before any more developments of real note come along, and the authorities will find they need another plan, to reinvigorate what was one of the world's workshops.

And yet it all still feels a little desperate, for a once great and still proud city to be holding up a banner giving thanks to a faraway rich man. It may be only polite to shout 'Manchester Thanks You, Sheikh Mansour', for buying £450m of footballers for Manchester City fans to sit and watch, for the FA Cup and for all the attention to detail which has revived a hollowed-out football club. And for spending money on his best-ever training ground, in the contaminated depths of Manchester, which has suffered so much and lain derelict so long. For being the only person prepared to invest £1bn in anything located in sunken east Manchester, one of the poorest places in Britain. It is just that saying thank you quite so explicitly to a rich absentee does not seem quite in character with the independence, entre-preneurship, fighting spirit and radicalism of Manchester, whose roots also lie deep in the earth, and which have always, at least partly, been expressed at its football grounds.

CHAPTER 17

THE PEOPLE'S GAME

It was by accident, really, that I found myself on bonfire night, 2010, taking my young daughter to the Lancashire hill town of Rochdale, for what turned out to be the most astonishing night in FC United of Manchester's young history. I had followed the supporter-owned club, writing for the *Guardian* about their efforts, since the hard core of Manchester United dissenters formed it as their own club in May 2005, after the Glazer family won its hostile battle to buy United against the fans' massed opposition. United plc shareholders had sold out and cashed in, and the Glazers loaded all their borrowings on to the club to repay. While most United fans on the threshold of the most successful period in the club's history opted to put up sullenly with the Florida invaders, this group decided they were not going to take it any more.

I had been at the Apollo theatre in Ancoats, the air thick with rebel ghosts of riotous old punk gigs, when the campaign leaders on the stage asked the fans massed in the stalls to come with them to a new club, which they would all own, and run for the common good, not for personal profit. A core of 2,000 signed up, became members, one-man-one-vote, and started this new club at the base of the non-league football pyramid, in the North West Counties League Division 2. Privately, I am sure they always hoped it would be more, but however strong the objections to what the Glazers were doing, United fans were not prepared en masse to turn their backs on Old Trafford. At FC United, Manchester United fans suckled on the Busby babes, who had been in Barcelona seeing Ole Gunnar Solskjaer toe-poke their club to the treble, now went to Flixton, Leek and Eccleshall United; Darwen, Blackpool Mechanicals and Castleton Gabriels, supporting a club to which they wanted to belong. They surprised themselves at how much they relished the experience, of supporting their team of triers and profes-sional academy rejects, at ramshackle Lancashire football places kept going by the efforts of committed volunteers.

The club was formed according to the principles crystallised by that first conference in London's Birkbeck College in 1999. There Andy Walsh, chairman of the Independent Manchester United Supporters Association, and Adam Brown, member of the Labour government's Football Task Force, sat next to the Barcelona group whose Elefant Blau campaign would cul-minate in Joan Laporta's election as president of one of the world's greatest football clubs. Walsh always dreamed of 'rolling back the plc' and somehow establishing United as owned by and run for the supporters. They, after all, had been standing on the Stretford End for decades while Malcolm Glazer was making his money in US trailer parks.

At United, the Glazers' leveraged buyout, using the bor-rowed money which the club, and fans, would then have to repay, meant instantly increased ticket prices. United season ticket holders soon had imposed on them the 'automatic cup scheme,' which meant season ticket holders were automatically charged for cup tickets even if they could not go to the match. Walsh, Brown and IMUSA had been at the forefront, with the shareholders group, reformed as the Manchester United Supporters Trust, in the fight against the Glazers. The club's board, including the chief executive, David Gill, made statements opposing the takeover, saying the plans would put a 'strain' on the business, until the major Irish shareholders, John Magnier and J.P. McManus, former friends of Sir Alex Ferguson, with whom they had fallen out over the racehorse Rock of Gibraltar, suddenly sold their United shares to the Glazers, at a huge personal profit. Gill has since argued that the structure of the Glazers' deal was reworked, and the borrowings lessened in severity, so he no longer had to oppose the takeover, and he stayed on to be the United chief executive for the Glazers.

Walsh faced the painful realisation that rolling back the plc was going to be done not by the fans, but by a family of American speculators, who had raised £810m, and now would turn Manchester United back into a private company, owned completely by them, via Delaware. Fans at English clubs are consumers, not members, they cannot vote for how their club is run, nor can they wield the money necessary to buy out those in charge. So Walsh, Brown, and a committed group who took all this seriously enough to do something about it, opted to start again. They were guided partly by AFC Wimbledon, formed in 2002 by fans who refused to follow the takeover and removal of their club to the new town of Milton Keynes, which had been sanctioned by an FA panel. They too had formed a club owned according to its constitution by the fans, one-member-one-vote, not-for-profit, and they too had started again at the base of the non-league football pyramid, in the Combined Counties League. In 2011 AFC Wimbledon completed a monumental phase of their supporter-owned journey back, winning the play-off final of the Blue Square Conference, on penalties at the City of Manchester Stadium, and being promoted into the Football League.

You could expect a club formed on principles, to establish community, mutuality, equality, to be worthy and solemn, yet when I first went to FC United's games, there was something in the way the fans were supporting their club which was hugely emotional. It was the raucous rebellion, the defiant humour, the fire and glee with which they had embarked on the adventure. FC United fans all signed up to the ideal, but most had also wanted a different experience, more raw and heartfelt as they remembered it from the cheaper 1970s and 1980s, to break free of the high prices, compulsory seating and corporate wrapping of a twenty-first-century afternoon at Old Trafford. Standing throughout at Gigg Lane, Bury, which they settled on as their home while harbouring ambitions for their own stadium, and away in the narrow grounds of the lower non-leagues, they let out their joy, relish and defiant anger, as if released from suffocation.

A banner at Gigg Lane proclaims 'Punk Football', the way FC United fans like to think of it: anti-authority, doing it for themselves. It is also shot through with pride in Manchester, celebrating the Manchester tradition of protest. One of their anthems is sung to the tune of the Sex Pistols' punk anthem 'Anarchy in the UK':

> *I am an FC fan,*
> *I am Mancunian,*
> *I know what I want and I know how to get it*
> *I want to destroy Glazer and Sky*
> *Cos I wanna be,*
> *At FC.*

Another is sung to the tune of Woody Guthrie's 'This Land is Your Land', the famous dustbowl protest song claiming the rights of the people in America:

> *This badge is my badge*
> *This badge is your badge*
> *Three stripes and three sails,*
> *Oh what a fine badge*
> *They tried to take it,*
> *But we replaced it*
> *On the shirts of United FC.*

And this song is one of defiance, which goes to that favoured football tune, the hymn 'Lord of the Dance':

> *Glazer, wherever you may be*
> *You bought Old Trafford but you can't buy me*
> *I sang not for sale and I meant just that*
> *Fuck off Glazer you greedy twat.*

These are not, it is fair to say, a breed of football fans who would laud Thaksin Shinawatra, or club together to put up a banner thanking a sheikh in Abu Dhabi in the name of Manchester. Even if he had put millions in, rather than taken millions out. One of the banners, a reference to Roy Keane's famous complaint that the atmosphere at Old Trafford had been sedated by people coming for 'the prawn sandwiches', proclaims simply: 'Pies Not Prawns'.

Supported by crowds of up to 3,000, unprecedented at a level where clubs might be happy with 50, FC United ripped through to promotions in their first and second seasons. Although Walsh, reinvented from Militant firebrand to the club's general manager, in impeccable club tie and jacket, said they were not paying players more than other clubs, players evidently wanted to join for the experience of performing in front of such a crowd. At a game against Formby in 2007, I talked to an FC United founder and board member, Mike Turton, an electricians' supervisor in the National Health Service. Turton had been a regular at Old Trafford for thirty-one years, and he turned away on the day the Glazers bought United.

'I didn't leave because of the takeover,' he said, as the fans sang 'Sloop John B', the anthem whose adoption he is credited with having started, in a pub karaoke while waiting for the train back from an away match. 'That was just the final push, gave me the kick up the arse I needed to finally get out.'

He said he had stopped enjoying going to Old Trafford in the 1990s, even as the trophies were serially brought home. Ticket prices were rising, and Turton said he was very conscious that the money he was paying went straight to the escalating players' wages. In describing his feelings for FC United, he paid conscious homage to Manchester's radical spirit, saying that was the Manchester with which he wanted to be associated:

'I love what we've built here, I'm really proud of it. I like to think it's in the best Manchester tradition of protest, along the lines of the suffragettes, the trades union and co-operative movements, which have their roots here.'

From the beginning, the club determined it would charge the sort of affordable prices with which fans grew up: £7 for adults, £2 for U16s and pensioners, although this was to watch football down in the non-leagues. Democracy, affordability, involvement with the community and being not-for-profit were principles written into the constitution. The club also invited its members to vote for the price of season tickets, and the members actually voted for an increase, to £160.

FC United developed extensive community work, because its members are committed to football's social role. Programmes include working with Barnardo's charity, with groups of children in care, Street League, which provides football as a constructive force for the long-term unemployed, and a well-being project, which brings older people, who have become isolated in their own homes, to matches and social events. A leader of this work with marginalised groups around Manchester is Vinny Thompson, an Old Trafford veteran who speaks with amazement himself at his conversion from a warrior of United's European campaigns to 'a lentil-eating social worker'. For the community programmes, matchdays, and all jobs around the club, FC United are helped by 300 supporters acting as volunteers, contributing to an endeavour they have built themselves, after feeling that their loyalty was exploited at Old Trafford.

In the summer of 2010 FC United launched a community shares issue, to raise money for the building of their new stadium, for which they also applied for grant funding from Manchester City Council and the Football Foundation. Subscribers can invest as much money as they want to; they must commit to it not being withdrawn for three years, and after that only in 10 per cent chunks, allowing security for the stadium to be built. After that, the club's business plan projected it would make a surplus big enough to pay interest to the community shares investors, provided that FC United's 'primary commitment to community benefit' was being met.

The share offer was designed to maintain the democracy of FC United; however much investors put in, as members of the club they would still have just the one vote on all the issues members decide. They are all adherents to the founding values of football, which they believe were sold out when the FA sanctioned the Premier League, the clubs were allowed to float on the Stock Market and became vehicles for the shareholders to make money.

When I cleared a day to go along and report on this community shares initiative, which could be a blueprint for other smaller football clubs, it was shortly after Wayne Rooney, helped by his agent Paul Stretford, had withdrawn his threatened transfer request from United, and emerged with a reported £180,000 a week salary. It was shortly before Liverpool, on whom the Americans Tom Hicks and George Gillett had perpetrated a £200m debt-loading takeover, would be dragged close to administration into the High Court, as three English directors tried desperately to sell the club to another group of US buyers.

Going to FC United, in that environment of general football gluttony, was like a cleansing of the palate. I suggested to my eleven-year-old daughter Isobel that she might like to come because I thought she might be interested in watching some football, and in the principles behind the club. I knew that in the more relaxed atmosphere of the non-leagues, I would be able to see who I needed to see at FC United with Izzy in tow, so she came to Gigg Lane with me and we stood up together in the seats in the main stand. The FC United fans all want a new stadium within Manchester, and think Bury, where they ended up, is up in the sticks, but as I went to school there, it is always a nice nostalgia trip for me. We stood with Adam Brown, who talked me through the details of the community shares scheme, and as the fans struck up their songs with 'fuck off', 'twat' and 'I can't hear a fucking thing', he eyeballed Izzy and drew on a lesson delivered to him by the adults at football when he was a kid:

'What you hear at the match, stays at the match,' he told her, with a smile, and she grinned impishly back.

When I arrived at the ground I hadn't even known it was the final qualifying round of the FA Cup. FC United had won their way through to play Barrow, who were in the Conference, two leagues higher, and the winner would make it to the first round proper, in which the clubs in the Third and Fourth

Divisions (by now called Leagues One and Two) enter the draw. The crowd was 3,263, standing up all the way through, Izzy standing on a seat and soon gleefully entering into the spirit of the songs being ceaselessly sung. There were the anti-Glazer songs and the proclamation of being not for sale – one of the banners opposite simply says: 'Against Modern Football' – then in the 76th minute, Carlos Roca, a twinkle-toed non-league Kinkladze, scored. Izzy had that overwhelming experience then, of being a child in the midst of adult joy at a goal being scored in a football crowd, and suddenly the afternoon was less about something constitutional and ideological. FC United were giant-killing, into the first round of the cup, to face Rochdale.

After the final whistle, as the FC United fans celebrated a major step for their club, we walked down and stepped on to the Gigg Lane turf to talk to Roca. Having played in the league with Oldham Athletic, Roca said it was a privilege to play in front of the FC United supporters. He said that the players understood what the club, supporter-owned and run, meant to the fans who had formed it. He told us he was back at work on Monday, at a call centre in Wilmslow, south Manchester, dealing in debt consolidation (which seems to be a growth industry in Manchester), and that the women he worked with didn't know anything about football and would not care a bean for what he had just achieved here. On the way home, Izzy suddenly mentioned that, and said she thought it was sad.

For Walsh, Brown, Thompson, Jules Spencer and the other FC United stalwarts, making it through to play Rochdale of

League One in the first round of the FA Cup was an emotional landmark. Other Old Trafford veterans found themselves wondering at it again, at the way their football sympathies had mutated, into finding it so huge a thrill to be going to Rochdale, as underdogs. Izzy, quite taken with it all, assumed we would go to the game. So I said okay, we would.

That is how we ended up amid a seething crowd of 3,000 FC United of Manchester fans letting out their pride in their achievement, and anger at the Glazers and modern football, along a whole length of Rochdale's Spotland stadium, on 5 November. It was an evening of relentless, uninterrupted singing, chanting and noise, an expression of support for more than a football club. The match had been selected by ESPN for live television coverage and friends who watched it said the commentator, Jon Champion, himself a York City fan who had given support when his own club had been threatened with extinction by its chairman, said by way of introduction:

'FC United, owned by their supporters, play Rochdale, the club where the co-operative movement was born.'

The game had the sniff of former and more earthy times; I was late, had to park miles away, and ran with Izzy round the ground to find the right turnstile. Once we struggled our way in, we could hardly move inside and it was difficult to find somewhere to stand in the unreserved seating. But eventually we did, along to the right in line with the penalty area, and Izzy stood on a seat again, a lady smaller than her sat in the row behind, just smiling. Everywhere was goodwill, celebration and defiance. There were flares and the rebel songs. To a constant drumbeat of 'I am Mancunian' and 'Sloop John B', the fans ran through their repertoire. I had tried to explain them to Izzy at the Barrow game, why they sang 'Glazer, wherever you may be / You bought Old Trafford but you can't buy me.' I told her that the people here had supported Manchester United all their lives, that it was cheap when they used to go, in the '50s, '60s, '70s and '80s, so people of all classes went and they grew up with it, not like today when none of the boys at her school go regularly to any football. Then, I told her, a family from America had been allowed to buy the actual club, Manchester United, and I tried to explain the dire details of how they loaded it with debt.

She asked me what on earth that banner opposite meant, which said 'Pies Not Prawns', and I had done my best to explain. It took quite a long time.

At Spotland, the acrid smoke of fireworks and bonfires drifted across the crackling action. I explained to Izzy that Rochdale were four leagues above FC United, they were full-time professionals; they did it for a job, they didn't have to work in a call centre with uninterested middle-aged women like Carlos did, so they would be fitter and stronger. That was true, they were, but FC United had a desire you could touch, and playing with great appetite, they went 2–0 up, the second a truly magnificent strike, lanced in off the crossbar, by their midfield player Jake Cotterill.

Rochdale were industrious, professional, and they did come back. The FC United fans were singing 'Are you watching David Gill?' and I was struggling with knowing how to start explaining that to Izzy – you needed to tell her who David Gill is, that he opposed the Glazers' takeover at first, but had stayed on to take their money and repeatedly claims the hundreds of millions taken out do not affect the club – when Rochdale scored. Then, unmarked at a corner by an exhausted FC United defence, Rochdale equalised, 2–2. That, I was explaining to Izzy, was surely the end of the romance for a team of part-time young lads playing a long way above themselves, but in the 90th minute, centre forward Mike Norton broke clear. He did seem to poke the ball out of the Rochdale goalkeeper's hands, although we could not see that from where we were because it was up the other end and there was a lot of smoke, and then, utterly improbably, he scored. FC United had come back in the final minute to win 3–2, and all around us, the FC United fans went absolutely, jumping-up-and-down-and-hugging-each-other mad.

FC United of Manchester supporters at Rochdale, first round of the FA Cup, November 5 2010

It was being there, that night, among people who love football, had supported Manchester United all their lives, which
convinced me that standing should never have been outlawed,
and brought home to me why so many supporters still cleave
to wanting that experience back. The joy of the last-minute
winner was intensified by the rebellion against everything which
these people felt football should not be about. In the middle
of those fans leaping about, I did hope David Gill was watching.
I found myself thinking of Sheikh Mansour and wishing he
could be there, standing up with everyone at Rochdale, seeing
the joy at a club like this, having its greatest moment. I thought
in those moments also of the prime movers and apologists for
the Premier League and its breakaway, those who defend the
transatlantic pillage of a great club by the leveraged buyout,
the random buying and selling of all England's great 'clubs'. I
thought of those who argue that football clubs are indeed fair
game for businessmen to buy and profit from, those who argue
that ticket prices are only a matter of supply and demand and
that nobody, at £40 a ticket, has actually been priced out – and
wished they could all be there and see if they, too, would get
just a little carried away.

Walsh and Brown reflected later that they had only ever
really thought about starting a club which would embody the
values they felt had been drained from Old Trafford; they had
never envisaged a night like this. Afterwards, the fans were
on the pitch, jumping about, not knowing what to do with
themselves. Izzy asked to go on, but I was solemn. No, I told
her, it isn't allowed, those people should not be on there; there
used to be a lot of trouble back in the old days before you

were born and the rules are there for a reason. But the fans stayed on the pitch peacefully for a long time – they ran across to the television studio low down on the far side, to wave at the telly, then they ran back again – and no stewards seemed to be moving them off. Izzy kept asking, so in the end I said: 'Go on, then, we will.'

We stepped on to the floodlit turf at Spotland, and immediately some fan came up to me, smile across his face, and gave me a bearhug. Some fans had a banner, so we walked round to see what it said, if it was another witty rebel slogan like so many others, and when we got to the other side of it, we saw it read: 'FUCK OFF CITY'.

You cannot change the club you support – that element of the football supporting rules is correct, I think. When the FC United fans start up their anti-City derby songs of yore, I am reminded that I am in the middle of the Stretford End, really, sometime in the 1970s, where I do not belong. But you can admire a club, for what they are and what they have achieved, and you can wonder at the stories which football can produce.

After the match Rochdale's coach, Steve Eyre, disbelieving that they had been defeated, mused that he had never known an atmosphere like it. He said: 'The FC United fans were singing for a cause.'

I thought the momentum they earned, the coverage they received, the word of mouth around Manchester about the anarchic glories the fans enjoyed at Spotland, could see Gigg Lane filled if FC United had a decent home draw. They were drawn away to the League One leaders Brighton, but in the game, Brighton played several reserves and were held by more miracles. FC United were leading from the 40th to the 83rd minute, then their goalkeeper, Sam Ashton, saved a penalty in injury time. I took Izzy to the replay at Gigg Lane, under floodlights in midweek, 6,700 people turned up, in the depths of that freezing winter. So new people were introduced to pies not prawns, and to the songs:

> *This badge is my badge*
> *This badge is your badge*
> *Three stripes and three sails,*
> *Oh what a fine badge*
> *They tried to take it,*
> *But we replaced it*
> *On the shirts of United FC.*

Brighton's manager, Gus Poyet, played a strong side this time against the crazy non-league team he had underestimated, and they, who would win League One and be promoted to the Championship, the division below the Premier League, produced a very professional piece of work, including kicking Mike Norton extremely hard quite early on, and they won 4–0.

As time ran out, somebody started a song to the FC United players:

> *Every single one of us,*
> *Is fucking proud of you,*
> *Is fucking proud of you,*
> *Yes every single one of us,*
> *Is fucking proud of you.*

As a dad, I have to admit I was a bit irked that they could not use the word 'very', and I spent the next week singing 'jolly proud of you' to Izzy, for a laugh. But it was still moving, this tribute from supporters, who had given up Manchester United to shape their own experience, to their bunch of willing lads.

FC United of Manchester invited me to their end-of-season dinner, because I had written about the club, which they held at Manchester's Museum of Science and Industry. Its story of Manchester, and artefacts of the industrial heyday, had been revamped, in spruced-up Castlefield, at the opposite end of Deansgate to where City had put up Carlos Tevez as their Welcome to Manchester display. Martin Buchan, United captain of the 1970s, made a fairly amusing after-dinner speech, but there was no mention of the tackle for which City fans will always remember him, on Colin Bell's knee.

There was a good crowd of paying tables, to raise money for the club, sitting within the museum, among the memorials to Manchester's industry. On the story boards around us were the innovations which made Manchester a worldwide wonder: the Bridgewater Canal, the world's first wholly artificial waterway; Richard Arkwright's steam-powered mill, opened in 1783; the first passenger railway, which operated from this spot, to Liverpool, beginning in 1830; the first mechanically powered submarine; cotton and engineering; Charles Rolls meeting Frederick Royce at the Midland Hotel in 1904; Ernest Rutherford discovering how to split the atom at Manchester University in 1919, and in 1948, the world's first computer with a stored programme and memory. After that, Manchester City Council's list of 'firsts' dribbles into hosting the first recording of *Top of the Pops*, the publicly funded projects Metrolink, G-Mex and the Commonwealth Games, and two obscure surveys, one of which apparently voted Manchester 'Britain's best city for business' in 2006.

The small core of rebels who founded FC United, in a city whose great, world-famous historic football clubs are owned by a sheikh in Abu Dhabi and some American speculators, have a long way to go to solidify their club. The new stadium project has presented many hurdles, and even at their level of non-league football, the Evo-Stik Northern Premier League, they play some clubs with local rich men pouring fortunes in. That gala night, they ate, drank and sang in their smart clothes, among the museum pieces of Manchester's greatness, cheering the fact that they had stood up for what they believed in. They celebrated enduring pride in Manchester, and their defiant vision of football, which they believe they share with the game's industrial pioneers: as a sport with collective, democratic values, forever the people's game.

CHAPTER 18

THE BEAUTIFUL GAME

On a stretch of grass, up some concrete steps behind a breeze-block school, sixteen men are running about, deep into a game of football, between a pair of broken-down plastic goals called, optimistically, Samba. The team in white is attacking, passing, running into space, attempting one-twos; the big lads in red are defending determinedly, the diving goalkeeper pulling off wonder-saves to his right. It's raining, chucking it down, and the pitch is churning into mud. Or it's a clear summer evening, the sun gone down, the sky still a perfect blue, the first star just appeared. Either way, we're always out there, every Thursday, whenever we can make it. Playing football on grass. In the winter, which lasts a long time where we live, we have to move inside to the sports hall, playing an intense hour of five, six or manic eight a side and the reds tend to win then, with two six-foot-four brothers parked in front of the D – the twin towers, I call them.

When you are tired and jaded by modern football, what you need most, if you are able to, is to play football. Out on that field, there are no leveraged buyouts, tax-avoiding speculators (at least in our game, I can't speak for London) or human rights abusers, the odd trailing leg excepted. Nobody is using it to make money, nor is any rich man seeking to control or manipulate the experience. It is not a vehicle for getting rich or a marketing show for a nation – and you would never describe it in terms as crude and lifeless as an entertainment product. It has nothing at all to do with money, and, although both sides like to win, it is not 'about' winning. There is the ball, the pitch, and the beguilingly simple yet endlessly intricate, most natural of games.

I have played on Thursday nights for years, after spending the day as a journalist researching and talking to those involved in some of the murkiest waters of football. I played the night Adam Crozier, a bright young chief executive of the Football Association, was pressured and resigned after trying to resist the Premier League's constant campaign for more control of the game. I remember playing after spending the day researching the record of Keith Haslam, owner of Mansfield Town, who had borrowed £585,000 from it over the years, in breach of company law. Once, I had just written an article in 2007 lamenting the takeover of City by Thaksin Shinawatra, accused of corruption and sanctioning state murders, when I ran up the steps in my moulded studs and out on to the field to play.

When you play the game, the essential rules and values still stand, untouched and undisputed, as they have for 149 years, while the arguments, scandals and battles have raged over efforts to make money or otherwise exploit its appeal. There is the simplicity of a ball at your feet, the freedom of running, the need, that lesson for life you learn as a child, to play as a team, the challenge of reaping a reward from the effort you put in. There is the tackling, the trying, the things which do not work, then there is how you feel when you stroke the ball successfully, when you make a pass which splits the defence for your striker moving on to it, or the odd time, which you may always remember in your own mind's eye for a great many years, even if nobody else ever will, of curling one into the far corner, beyond the reach of a diving keeper.

It was a wise old man somewhere along my journey in football who stated to me as a matter of fact: 'Of course, it is more enjoyable to play than to watch.' For years, I did not feel that way. As a boy I loved to play but struggling on the outsize pitches in the cold of Manchester did not compare with 40,000 people rising at Maine Road to acclaim a goal from a still-sparkling Manchester City. Gradually, though, it has come upon me, to the point where you cannot compare the enjoyment and fulfilment of playing the game, with the pleasure of watching other people doing it, however good they are.

As this feeling came over me, I resisted it as if it were another strange reaction, like falling out of love with supporting Manchester City. All around us is a celebration and injunction to watch other people playing sport, the hype that supporting a professional football 'club' is compulsory, Sky TV's relentless persuasion that paying £50 per month will provide endlessly exciting hours on the sofa, the newspapers, whose sections entitled Sport are wholly about following the skills of a very few, and almost never about helping people play sport themselves.

While we are living through the unprecedented boom in millions of people paying to watch football, in the stadiums and on television, in Britain and around the world, and the Premier League is seen as an untrammelled success and worldwide advertisement for England, football has limped into decline as a game to play. Up to 1997, after the Premier League clubs had feasted on the first £305m from forcing fans to buy Sky subscriptions if they wanted to watch live matches, 10,000 playing fields in England are estimated to have been sold for development. The adult eleven-a-side game, always the backbone of football in the country where the game was first defined, has declined dramatically throughout the years of spectator boom, from a high of 43,000 teams, to 30,355 registered by the Football Association in 2010–11. In December 2010 Sport England, which gave the FA £25m in grant-aid in 2007 to grow by 150,000 the 2.1m people who play football in some form, reported that in fact there had been another drop, of almost 30,000.

'The Football Association is not on track to achieve its target for growing participation,' Sport England lamented. 'This is a concern and is due largely to the loss of players between the ages of 16 and 19.'

At the same time, the Premier League was in the first year of its 2010–13 television deals, which brought in £3.5bn to the 20 clubs. That included £2.1bn for exclusive domestic live rights from the pay-TV channels Sky and ESPN, and the frustratingly brief highlights the BBC shows on *Match of the Day*. The Premier League clubs overall made £2.1bn in 2009–10, from television, fans buying tickets and eating and drinking at the matches, and sponsorships, often by beer and betting companies.

These two modern tendencies, the boom in watching football, sitting down in the new grounds or on bigger and better televisions, and the decline in numbers of people knowing the joy of playing the game, are related. We are becoming a more sedentary society. We think of ourselves as sports mad, but increasingly that means we watch other people doing it. We have a new health problem, being overweight, which has increased at a frightening rate, coinciding with the years of football's boom. In 1993, according to the Health and Safety Executive, 13 per cent of men were categorised as obese (a body mass index of 30 or more); by 2009 this figure had almost doubled to 22 per cent, nearly a quarter of British men. The proportion for women was worse: 16 per cent were obese in 1993, by 2009 that had grown to 24 per cent. At that rate of growth, the Foresight survey of 2007 predicted that by 2050, 60 per cent of adult men will be obese, 50 per cent of women, and 25 per cent of children.

'Obesity is associated with health problems which include type 2 diabetes, cardiovascular disease and cancer,' a government collation of the evidence warns. 'The resulting National Health Service costs attributable to overweight and obesity are projected to reach £9.7bn by 2050, with wider costs to society estimated to reach £49.9bn per year. These factors combine to make the prevention of obesity a major public health challenge.'

As my support for Manchester City loosened and weakened, and my opposition to the financial carve-up of professional football grew, I have found my love for playing the game deepened. I myself had been part of the drop-off in adult eleven-a-side football; in 1999, when we had Izzy, I found responsibilities as a dad meant I could not justify being out for the best part of Sunday playing for my mates' team, Dynamo Thursday, and I nobly retired, although the buggers did not give me a testimonial.

With a wife and young baby, and working hard, I found myself not playing football for the first time in my life. Playing and training had always been my fitness too, and soon, with eating and drinking rather too much to soften the nerve-jangling edges of fatherhood's indisputable wonders, I think I may have sagged into a statistic in the obesity surveys. It took me time to wrestle with new grown-up realities and work out how I could squeeze in getting fit. After a few months, I started cycling and swimming, after dropping Izzy off when she started nursery. Both were fine, and my fitness improved, but there was too much time and fuss involved in changing, hauling the bike out or getting down to the pool, before the exercise began. One day it dawned on me as an unavoidable fact that I now had so little time, and to get the most fitness out of it, I was going to have to buy a pair of trainers, go out the front door, and run.

I had not been running for its own sake since I was eighteen, fit from playing football and training every day, and then I could skip the streets of Prestwich and surprise myself with the speed of a sprint finish. As a thirtysomething dad, I had to drag my reluctant tummy out of the house and take it on a run, just a mile and a half to start with, and it still nearly shattered as well as embarrassed me. I persevered, though, because I really wanted to be in something approaching shape, and feel fitter. It took around six weeks, of asking my body to go for a run with my willpower, before I had the next revelation. I was running, and I was actually enjoying it. I don't mean only that I was finding it easier, I mean just that: I was actually enjoying it, being out in the open air, feeling myself find a rhythm to do what our bodies are naturally built for, the physical joy of running, finishing with a push, not just collapsed relief. There is happiness in it, a basic human facility and impulse which somehow, amid the modern noise of marketing sport as an entertainment product, too many of us have lost.

Over the years covering the commercialised development of modern football, I have visited and reported on many social work schemes which offer sport, and particularly football, as an attraction to people and a means of helping them to rebuild troubled lives. Neil Watson, a pioneer of football community programmes at Leyton Orient, told me the same miracle happened regularly. They had schemes for people who had been drug addicts for years, and if they stayed off the heroin, and came to football every session, they could be fit, their bodies in good condition, within six weeks. More than the basics of becoming fitter and in better shape, the physical and psychological boost provided by exercise is a proven scientific fact. Dean Cartwright, coach in Middlesbrough at Street League, a charity which lays on football sessions, with life and confidence-building skills, for long-term unemployed young people, told me:

'When the endorphins kick in after the football, the young people start to feel better about themselves, and they want to do more, and that's when we can start to make some progress with them.'

Anti-depressants, for which 43.4m prescriptions were issued in 2010–11, an increase of 94 per cent in ten years according to the NHS, include some of the same chemicals as are generated naturally in the body after doing vigorous exercise. You do have to work hard, and sometimes think you can't face it, but, I have found, it is always worth it. Even when it's pouring down.

Before we moved to Yorkshire, I had found another weekly game of five-a-side, on a Tuesday night in Ardwick near Manchester Apollo, with some friends on Astroturf pitches run by Powerleague, a company making good money from the modern footballer's desire for clean and half-decent facilities. After we moved, it was too far to travel. I was running when I could, but I felt an almost physical craving to play football. When I was a teenager playing regularly for my Sunday club, the older guys, who were market traders or reps mostly, and who lived for football, used to say that they 'had the horn for it'. You'd see them in the summer, ask how they were doing, and they'd grimace: 'I've got the mad horn for a game.'

There I was thirty years later with, as they also used to say, 'the raving horn' for a game, but in the small town where we live, it took me months to find one. Eventually I realised I was being an idiot and should just ask in the sports centre. They told me that there was a game on a Thursday night, it was a group of guys including a couple of the local butchers. I knew one of them because my younger daughter, Emily, was in the same nursery class with his daughter; she had pointed him out once in the shop. So at the next opportunity I went to the butcher's, and there he was, hacking into the leg of a poor dead lamb which had never done him a moment's harm.

I asked him, over the counter: Do you guys play football?

He lifted an eyebrow, cleaver in hand: 'Yeh, why? Do you want a game?'

I said: Yes, I do, I'm absolutely bloody dying for a game.

And without hesitating, although he's lived here all his life and all the lads have been friends since school and playing together for years, he said: 'Thursday night, 7:30, on the field behind the school. Get yourself down there.'

That was six years ago, and I've been down every week I have been able to since. Everybody works, and we have all reached the sad stage in life where playing football, like you did when you were a kid, is a true highlight of the week. When I first ran out on that turf, I hadn't played on grass for years; I'd had to find my boots and fish them out of a box after two house moves. Then I had that incomparable feel again, for passing the ball on a surface of wet grass, stroking the ball wide, sidefooted, trapping it on your chest, directing a header, running as fast as you can for twenty or thirty yards and coming away with the ball, having a decent crack at goal.

I felt in that process I had rediscovered the benefits of sport for myself, and have become something of an evangelist for people to do more sport, not just watch it. I began to seriously object to the awful food for sale at football grounds, the rows of club-sanctioned burger vans ringing the City of Manchester Stadium for fans to eat, before an afternoon of sitting down watching other people run around.

I worried that this was strange, going so against the flow, in which all the marketing is for all us blokes to support a football club, and be spectators, and when the Premier League is followed as soap opera in 200 countries. Then, in January 2010, the *Guardian* published in its feature 'From the Archives' an article from the same day, 1923. It is written in praise of walking in the countryside, rambling, as they called it then, which was gaining modestly in popularity as a weekend recreation for people desperate to get out of the cities. It included the opinion that: 'To live submissively in great towns . . . is a deprivation, almost a creeping disease.'

It was an exhortation to people to get out more, walk and breathe fresh air, and it began like this:

'Anybody who is depressed by the thought of some fifty thousand able-bodied men, in every great English city, looking on at a few others playing football every Saturday afternoon . . .'

This is not a debate which is had any more, now sport as an entertainment product vanquishes sport as a life-enhancing physical activity, but in its early days, there was a great deal of agonising about it. The conflict the Football Association had over whether to sanction professionalism was the tip of much deeper unease among the gentleman amateurs for a game they founded, and for which they defined the rules, to play. They were horrified at football turning into an industry, to which working-class people in their thousands would turn up and pay to watch, the mass of amateur clubs coalescing so quickly after the 1888 formation of the Football League into a handful of great names powering football as a spectator industry, not participation sport. Television, of course, has hugely accelerated that process in recent times, coupled with the other modern tendencies towards more sedentary lives. 'Obesity develops from an accumulation of excess body fat, which occurs when energy intake from food and drink consumption is greater than energy expenditure through the body's metabolism and physical activity,' the government tells us, rather obviously. 'However the causes of obesity are more complex than this, and relate to a wide variety of societal and behavioural factors.'

When you look into it, there are several major reasons, not difficult to identify but which take determined effort to address: we drive too much in cars, we do not walk or cycle enough;

food is plentiful and too much is high-fat and processed; we have built into modern life too few opportunities to do exercise; the drive to commercialise leisure activities means that kids play the Fifa football game on a computer rather than play the Fifa football game in the park. Poor facilities are identified and recognised by the FA as a turn-off for people who might think of playing, or who give it up after experiencing the realities of Sunday mornings.

In 2005 a review of England's low levels of people participating in sport found that the country invested 37 per cent less in sporting infrastructure than the average of developed western countries. The Olympic Games, on which £9.3bn was spent for two weeks in 2012 with the stated aim of inspiring young people to do more sport, resulted in less money being invested in sports facilities. In the run-up to the games, overall participation in regular physical activity recorded by Sport England was falling. There is, in England, a dramatic drop-off by young people when they leave school, the late teenagers identified by Sport England as having given up football. In schools, sport is provided as part of the curriculum, however patchily and however much the investment has always been cut by the Conservatives whenever they are in the government. It is when young people leave school, though, and are presented with the poor and run-down facilities and difficulties of playing sport in adult life, that they tend to drop out and give it up.

In 1999 the Premier League agreed to put 5 per cent of its income to improving grass-roots facilities and programmes, in return for government support against a challenge by the competition authorities to the twenty clubs selling their TV rights collectively. The clubs won, and proceeded to make billions in television money, selling the live rights to Sky every season for twenty years, never allowing a single live match on terrestrial television. The Football Foundation was set up to administer the new millions which the Premier League would distribute to the grass roots for the first time ever, matched by the FA and government. The foundation carried out a survey of football facilities in England, the first ever, to assess the task ahead of them; it found that the vast majority nationwide were in an appalling and neglected state. Their consultants came up with an estimated figure, £2bn, which would be required to bring these playing fields and broken-down or absent changing rooms to a new generation of a decent standard. That was substantially revised more recently, once the foundation became more familiar with the degrading realities at the grass roots, to £7bn.

Since 2000 the Football Foundation says it has spent in total £313m on pitches and facilities, which it admits has been an improvement, but wholly inadequate, less than a twentieth of what it says itself is required. My friend Ric Demby, with whom I watched City as a boy and played in the Dynamo Thursday midfield years later, now coaches his thirteen-year old son, Cal, in a team at Chorlton Park, where we used to play. Still two miles from Old Trafford, where United have spent tens of millions of pounds in the intervening years, increasing the capacity to 76,000, and the Glazers have drained out £480m in bank charges, fees and interest, there are still no changing rooms. The place is as forlorn as it was fifteen years ago, in the world-famous football city where Sheikh Mansour is spending £140m on a new training ground for Manchester City's superstar players, and City's millionaires are preparing to overcome United's.

The other social factors which the experts say determine low participation in sport are poverty, inequality and poor education, of which Britain has large portions. In 2008 I visited Helsinki to see how Finland manages to encourage the highest proportion of people in Europe, 55 per cent, to do regular exercise, against England's sad figure of 21 per cent. Looked at the other way round, that makes 79 per cent of England's population, almost four-fifths, not doing regular exercise. The answer, I found, was not magic. Helsinki did not have gleaming sports facilities and many of its sports halls and swimming pools were also old. But those involved in the revolution in the nation's health since its fat, slobby and heart-disease-riddled 1970s, told me it had been hard work, gradually persuading people to change their habits and exercise more. Everywhere in Helsinki people were walking, cycling and exercising, unashamedly taking part in public aerobic sessions in a park, nordic walking in the winter.

Mika Pyykkö, executive director of Finland's Centre of Health Promotion, said that a reasonably prosperous and equal society was likely to exercise more, and watching professional sport in the stadium or on television did not encourage people to do so.

'We are a more equal society,' he had told me. 'We have rich and poor but not so extreme as you. We have a high level of education, and, generally, educated people exercise more. We still have a challenge but historically the Finns have always been close to nature and so the culture of walking, or "moving", is still there.'

That was, indeed, the British government's official finding, that people can actually be put off trying sport themselves by spectator sport, by the images of human perfection performing in the Olympics. Sport England, commissioning research into why people do not exercise, came to that surprising finding too, that watching great athletes perform impossible feats can be intimidating and people can be deterred from thinking they too can play, to their own levels. When Tony Blair was Labour Prime Minister, his strategy unit produced a research document, 'Game Plan', to help develop a vision for seeing more British people taking part in sport. They reviewed all the evidence and concluded:

'It would seem that hosting events is not an effective, value for money method of achieving a sustained increase in mass participation.'

Then Sebastian Coe and his team went to the International Olympic Committee in Singapore in 2005, promising that the games in London would inspire young people to do sport, the precise opposite of what the Prime Minister's research had found. Blair himself, despite his own strategy paper, vowed to the IOC that a London Olympics would 'see millions more young people in Britain and across the world participating in sport and improving their lives'.

The need to build an 80,000-seat stadium and massive arenas for minority sports like handball, for the two-week event in the summer of 2012, sucked hundreds of millions of pounds away from funding facilities and initiatives for ordinary people to play sport themselves.

Arriving at Manchester City, and all the other stadiums, to

find the burger vans lined up and some seriously unhealthy-looking middle-aged fans in extra-large replica shirts, who look like they have not broken into a jog for years, has become part of the landscape of football's boom. Its flipside are the rotting public pitches and decline in people exercising. And it is seen as a great credit to England that we are exporting around the world our multi-million-pound Premier League, for more people in more countries to watch on television.

In Germany and Holland, particularly, the professional football clubs have always been at the centre of true community sports complexes, running dozens of amateur teams themselves across many sports, with the senior football team in the stadium at its apex. If English football was organised like this, the clubs owned by the member-supporters and devoted, truly, to being leaders in sports participation in an area, my club would be one to which I would still be proud to belong. But I do not want to live submissively, giving thanks for some superstars, bought by Sheikh Mansour's millions, who would otherwise never have come to Manchester City except, possibly, for an away leg of the Europa League. Even as City are restored by the power of Abu Dhabi oil money to the success we all believed we craved, I have found myself reaching the point the wise old man at the FA stated to me as a matter of fact when my education into football began. It is more enjoyable to play than to watch.

CHAPTER 19

THE COLOSSUS

The Premier League's twentieth season, 2011–12, turned out to be extraordinary, voted the best ever, in a series of anniversary celebrations organised by the league's marketing people. Fans were invited to vote for their greatest team since 1992, the best goal – that was Wayne Rooney's awesome overhead kick to win the derby at Old Trafford 2–1 in February 2011 – the most stylish goal celebration – Eric Cantona's famous Jesus stance after a floated chip against Sunderland – the best TV moment, and sundry other enthusiasms. At no point did the Premier League state what we were in fact commemorating, and why dating the top flight from 1992 was a landmark after the 104 years of the First Division which went before. The official history of the Premier League, which congratulates itself on rising crowds, from grounds 69.6 per cent full to 92.9 per cent full in 2010–11, begins with 1992–93 and states baldly:

'The competition is formed as the Premier League, 22 teams compete in the first season.'

They never held a vote for which English club owner had made the most money, after voting to break away from the Football League.

With just the final game to go of 2011–12, and Manchester City and Manchester United still tangled in deciding which club would win it, a Premier League-appointed panel pronounced that this had been its most compelling and exciting of the twenty seasons. City had started with aplomb, swatting opponents away, winning 4–0 and 5–1 as of old, not losing a match, except in the Uefa Champions League, until they lost 2–1 at Chelsea on 12 December. The highlight not only of that mesmeric early season but arguably of City's whole history came on 23 October, when Roberto Mancini's team went to Old Trafford and beat Sir Alex Ferguson's United, an absolutely we're-not-really-here 6–1.

'That,' a senior figure at City told me subsequently, 'was the day the world changed.'

It looked like it had, at that point. The final quarter of 2012 was the period in which the money drained out of United by the Glazers' takeover in interest, fees and bankers' charges reached an unconscionable £500m. Sir Alex Ferguson had not signed an established international for years, and while Brian Marwood was presenting fifty-page dossiers on major talents to a willing board at City, Ferguson was grumbling about the price of players, like my grandma used to do when dumbfounded by her rates bill. In 2009 United had been paid a barely comprehensible £80m by Real Madrid for Cristiano Ronaldo, and I always felt it was emblematic of frugal, reduced ambition that they signed to replace him, for £16m, Antonio Valencia, a good Premier League performer, granted, from Wigan Athletic. In the summer of 2010, when Mansour, Al Mubarak and Marwood were furnishing Mancini with the silk of David

Silva, Yaya Touré, Mario Balotelli, James Milner and Aleksandar Kolarov, Ferguson signed for United the promising young potential of Mexican striker Javier Hernandez, centre half Chris Smalling and – still baffling now – spent £7.4m on a Portuguese lad, Bébé, whose only competitive football had been a single season in his country's third division.

So, after Jonny Evans was sent off with City winning 1–0, when Silva wove through United's fraying heart and he and Edin Džeko scored three in the last two minutes, it did seem then that football power in Manchester had swung, from the club which had £500m taken out, to the one whose owner was putting in £1bn.

Yet the season was not determined in anything like so absolute a way. United, still patchy, nevertheless drew on their backstory of success and kept winning. City shivered at Sunderland on New Year's Day and lost 1–0, then with the Touré brothers away playing for Ivory Coast in the Africa Cup of Nations in Equatorial Guinea, on 31 January lost 1–0 at Everton.

United, who had been knocked out of the Champions League in the group stage, Swiss club Basel qualifying instead, brought back Paul Scholes into centre midfield, in January. He said, having retired: 'I just love playing football and I have really missed it.' Ferguson, lacking players of authority for United, was glad to have Scholes return, aged 37, dragging space around with him and arrowing gorgeously accurate passes. City remained top of the Premier League, though, from 15 October until Sunday 11 March. Then, with the captain and immense defender Vincent Kompany suspended for four matches after being sent off in the 3–2 FA Cup defeat by United, Scholes' first game back, City went to promoted Swansea City with a hole in central defence and lost 1–0.

Swansea was a club I wrote about. In the league of billionaire overseas owners, they were owned by the same five shareholders who had rescued the club from a tawdry, terminal-looking crisis in 2002. A 20 per cent stake was owned by the supporters' trust, and they had an elected supporter-director on the club board – Huw Cooze. I had written about their crisis eleven years earlier, when the Swans were bust and broken, stuck in their dingy, decrepit ground, Vetch Field, and the club had been sold for £1 to a man called Tony Petty, who lived in Australia.

The fans and local businesses had galvanised a salvage campaign, eventually wrenching the club from Petty for £20,000, then putting Swansea into a company voluntary arrangement to structure the settlement of the debts they inherited. From there, they had rebuilt their club, from fourth division penury to the Premier League's 2011–12 good news story, with time, effort and commitment.

Plus they had a new stadium built by the local council – it had been important to the authority that the supporters' trust owned a substantial stake, because with £35m public money spent, the council wanted to be confident the owners were there to serve the club, not themselves. Nobody had yet sold up and cashed in. Cooze said there was mutual respect, and he was always completely involved in all decisions at the club. That included the crucial selection of managers, which had been enlightened. Roberto Martinez, appointed in 2007 with Swansea in the third division (League One), had first shaped their pleasing, passing method, and won promotion to the second division (the

Championship). Then, from 2009, Brendan Rodgers turned out more Spanish in philosophy than the Spaniard, and lifted the Swans to surprise everybody in the Premier League.

Cooze insisted that football could be shaped, and was better off, without foreign owners taking over and trying to buy their clubs success as quickly as possible:

'At this club, the supporters are integral and that strengthens its soul and character,' he'd said. 'We see the big clubs owned by Roman Abramovich or Sheikh Mansour, and we don't want that ever to happen; that isn't what our football club is about. We feel we can be successful, go a bit further, ourselves, with hard work.'

Rodgers would cite the 1–0 defeat of Sheikh Mansour's Manchester City acquisitions, the goal scored by £850,000 signing Luke Moore four minutes after coming on as a 79th-minute substitute, as his greatest achievement. City, having been top of the Premier League for nearly five months, taking in the 6–1 over United and sundry other thumpings, slipped to second after that defeat, and into the decisive closing chapters of the season.

United had won every single league game since Scholes returned, although they were wiped out of the Europa League by a spirited Athletic Bilbao, a Spanish club owned by its members, whose policy is to recruit only players of the Basque region or tradition. On the day City lost to Swansea, United went top by beating beat West Bromwich Albion 2–0, both goals scored by Wayne Rooney in front of 75,598 people at Old Trafford.

'We will hold our nerve,' Ferguson promised.

Carlos Tevez, the £45m Welcome to Manchester poster boy, had seriously disrupted City's season, effectively going on strike after he was fined two weeks' wages, £400,000, for the Munich disobedience. He was photographed lounging on the beach in Argentina while his team mates were faltering in a damp English winter. Joorabchian, still his adviser, tried to strike deals in the January transfer window, to see Tevez leave City. Principally this boiled down to AC Milan, whose president, Adriano Galliani, was aiming to take Tevez off City's hands without it costing his club, owned by the recently resigned Italian prime minister Silvio Berlusconi, too much.

On 25 January City broke a long silence over Tevez's absence, and informed the world they had taken firm action. They had treated his absconding as gross misconduct, fined him six weeks' pay, £1.2m, and stopped paying his wages. City made it known that for asking to leave City previously, Tevez had forfeited loyalty bonuses of £6m. He was down £9.3m, and counting.

Khaldoon Al Mubarak then went public in the Abu Dhabi English language newspaper, *The National*, to suggest that AC Milan had not been 'professional' in their negotiations. He warned that unless Milan made a serious offer, City would not sell.

'If they want to be a consideration in this transfer window,' Al Mubarak said, 'they would do better to stop congratulating one another and begin to look at how they would meet our terms. Unless we receive an offer we deem appropriate, the terms of [Tevez's] contract will be enforced.'

They did not, so Tevez went nowhere. His options were narrowed to returning to City, or not playing football at all. Negotiations continued, with Joorabchian and Tevez himself, the affair swallowing up hours of City's senior executives' time every day, including the acting chief executive, John MacBeath.

City did not permanently replace Cook all season; their preferred candidate, former FC Barcelona vice-president Ferran
Soriano, having decided against leaving Spanair, the Catalan
airline of which he was chief executive.

Roberto Mancini, too, needed to be persuaded he would
accept back the player he had announced would never play for
Manchester City again. Eventually they reached a truce, and
Tevez did fly back from the beach to the grey English city he
said he could not stand. He very nearly violated the ceasefire,
saying in an interview with Argentinian TV channel Fox Sports
that in the Bayern Munich spat, Mancini told him to warm up
in a bad-tempered tone, because the manager was having a
heated argument with the substituted Edin Džeko. Mancini,
Tevez complained, had treated him 'like a dog'.

But they cajoled all over again and finally, on Valentine's Day,
had their tentative reunion at Carrington, with Tevez met by
medical staff whose most obvious pressing job was to weigh
him. After a month on the exercise bikes, he was picked by
Mancini, selected as substitute for the first league match after
City lost to Swansea, at home to Chelsea on 21 March.

The evening Carlos Tevez, still with extra padding, returned
to play for his £200,000 a week, was the day Britain's budget
was announced. Its centrepiece, which did not go down well
with a general public suffering recession, higher food and fuel
prices and biting public spending cuts, was to reduce the top
rate of tax for the richest earners, from 50p to 45p. The Conservative chancellor, George Osborne, a millionaire himself,
said in effect the very rich had found ways to avoid paying the
50p rate, so it had not been worth keeping anyway. On 1 March

the chairman of the Professional Footballers Association, Clarke Carlisle, who was playing for Northampton Town at the bottom of the Football League, had acknowledged on the BBC that many of his members earned enough to pay the 50p rate, and argued it should be reduced.

Knowing Tevez's single-minded fixation on winning, despite everything, allied to his determination to write himself into a central role in every story, I thought it was now scripted for him to deliver City the Premier League, probably with the ultimate revenge against United, in that derby timetabled for 30 April. Against Chelsea, City were losing 1–0 until as late as the 78th minute, with the supporters suffering that queasy expectation of let-down, when Sergio Agüero scored a penalty. Then with five minutes left, Tevez played a tidy pass into the stride of Samir Nasri, who dinked the ball over Chelsea's goalkeeper Petr Cech and City won the game.

Yet Tevez's comeback did not quite spark the neat tale of ultimate redemption the comic strips I read as a boy would have picture-boarded. They were held 1–1 away at Stoke City, then Martin O'Neill brought his Sunderland revival to Manchester and his team were 3–1 up until the 85th minute when City scored two to grab a draw. The deepest pit of Manchester City's season was dug on 8 April, at Arsenal's Emirates Stadium, the 60,361-seat temple to football, top whack ticket prices and corporate dining, built in 2004 so Arsenal could make enough money to compete with United on the field.

Arsenal had projected themselves as a kind of model for old-fashioned dignity, a board of custodians amid the speculators, outraged that Sheikh Mansour's vulgar cash had lured away

Nasri and Gaël Clichy, after Arsenal's conductor, Cesc Fabregas, had returned to Barcelona. That halo had been tarnished somewhat, for me, when Arsenal's long-standing shareholders cashed in. David Dein, who bought his first 16 per cent Arsenal stake in 1983 for £292,000, famously described by the chairman, Peter Hill-Wood, as 'dead money', sold his shares for £75m to the Russian-Uzbek billionaire, Alisher Usmanov.

With Danny Fiszman, another major shareholder, suffering terminal illness, just before he died the decision was taken for him and others to sell to the US Walmart investor, Stan Kroenke. In that final bout of selling in April 2011, Hill-Wood banked £4.7m, Lady Nina Bracewell-Smith, third-generation inherited shareholder, £116m, and Fiszman £117m, which went to his estate, when he died soon afterwards. At the same time, Arsenal had sighed, financial pressures in the Premier League meant ticket prices for fans had to go up another 6.5 per cent.

Arsenal had rallied well after the manager Arsène Wenger's shell-shock at losing three of his graduates, and City, on their wobble, lost at the Emirates Stadium 1–0 to a glorious 87th-minute winner by Mikel Arteta. The slump into haplessness, though, was created by Mario Balotelli, always a liability since Mancini had requested his £24m acquisition by City in the summer of 2010.

Balotelli had drawn oceans of notoriety for erratic behaviour since he had arrived at just twenty on a multi-millionaire's pay packet to the global village of the Premier League and a house in Alderley Edge in a country whose language he did not speak. Most Manchester City fans took to his idiosyncrasies, coupled with a talent you could see not quite being wholly fulfilled. In January he had parked his Bentley in Rusholme and popped into Xaverian College, to have a wee. Balotelli's complexity, I always felt, was too little understood in the bubble of football, obsessed as it is by performance on the pitch. He had a difficult, disrupted life, his Ghanaian immigrant parents gave him up for fostering when he was three; Mario felt they abandoned him and wanted little to do with them.

At the Emirates he lost his focus, should have been sent off for a horrible tackle on the Arsenal midfielder Alex Song, then was booked, and finally sent off on 90 minutes with City losing 1–0. Balotelli's behaviour had reminded me of something and a day or so later it dawned on me: it was how some of the more temperamental boys used to behave when we first started playing football, barking frustration at every mistake, kicking the air or a post, before they learned to channel their efforts and not argue with referees. The television cameras fixed on Al Mubarak in the cushioned directors' seats, watching Manchester City's season imploding, looking glum, furious and let down.

United won yet again, 2–0 against QPR, so City, who had led for so long and by five points until so recently, sank to eight points behind. Mancini, looking more gaunt than when he first swished into City, afterwards insisted flintily that City could still win the Premier League. But few, including City fans, believed United would blow a lead like that with only six games left. During the week, we journalists were all asked to speculate again about whether Al Mubarak would sack Mancini in the summer, and for all the money spent, hire a Jose Mourinho to actually acquire a trophy.

The attitude I discovered among senior people at City towards

Mancini was enlightening. I was assured they would not react to the Emirates embarrassment by sacking him summarily, but expected him to improve, 'evolve', as they liked to term it, as they did of all senior employees running any of the businesses they own. Al Mubarak and Mancini had an excellent working relationship, talking almost daily, unlike Mark Hughes who admitted when he started at QPR that he had 'made mistakes' in his 'communication' while at City.

The men in charge were not under the illusion that Mancini was perfect or the greatest manager in football, but they did assess him to have great qualities. Al Mubarak and the City hierarchy believed from the beginning that with Mancini they had a top-rank football man, an obsessive winner. They observed that in the crucible of rapid, intensely unfolding action on the pitch, Mancini's tactical decisions, his substitutions, were invariably spot on. Mancini's identification of players was considered excellent – although not immaculate. Balotelli, who had played for him at Internazionale, had been particularly favoured, as had Stefan Savic, a 21-year-old Montenegrin centre half who had caught a dose of Cityitis when he had to replace the suspended Kompany, including in that D-day Swansea defeat.

Mancini's principal area of weakness is surprising to the media, who find him charming, and to the fans who took to singing his name whenever sacking talk came round again. He was not a people person with the players; he could be cold, haughty and steely-fixated on winning. He was abrasive, could lose his temper, as Tevez had pointed out, although the insight was lost because Tevez had drained his credibility for saying very much about anything.

The more personable chatters, David Platt and Brian Kidd, had been embraced as coaches who would compensate and handle more reassuringly the players who needed it. But in the fallout with Tevez, Balotelli's strops, and the sharp way Mancini talked about some of the younger players, most notably Adam Johnson, the cracks in this design gaped at times.

Most obvious to Mancini's bosses, though, was that in his zeal to win the Premier League, their manager was loading the pressure on his players, which was hampering their confidence. Al Mubarak, who looked speechless at the Emirates, in fact revealed later he had been to see Mancini afterwards and they had one of their talks. When I interviewed the chairman the day after City extraordinarily did win the Premier League, City fans outside the Lowry Hotel streaming to the Albert Square victory parade, the chairman recalled that meeting:

'Roberto said there was a huge mountain to climb, but he still had a feeling we might win it. Part of me wanted to say: no, it's over. But I agreed, it was still possible. The pressure had got to the team, so we discussed ways in which he could take the pressure off the players.'

The title challenge enabled by Sheikh Mansour's purchase of Manchester City, his £900m cash-injection and the further £140m to be spent on the training 'campus', was turning into fascinating soap opera. As a writer, I found it compelling. As a supporter, emotionally, I felt no closer to it. I was not spending my days desperately hoping the club of my youth would claw United back. Instead, I was waking up in the morning questioning how I had come to feel so detached.

Constantly wrestling with it, I had come to realise that there are some practical reasons which created a distance between the football club which so blessed my childhood, and my grown-up self. Becoming a journalist separates you to some extent from the marriage of being a fan. As a writer, you have to have some critical distance to assess, write fairly, report what is going on. Being in a stadium press box is a privilege, ushering in live access to the greatest of sporting events that fans must economise in other areas to afford. But you do actually have to work in there. Even at the club you support you are sealed in a bubble whose atmosphere, by necessity, is essentially that of an office. Football, that altogether more splendid world, becomes work, not the great escape from it. And because you get to think and write about football all week, even if I was mostly investigating its new profiteers, takeovers and commercial rapaciousness, you get that hit which you would otherwise still need more elementally if working in a job away from football.

As my friends grew older and began to take their kids to the match, I also realised that if my wife and I had had boys rather than our lovely girls, they could have become addicted like I did, and demanded to be taken, not, like my girls, needing to be bribed into going.

Inescapably, though, I knew that my detachment went further than that, and had begun with Francis Lee's takeover in 1994, and the discovery that 'we' were a company, which anybody could buy. It had led me to investigate the long, great and tangled history of English football, the battles over its soul and purpose, and what I considered to be the sell-out of the Premier League era. It was a bloody, fundamental awakening for me to understand my club was not a club at all. I had never managed to make my peace with that realisation, place it in some compartment of my mind, and keep my heart with City. I wrote and campaigned passionately against the financial exploitation of football clubs – of the loyalty of supporters – for magnates, here and overseas, to profit from, overcharging people for tickets that had been cheap for 100 years before. I had become convinced by what I considered to be the very simple principle that if a club is called a club, it should be a club. I believe football clubs should embody the emotional belonging of supporters, and be beacons of sport's best collective values, in a mean and greedy world. I never found how to set that aside and still support Manchester City with the innocent belief – in part the ignorance – I'd had before.

But it was equally true that in all these years I have never been happy with that detachment, and missed the roaring involvement of supporting my club which had been so nourishing, even in the years of inflatable doom. I would see friends who knew the truth about the game but were still there every week wrapped up in their clubs. I'd agonise, worry about whether actually my heart had just turned cold, that I was taking the values and money stuff too seriously, that I'd over-analysed it all into unnecessary misery.

I do not truly believe that, though, because I trust that what I discovered was all true, important and in fact more fans should also wake up to it. You have to stick by your beliefs. So I had to conclude that from roaring in St Francis's Second Coming at the age of twenty-nine, to believing football clubs should be communal, supporter-owned institutions, dedicated to encouraging involvement in sport, for all sections of society, had been a good part of my growing up. Perhaps it was not so un-natural for me to feel very differently about my football club as an adult than I did as a boy living the sky-blue dream. There are not many things you did in carefree childhood which you consider the same as a thinking adult. I concluded it was valid, if not very usual, to challenge the overwhelming orthodoxy that we English blokes must pledge unquestioning loyalty to a football club, from infancy, when as grown-ups there is now so much to question about it.

But I have never actually been very happy with that, alien-ated from the feeling of belonging to the club which meant so much to me. I still tangle with it all inside, constantly. And at some point I realised that, in all these years, I have never had any such agonies about drifting away from my actual religion. In thirty-odd years, I honestly never once woke up with a start, sweating about not going to the synagogue, attending football matches on the holy sabbath, or sampling the sweet and sour pork at a Chinese buffet. In my wrestling with the Manchester City faith, though, I have never found peace. The football reli-gion, I'd venture, is stronger than real religion. I'm not sure life is sweeter without it.

As for Sheikh Mansour bin Zayed Al Nahyan and his far-fetched purchase of Manchester City, that, obviously, is the very extreme opposite of how I wanted my club to be incarnated. If City were owned by 45,000 diehard supporters, I have always felt I'd be a proud and active member. A takeover by a sheikh, who inherited money too huge for a sane world, then poured it into City but came to only one match, was a hard thing for me to be thankful for.

Yet in actually talking to Al Mubarak and his lieutenants since the takeover, and, more importantly, seeing how they operated, the thought-through thoroughness and sound sense of how they went about things, I had found the strangest of contradictions. They were really very good at it. They were world-class business people at Manchester City. They seemed to be the first owners in my lifetime who really understood what they had, how precious it was to own a football club, and what responsibilities came with it.

Those who characterised it as the ultimate wrong were, I felt, misinformed. Perhaps they did not realise that Sheikh Mansour had not bought a friendly neighbourhood community institution; he had bought a company up for sale, from Thaksin Shinawatra. His tenure was the greatest outrage for me, yet Thaksin had been welcomed by the Premier League, which allowed him to take over the club, and by the FA, who had had nothing whatever to say. Thaksin had made £90m personal profit when he sold, in large part due to the stadium built for Manchester City plc with public money from the poor and benighted local council now making painful cuts. Not one voice was raised in protest at that. Before Thaksin, John Wardle and David Makin would surely have made fortunes from their investment in Manchester City if they could, and the attempted flotation of my football club had started with the icon who should have been our deliverance, Franny Lee.

Of the broader arguments, that it was 'not football' to have a sheikh pour money in to buy a team to win the league, rather than building a team on its own resources, I do agree. It also puts further out of reach the necessary dream for clubs once similar to City: Everton and Sheffield Wednesday, for example, who could never happen on a manager who might assemble the players to rise to the top again. Now, you needed a billion pounds to raise a club from ninth to first. I had less sympathy with the Arsenal complaint, though, that City, luring away Nasri and Clichy, were inflating wages and making Arsenal's 'self-sustaining model' more difficult to maintain. From a club whose model was based on some of the world's highest ticket prices, and directors who made multi-millions for themselves while solemnly declaring they must not ever put a penny in, criticism was hollow.

It is against football's traditions for an owner to throw money in, to buy a team and subsidise massive wages. Those who argue it was always this way are simply wrong: Jack Walker, the tax exile, was the first to do it, at Blackburn in 1995. Before that, 'owners' were always criticised as skinflints. At smaller clubs the directors did put money in of course; it subsidised losses and wages, but to keep up, not blast the other clubs out of sight. At the bigger clubs, United, Liverpool, Arsenal, Tottenham, City, Aston Villa, owners might have put money in to subsidise a loss or bail out a crisis once, at the beginning, then they sat in the wood-panelled boardrooms for years, never putting in another penny. The clubs rose and fell on their own resources; the bigger clubs made it to the top because they made more money from bigger crowds and their rudimentary commercial operations, if they appointed the right manager and signed or trained good players. What Uefa were seeking, the principle behind the cheesily named 'financial fair play', is true to the tradition and concept of football we grew up with, for clubs not to rely on owners putting fortunes in.

Yet since understanding the change in culture which bypassing the FA rules to float the clubs represented, I always had much more of a problem with those seeking to make money out of clubs than those few, like Walker, who put money in. And from first seeking to understand what the Abu Dhabi project was about, even if it was all Premier League and Champions League and they knew nothing of windy nights in Chesterfield, I had found myself very impressed. The simple fact that the first thing they did, supervised by Simon Pearce, was employ consultants to examine every area of the football club's operations and assess the improvements needed, seemed startlingly sensible, compared to the blunderings of previous regimes.

Then, when they had their plans and targets, they did set about rejuvenating every area of the club's operations. Of course buying the players and paying their unholy wages was the most aggressive element of what they did, and it is inflating wages across Europe, and of course it is to satisfy the desire of a young sheikh to own a football club he could watch lift trophies. But they showed an appreciation, too, of the fabric of the club they bought, recognising it had only lasted because it had been supported out of loyalty through decades of disappointment. They celebrated the history, back to its foundation by the vicar's daughter in West Gorton, who wanted to encourage a better life. They tried to humanise the stadium and communicate with supporters as if they actually cared. After years of dire talk that football clubs were 'just businesses', they understood that actually they are more precious than that. I got the sense that, beyond the unshakeable confidence imbued by money, they were, in many ways, genuinely thrilled to own a Premier League football club, and that it had turned out to have as much depth, character and complexity as Manchester City.

The men from Abu Dhabi, another world, another culture, treated Manchester City's homespun former players with more respect than had been the case in some dispiriting times under previous owners. They understood their value to the supporters, the customers, the brand; this was intelligent business sense which in itself often represents the best practice. But I also sensed they did genuinely respect men like Bell and Book who forty-four years earlier had performed the greatest sporting feats.

I still would not have put up a banner to express the thanks of Manchester to Sheikh Mansour. It is difficult to accept that in a world where so many people live in poverty, around Abu Dhabi's region and next door to the Etihad Stadium, one sheikh should have personal billions and spend one of them on footballers' wages to win shiny cups. Yet aside from all the money, in the expertise Al Mubarak and his men had applied, their intelligence, their attention to detail and honouring of the heritage and loyalty of fans, they were undoubtedly the best owners Manchester City had had in my lifetime.

Which, given the history, was not, in truth, that difficult.

At the first home match after that hideous defeat at Arsenal, when City played West Bromwich Albion on a drizzly Wednesday night, 11 April 2012, I had a kind of epiphany. City had stumbled to eight points behind United, who faced an easier six games left, including against strugglers Wigan Athletic, that same night. There was even the Typical City possibility that United could wrap up the Premier League before the 30 April derby, and City's players would be forced to stand in their own home and applaud United's players on to the pitch as champions. The dream had died, again.

But inside the ground as the rain tipped down, 46,000 City supporters were not shattered or angry or feeling cheated. A strong sense of anti-climax hovered in the stadium, but there was support, not indignation, for Mancini and the team. Five minutes in they launched the song which has spanned the journey from third division ignominy to these pinch-yourself heights:

> *We are not, we're not really here,*
> *We are not, we're not really here*
> *Just like the fans, of the invisible man,*
> *We're not really here.*

They were in the pristine bowl of their new stadium, given a lick and entitled Etihad by the slick new owners and they sang old songs, including this one:

> *We are City / Super City*
> *We are City / From Maine Road.*

The supporters in the crowd, on the evening they believed that winning the Premier League to be gone for yet another year, were paying homage to their club itself.

I felt a very strong reminder that City supporters were there for the loyalty, not the winning. If supporting their club was about winning, they would have drifted away and not outlasted the Franny Lee–Alan Ball partnership. These people stayed steadfast when their club fell to the third division, watched City play Lincoln City, Mansfield Town and Wycombe Wanderers. They held fast to it as a temple of belonging, a constant in their lives. They never really asked for all that much in return, just for the football not to be humiliating and to be allowed to yearn for better. They had willingly stood on the gloomy old Kippax – most people in the gleaming new stadium still miss Maine Road. In the face of yet another disappointment, they were restating their loyalty again. They had, just in my time, outlasted hundreds of players, a sad litany of seventeen managers, owners had come and departed and no doubt Sheikh Mansour will be gone at some point, in some future event impossible to envisage now. Whatever happened, they would still be really here.

With Balotelli suspended following his tantrums at Arsenal, Mancini had made best practical use of the resources available, and picked Carlos Tevez to start for the first time. There was restrained applause when his name was announced, and they sang a song to gently rib him about his weight – 'He eats what he wants' – as the game started.

Manchester City played beautifully that evening, restored to the sumptuous football of the season's early months. Kompany and Lescott, in the centre of defence, were in unruffled control. Nigel de Jong was terrifying, as normal. David Silva was back to weaving about in small spaces between bigger men, the football almost carried on his left foot. Sergio Agüero, one of those players whose thunder thighs give him a speed part human, part motor vehicle, was unplayable and scored after just six minutes.

Still there was subdued resignation to what might have been, when five minutes after half-time the news came through that Wigan, improbably, had scored against United. Then Agüero bulldozed in, scored again, the mood changed and City fans decided that actually, this time, they really did want to win it this season. On 61 minutes, Tevez scored. He ran behind the goal, and a section of the crowd sang their Mancini song, to affirm their allegiance in the dispute, but the players chased Tevez down, clasping him to them. Welcome (back) to Manchester.

Silva scored a lovely chip with that blessed left foot just three minutes later, 4–0. West Brom, who barely penetrated City's half all match, were managed by Roy Hodgson, who not four weeks later would be appointed manager of England. Then everybody waited until it was all confirmed: Wigan, managed by Roberto Martinez, had held on to win the game with a goal from Shaun Maloney that we later saw on television had been a thing of curling, far-post excellence.

The Premier League was suddenly that night a possibility again; if City could beat United in the derby, the difference would be two points. City had a better goal difference, partly, as Ferguson had lamented, because at Old Trafford after Evans was sent off, his team had poured forward at 3–1 and Džeko and Silva had scored the three late goals to make it 6–1. So if City managed to win all their remaining games including the derby, United had only to draw one, drop those two points, and City would be champions.

In the press room after that game, when Mancini came in, that was when he insisted for the first time: 'No, the title is United's. They have easier games and a fantastic spirit, better than us.'

Grey slightly of face as well as hair by now, the knot in his blue and white scarf almost scruffy, compared to the flourish with which he wore it when he first strode in, Mancini stuck resolutely to that line. Some journalists were close to banging their heads on the desks: if Mancini had insisted on the Sunday after the Arsenal defeat, with City eight points behind, that they could still win it, how could he possibly argue now City had just closed the gap by three points, that the title was gone? It was so transparently a tactic, to play 'mind games' on Ferguson, we all assumed, pile the pressure on United, but whichever way anybody asked him, Mancini dug in: the title was United's.

On the Sunday before the derby, United were until the 83rd minute winning 4–2 against Everton at Old Trafford, and United fans were running through their practised repertoire of victory songs. Then Nikica Jelavić, a Croatian whom Everton signed from financially collapsing Rangers in January, scored his second expertly crafted goal. Just two minutes later Everton's Steven Pienaar, unmarked in United's penalty area, prodded the ball in and that goal, after 85 minutes, to draw 4–4 in the fourth from last game of the season, meant City would win the Premier League if they won their final three games including the derby.

The previous week, City went to Norwich, who had played

exceptionally well since their promotion to the Premier League, and won 6–1. Tevez scored three, greeted gleefully by his team mates again. Now knowing that they had the chance to reduce the gap between the two clubs to three points, City went to depressed Wolverhampton Wanderers, who were heading down, and beat them 2–0. With Tevez, all diligent effort, playing like a schoolboy who had promised his parents he would behave at school this term, it occurred to me that the damage to Manchester City's season was like an Agatha Christie whodunnit. We all thought the villain was Carlos, in Munich, but in fact it had been the lovable Mario all along.

As Manchester City approached this most elevated derby, unexpectedly, remarkably, closing in on the Premier League, I surprised myself by becoming quite emotional. It was not that I suddenly found myself a fan again. I could not claim to be mad for it like the 45,000 who had never felt a separation. It was to do with the momentousness of it, with the club which had been so integral to my life hoving so hugely into national life and a reshaping of its destiny. There were constant remembrances of 1968, and so it connected me to my childhood, to thoughts of growing up, Manchester and all it had meant, and the football club which played so great a part in what formed me. Whatever happens, whatever the ups and downs in a family, there are few more ideal moments to recall than a dad taking an eager ten-year-old son, hand in hand, half skipping to the floodlights of a football match.

On the day of the derby, I found myself in the car on the way over, welling up. As I approached the turn-off for Middleton on the M60, I drew level with a small silver Nissan Micra, three

City fans inside, a woman and young girl in the front with sky-blue hats on. I instinctively lifted a fist to them, and gave it the thumbs up. They waved back, and I nearly burst out crying.

It was golden dusk sunshine that evening in east Manchester, and the whole inside of the stadium was a canvas of sky-blue, interrupted by the segregated ranks of United supporters. Mancini had boiled his selection down to his very best team. Tevez was in. There was no room for Micah Richards, the only player who had come through City's academy – and even he had come at fourteen from Oldham, who had not been happy with City taking him. Joe Hart was signed from Shrewsbury Town aged twenty, so was not a City youngster. It is the one promise made in that 22 September 2008 letter in the name of Sheikh Mansour to 'fellow Manchester City fans' which they have not kept so far – to balance the multi-million acquisitions of ready made stars from other clubs with academy graduates. Now they are building their 'campus' to attract the best youth from around the world whom they might burnish into players worthy of places. Those graduates who had been there when Sheikh Mansour arrived were nearly all gone now, to other clubs, where few had truly flourished.

While the media had been dwelling on the parallels with the importance of the 1968 derby, which City had won 3–1 at Old Trafford on their way to winning the championship, I was struck by the differences. Jamie Jackson had written an article about the game in the *Guardian*, citing that the crowd of 63,004 had paid five shillings, 25p, on average, to watch the match. City had risen from the Second Division in 1966 not because owners had put huge money in to buy top players, but because they had shrewdly appointed Mercer and Allison, and supported them to spend modestly on prospects from humbler clubs. City's team was full of young Mancunians who had cost nothing. Even in the greatest match of my childhood, the 1975 derby in which Colin Bell had suffered his knee damage, five of City's players, plus Tommy Booth the substitute, came from Manchester or near by and were described nicely in the programme as 'local discovery'.

The Abu Dhabi-owned Manchester City in April 2012 fielded no local discoveries in this derby and just three British players: Hart, Joleon Lescott and Gareth Barry. United had more, a majority, which was laudable of Ferguson, but, although he snorted at the accusation later, it looked to everybody that he was intimidated by the power he now faced at City, and had come to play for the draw United needed. Wayne Rooney, who the season before had accused United of 'lacking ambition', then was persuaded to stay for a salary said to be more than £200,000 a week, was left up front on his own, with Vincent Kompany determined to dominate him.

The City fans rumbled into a loud rendition of 'Blue Moon' – still, three wins from a modern football triumph, without a dream in their heart, without a love of their own. As they play their precise football across the floodlit green, I always like watching the advertising hoardings around the Etihad. Apart from Barclays, the unlovable bank Mansour propped up, which is the Premier League's sponsor and gets its name all over it, all the adverts are paid to City from Abu Dhabi companies, for the marketing of Abu Dhabi. There is Etisalat, a telecommunications operator in the Middle East, Africa and Asia. The Abu Dhabi grand prix, which Al Mubarak and Pearce brought to the racetrack built on Yass Island, coming up in November. There is Aabar, an oil and gas investment company backed by Al Mubarak's Mubadala fund, rolling round next, in the stadium in Beswick. And there is the one which simply advertises the country itself: Abu Dhabi, Travellers Welcome. A top Premier League football club, Manchester City now the most extreme form, has a dual personality. There are the fans in the ground, still mostly local, the club a fundamental part of who they are and their family life, City till they die, forking out, as long as they can afford it, to follow whichever team is put in front of them. Then there is what is seen on television around the world: iconic star footballers, promoting a global brand, in City's case the image of one of the richest countries on the planet.

When the 'mind games' between the two clubs had begun, City's Patrick Vieira, who had stayed on after retirement as an ambassador, had said United were a bit 'desperate' to bring back Scholes to anchor the midfield. Ferguson had retorted that bringing back Tevez, whom Mancini had said would never play for the club again, was rather more desperate. Yet as Scholes joined battle with Yaya Touré in the biggest football match of all, it did look genuinely quite desperate for Manchester United to be relying so heavily on a great little footballer, at the age of thirty-seven. In one tangle with Touré, Scholes had looked a foot smaller, and suddenly tired, against a player I described as a 'colossus' in an article the following day about United's depletion under the Glazers. I had thought it was my clever observation, but then as Touré, 6ft 3ins, 14 stone, began to dominate these defining matches, I saw that everybody was labelling him as a 'colossus'. It was not my brilliant observation, just the only way to describe him.

Just before half-time, City scored. They had done what they were at times habitually guilty of: having a great deal of the ball, but doing too little with it, passing it square across, forward, back again, not creating chances, pressed on the edge of United's penalty area but reluctant to shoot because they did not think they would score and that would count as giving the ball away. But United had just defended, with Rooney lost up front, and City deserved to go ahead. David Silva floated over to take a corner from the right, looped the ball in left footed, and Kompany lost Chris Smalling, the youngster Ferguson had signed that summer when City bought Yaya Touré, and Kompany thumped the header in.

After 78 minutes, Scholes was brought off, panting, looking defeated, his brilliant return from retirement finally undone by colossal competition. Antonio Valencia came on, and this is where you see how his talent compares to the very great; he could make no difference.

On the touchline, Ferguson, red-faced and chewing, was prowling the line, and so was Mancini, overseeing it all. They got into an argument, Mancini wasn't having it and waved him away. Ferguson lost his temper and started to abuse Mancini. I was with the people who read it as Sir Alex Ferguson, now seventy, manager of Manchester United since 6 November 1986, seeing the empire he built overcome by the long-term inferiors who were finally spending money he had persuaded himself he did not need. He seemed, on that touchline, to be raging against the dying of the light.

When the final whistle went, and City had won 1–0, men hugged their sons and mates grabbed each other. You could see in the reactions the release of people who had been with City down in the dumps and, in the Premier League era, been blinded by United. In front of me a youngish man put his scarf over his head and looked up at the sky for a long time, unable to believe it.

Mancini came into the press conference afterwards and said United were still favourites because they had two easy games, Swansea at home and Sunderland away, while City had to take on Newcastle, excelling this season, away, and QPR, fighting to stay up, at home. It was still transparent, but talking like this had, without question, taken the pressure off the players, as he and Al Mubarak had discussed in the aftershock at Arsenal.

The Newcastle match on Sunday 6 May in front of 52,389 people, 3,176 of them Manchester City supporters, was a wonderful game of football. I was again struck by the differences between the images of 1968, that famous picture of Franny, taking the acclaim, young boys reaching up to touch the hem of his shirt. This time, few City fans I saw were young lads, given the prices, and their seats were high up in the gods.

Newcastle had been turned round. The club's owner, Mike Ashley, bought the club in 2007 and made a stinking, lumpen mess of it, leading to relegation in 2009. Then he and the managing director he appointed, Derek Llambias, took it in hand, made clear-eyed and ruthless decisions. They sold centre forward Andy Carroll to the new American owners of Liverpool for an outrageous £35m, and spent the money on shrewdly scouted overseas performers. The one major move which still

grated on the Newcastle supporters was the branding of St James'
Park into the Sports Direct Arena, after the pile-it-high retail
company where Ashley made his £1bn fortune. Llambias had
said it was to prepare the crowd for a genuine naming rights
deal, but when you sat in there you realised why it jars with
the fans. The branding, huge on the stands and on hoardings,
is in your face. It occurred to me though, that there was something sadly appropriate in it, in football itself and one of its
most evocative names, becoming just a vehicle for one of the
companies which flogs its replica gear.

On the pitch it was a great contest, between Mancini's
unchanged team – no Micah Richards again – and those clever
talents playing for Newcastle, Hatem Ben Arfa, Davide Santon,
Papiss Cissé, an authoritative Cheik Tioté and Yohan Cabaye.
Newcastle threatened, City held firm, then they did that act
again of monopolising possession, but creating almost no pen-
etrative chances to score. Then with 62 minutes gone, Mancini
strode forward, arm aloft, called Samir Nasri from the right
wing to come off, and sent on Nigel de Jong to be a bully in
midfield. He had broken Ben Arfa's leg in a tackle the previous
season, so was not warmly welcomed back.

It looked defensive, but in fact it was so the colossus could
go forward. Just eight minutes later, Touré played a one-two
with Sergio Agüero, and moving to his right on the edge of
the Newcastle area curled a shot around, inside the far post,
to be cushioned by the net. City had scored, and the fans high
up there went wild. Touré scored again in the 89th minute, a
classy lifting of the ball over the goalkeeper, Tim Krul, and
Manchester City had come through the hardest challenge of

their final matches and won authoritatively, 2–0. Afterwards Mancini's substitution was recognised as a master's move: done at just the right time, exemplifying his employers's assessment of his tactical cool. They, and Brian Marwood, were proved right about Yaya Touré, too. So Manchester City were heading towards a very big story indeed, at home to Mark Hughes's Queens Park Rangers the following Sunday, which if they won, would mean they would win the twentieth Premier League.

The European Champions League final was to be played the Saturday after that, between Bayern Munich and Chelsea, and I was asked to write for the *Observer* about the different visions of football embodied by the two clubs. Chelsea was owned by Roman Abramovich, the oligarch, who had funded Chelsea with £800m of Russian oil money he acquired in rigged auctions by attaching himself close to the then president, Boris Yeltsin.

Bayern Munich, by complete contrast, were 82 per cent owned by their members, of which there were 130,000. The German Bundesliga clubs had repeatedly voted to keep their rule that they must be majority owned – 50 per cent + 1 at least – by their members. Bayern, one of the great clubs, could never be bought. In their new Allianz Arena, which holds 70,000 people, 13,500 places were available for fans to stand, for €15, €12.50 to members. The cheapest Chelsea ticket for a top match was £56. The German game had also suffered a decline in the 1980s, when its crowds were down to an average of 17,000, but they had not based their revival on throwing out the tradition of being the people's game.

In 1993, contemplating hooliganism, whose prevention was

the real reason all-seat stadiums had been recommended by the Taylor Report after Hillsborough in England and made compulsory, the German football authorities decided to keep standing areas. The German football association issued a statement which our Football Supporters Federation has always cherished.

'Football, being a people's sport,' it stated, 'should not banish the socially disadvantaged from its stadia, and it should not place its social function in doubt.'

Understanding the German vision more fully unveiled a fundamental truth. We had always been told there was no alternative, that the success of English football now, the increased crowds and great action, was due to twenty years of the Premier League and all that went with it: the breakaway by the top clubs, the selling out to overseas buyers. Yet Germany had had its own remarkable revival, average crowds were now up to 45,000 per match, the world's highest average, but they had done so with continuity. They had reaped the benefits of pay-TV, but retained supporter-owned clubs, standing areas, tickets which young people could afford. Ownership of a football club which stood for a town or city and community of fans, by a sheikh or oligarch from far away, was anathema to them. If a sheikh wanted to be involved in Bayern Munich, he could buy membership for €60, have an equal vote with 130,000 members, and buy a ticket to stand behind the goal for a tenner.

CHAPTER 20

WE'RE NOT REALLY HERE

On Sunday 13 May 2012, when Manchester City sensationally won the Premier League forty-four years after Bell, Lee,
Summerbee and Book lifted City's last league championship in
1968, the sun came out, after a week of rain, and shone in a blue
sky. This most engrossing of Premier League seasons was to be
decided on its final day, when City's expensively constructed squad
had only to beat scratchy, struggling Queens Park Rangers, managed by Mark Hughes, to overcome United, on goal difference.

In the week, old friends I had grown into football with, first
turning out at Drinkwater Park as shivering ten-year olds, had
invited me to play in a tournament for over-forties – veterans,
as we never thought we would call ourselves. They organised
a training session in north Manchester on the Tuesday, and
when I got there, three were in new, old-style cotton City shirts,
Etihad across their chests. Contemplating the QPR match, they
said they were nervous. But really, that was for form, not to
tempt fate. They weren't nervous like the old days, when City
would face a relegation decider and everybody was truly terrified, hoping for deliverance but expecting Cityitis.

Joe Royle, the manager who wryly coined that word to describe the yips his players suffered when confronted up close with the scale of the club they played for, was on Radio 5 on the Sunday morning. He said, confidently, that City would certainly win the game and beat United to the league. He recalled another match, from his time, when City had to beat QPR and, he said diplomatically, had been 'badly affected by nerves' City fans could instantly recall the detail Royle spared us: at Maine Road on 25 April 1998 with City fighting to avoid dropping into the Third Division, Jamie Pollock, playing centre midfield for City, opened the scoring with a careful, looping, painstaking header – over our goalkeeper. It was an own goal of crafted self-destruction. City went down then, of course, at Stoke, and Royle dragged them up again, but now, Royle said, with the world-class, big match-winning players bought by Sheikh Mansour for an investment now up above £900m, 'This is a different Manchester City.'

For some reason I started heading over as if the matches were all kicking off at one, not three, and when I stopped at a garage halfway, near Burnley, I realised I'd have hours to spare. It was too late to go back, so I decided to make a pilgrimage to the site of Maine Road, where I had never quite managed to go back since City moved out to east Manchester in 2003. I came off the motorway at Whitefield, and drove straight down Bury New Road, through Prestwich where I'd lived for a while with my mum and brothers, then into Salford 7 where we all grew up. I passed the end of the road we'd lived on, where sometimes I'd wait for my friends the Dembys, whose dad, Carl, took the three boys to City, to pick me up and squeeze me in. I welled up then, for the boy I was who would have loved to see City winning the league.

Down into town then Rusholme, I turned right alongside

Platt Fields and City's academy, then turned right again into Yew Tree Road. As you go along there, past the rows of red-brick Moss Side terraces and long back alleys, you cannot quite believe Maine Road is not going to loom above the houses just past the row of shuttered shops, like it always did. Then there is a space and you see the ground right there, gone. I had only been dimly aware of what had happened to it – turned into housing, they said, and that was true, up to a point. A new primary school had been built, Divine Mercy RC, near to the site of the old Platt Lane stand, and very nice and modern it looked. A lady in the developer's office – 'The Maine Place' – explained that the planned new housing estate was about half built. There were some nice new houses and apartments, named after former City players – the Doyle, three bedrooms; the Rosler, four bed-rooms; the Corrigan, Coleman, White and Goater. But fully nine years since City moved out, half of the planned houses have not been built because of the recession and housing market slump. Behind the site office, where the pitch was, and the Kippax, it is a very big and wide wasteland.

That has always been my question about the idea that spending £400m or so on the Commonwealth Games, including £127m on the new stadium, and moving City into it was going to spark regeneration there. I understand it has, in investment terms, struck the jackpot with Sheikh Mansour, and some of the £1bn he is putting into Manchester City has found its way into the post-industrial muck and earth of Manchester. But I have always been unconvinced by the claim it could spark the 'reinvention' of Manchester, possibly begin to replace all the jobs lost when we allowed the industry to die. Germany had never done that.

Just as it had not had a year zero in its attitude to football's development, Germany had modernised its industries, not destroyed them, and now it was Europe's powerhouse again, based on quality manufacturing, serviced by banks, while we were on our over-borrowed knees, begging to be bought.

A woman came out of one of the houses to tell the lady how much she was enjoying living there. Her name was Zahra Alijah, thirty-eight; she said she had moved from Solihull for a job in Manchester, and she loved the area, which was so diverse. There were Arabs in hookah bars on Claremont Road, then a group of Somali shops, then Caribbean, she smiled. There was a bit of a separation between the buyers of the new houses who tended to be professionals, and the people in the terraces around what had been Maine Road since 1923, but never any trouble, Alijah said. Her house was a Lee, she smiled – named after Franny; four bedrooms, the biggest.

I told her I had grown up a City fan and had decided today, when they could possibly win the league at the new stadium, I'd pop down here to see where Maine Road used to be. My dad had brought me here first when I was a boy, I told her, and my voice began wavering.

She said she had moved up to be the operations director for an agency which funded mature working people to retrain as teachers, so ensuring schools had people with experience of life.

'Unfortunately the funding has been cut and we are being closed down,' she said. 'There will be nothing to replace it.'

Her job was ending on 31 August; she was applying for work. 'I've been looking round,' she said, 'but education has been hit so hard.'

The lady in the Maine Place said the commemoration of the football ground was going to be something called the centre circle, on the site which had been the Maine Road centre circle, including the kick-off spot itself. She pointed out where it was, so I walked round there to make the pilgrimage. I wasn't sure when I got there if that was where she had meant. You can sort of see its outline, but it is mostly in the wasteland, stones and a big puddle in the middle, with a half brick in it. The houses on Kippax Street look out on that now, on what was.

I drove from there to the Etihad Stadium, where vast crowds of City fans were gathering in the sunshine. It was a day of all days when people had got there early, and I bumped into friends more than I had at any game for a long time. City's organised entertainment, its bars and a raised stage, was in full swing to a mostly passive audience, but it was more raucous down at Mary D's pub, where people were queuing right up the street to get in for a pint, and opposite at the Manchester, where some lads were singing 'We're gonna win the league'.

On my way in, I recognised a bloke I used to sit next to in the Main Stand in the early 1990s, Peter Reid time, then under Alan Ball when, on a final day like today, Niall Quinn had run up the touchline to tell Steve Lomas not to waste time, before the word Cityitis was even invented. This guy and his dad, with people groaning and shouting around us, always had a quip on the unfolding disaster, insisting you had to laugh. I said hello and after a few seconds he recognised me. I told him it was doing funny things to me, all this, I was finding myself getting very emotional.

'It's all the memories,' I told him.

'I know,' he said, straight away. 'I was born in 1968, the year we won it, I'm forty-four. My dad has got terminal cancer, and all this year he's been saying: "You were born when we last won it. And this year we're going to win it again, and I'm going to die."'

All those years we sat a few seats away and I never knew his name, so he told me: Trevor Jones, and his dad, Alan: 'I'm still here though!' Alan grinned.

'I just know I'm going to be crying my eyes out at the end of today,' Trevor said.

Along from him a small group of younger fans was singing one of the old songs, from when City fans needed to find solace in self-mockery from all the disappointments: 'We never win at home and we never win away / We lost last week and we'll lose today / We don't give a fuck cos we're all pissed up / MCFC, OK.'

Mancini had picked the same team again, which had won so imperiously at Newcastle. It surely could not be Typical City this time, not with Yaya and Sergio and even, whisper it, Carlos in the team. When they kicked off in that bowl of expectation, Mark Hughes seemed to have set QPR to defend with all eleven men just about on the edge of their own penalty area and they did not get the ball into City's half for seven minutes. There was an episode on 24 minutes, when Shaun Wright-Phillips, City's brightest young hope for some years straddling Maine Road and the move here, scampered up the left wing, and Yaya Touré kind of stretched out his left leg, relieved Wright-Phillips of the ball, and started an attack. And that was it in a moment, the meeting of the old City with the new Abu Dhabi model.

It was only a question of waiting until City scored, surely, although they lapsed into that directionless comfort, going backwards, passing square and back, across the front of QPR's penalty area without penetrating. Playing too slowly, not really attacking, despite all the possession. And QPR, to be fair, were defending very determinedly, Clint Hill, in particular, who attached himself to Agüero. Finally Pablo Zabaleta, preferred at right-back to Micah Richards for these decisive games, scored. He took a pass from Yaya Touré, struck a decent shot from inside the area and Paddy Kenny, a classic and effective scruff in goal I'd first seen playing years ago for Bury, reached it but could not deflect it far enough away from looping inside the far post.

Then all around the Etihad Stadium, even the sedate sides where the pricier seats were, everybody did the Poznan celebration, turning backs to the action, smiling broad smiles, and singing:

City, City, the best team in the land and all the world.
City, City, the best team in the land and all the world.

You could tell from that they had all come to celebrate and were not really as nervous as they had been making out. Even after Yaya Touré went hobbling off, to a standing ovation, nobody really thought he would be missed too much, not against this lot. Still, some of the older hands at half-time said they really wanted another goal. And just after half-time, Joleon Lescott, who really had been flawless every time you saw him, always on his toes, got underneath a looping ball from Wright-Phillips, skimmed his header backwards, and suddenly Djibril Cissé was through for QPR's first chance and it was just him against Joe Hart and he did not flinch from smacking the ball very hard inside the near post to score QPR an equaliser.

It took a little moment for the significance of that to sink in. City really had won nothing yet. It was 1–1. United were already winning 1–0 at Sunderland; the two clubs had started level on points with City ahead on just the goal difference Ferguson had sighed about – the goals City had scored against United. If the results stayed like this, City would lose the title at the very last, to United.

After 55 minutes, Joey Barton was sent off, for an act of sneaky thuggery first on Tevez, then on Agüero, which rather demolished his recently made-over image from lad of violence to man of culture. City now had 35 minutes to score one goal against ten men of a team still at risk of relegation. But then 11 minutes later QPR broke down the left for their first actual attack of the match. Kompany, you could see, stopped himself checking Armand Traoré, seeming to realise just before he pulled out that he could be sent off if he took him down. Traoré surged past Kompany and suddenly there was James Mackie, a striker much more accomplished than he appears at first, hurtling unmarked into the box. Traoré found him with an excellent high and dipping left-footed cross and Mackie dived on the ball, headed it down, bounced it high up into Joe Hart's net and City were 2–1 down.

Even then it still took some time for the reality to be accepted that City, even this City, really could choke at the end of this glittering season. There were still 25 minutes left, but QPR had all ten men around their own penalty area and City could not wriggle free. Mancini was absolutely, gesticulatingly, body-jerkingly ranting at his players – but he still made good calls.

He sent Džeko on for Barry three minutes after QPR's second, signalling it was all-out attack to score two goals. When it reached 72 minutes it seemed to me properly serious, the first feeling there really was not much time left now, and City really might honestly not do it. They might lose, Ferguson would be standing at Sunderland and be handed the trophy, and nobody would ever forget the Sheikh's expensively bought club choked like this. After 76 minutes he brought off Tevez, who would not, ultimately, be at the centre of the fairy story, only a model of decent hard work after all the silliness, and Balotelli was thrown on, truly a clutch at the final straw of hope.

Balotelli made a difference, showed control and skill, but City did not threaten, and the scoreboard in the corner of the stadium ticked the seconds round with stomach-sinking inexorability. My friend Ric Demby told me that in the family stand where he sits with his two sons, his two brothers and their boys just up and around him, lifelong City fans, he had his head in his hands and could not watch. He said people were 'taking it personally'. It was like the Gillingham match, back when the old City were trying to clamber out of the third division at flaking Wembley. He said people were shouting: 'You bastards. You fucking bastards. You've done it to me. Again. You've gone and burst that bubble.'

The clock ticked round and this Manchester City of superstars seemed to shed layers of skin and discover the old City lurking within them. Gaël Clichy, splendid throughout this run, smacked a cross behind and out of play. Balotelli turned in space, looked up, and passed the ball to nobody and into touch. It was just the kind of football, with no bearings or confidence, we'd watched for so long at Maine Road. It was as if these players from all over the world were not really playing QPR, but the ghosts and baggage and history of Manchester City. They were confronting Typical City in a few last boiled-down minutes as the world was watching. They were clawing the spectres of Malcolm Allison's return, relegation in 1983 when David Pleat had skipped across the Maine Road pitch to hug a beaming Brian Horton. The sickness that had infected Jamie Pollock, an effective enough player with Bolton, to almost deliberately fashion the opposite of what he intended, was thick in the air, haunting world-class modern footballers whose winning mentality had been documented in lengthy dossiers.

When people started to leave, some in tears, I honestly made a note that it felt like Gillingham, the whole hideous atmosphere, the emptiness. Even being objective, it felt like a wrong ending to me. I felt that if Ferguson won it, after his owners had caused £500m to be drained out of United to pay for their own self-seeking takeover, it would draw the wrong and nonsensical conclusion, that the Glazers' machinations made no difference to United's ability to win. If Mark Hughes had truly been treated appallingly by City you could have lived with the idea that his revenge was just, but I did not think he had, in the round. City had arguably been ruthless, and the way the news leaked out was awful for him, but they had kept him on and given him £300m or so to spend on players of his choice, and if he had made mistakes in his communication within the new structure which the Abu Dhabi ownership had created, then he had jeopardised his own golden football opportunity.

On 90 minutes the clock stopped and the scoreboard went

blank, except to say City 1 QPR 2. When David Silva looped one of his perfect corners into the six-yard area and Džeko quick-stepped forward, then back, to lose his marker and score with a header, nobody reacted much, just as they hadn't when Kevin Horlock had scored his injury time goal at Wembley in 1999. Džeko ran back with the ball, QPR kicked off, City won it back, and the crowd, which had been so quiet, feeling the dread of all those collapses, did start to urge them on. Balotelli was scuffling on the edge of the penalty area, not losing his head – and that was a nice little sub-plot in the near-perfect sporting drama, a glimpse of redemption for Mario, who was on the floor when he nevertheless got his right foot to the ball and pushed it into the path of Sergio Agüero.

It was the 94th minute of the final game of the maddest season, and Agüero was free of Clint Hill for the first time. For £38m you want a young man who can look a moment of truth like that face on, decide he was having no Typical City truck with it, nick past his marker and properly smash the ball past a goalkeeper like Paddy Kenny. And that was the moment when everybody realised they had actually turned round the worst of all the let-downs, that in a second they had gone from the worst collapse to the greatest of triumphs in their lifetimes, that City were winning and there was no time for QPR to equalise and in fact they had done it after all.

People were throwing themselves up and down with such glee they did not really know what to do with their bodies. Ric said that in the family stand the dads were properly bearhug-ging each other, that a lot of people of all ages had instantly burst into tears. They had all travelled a long way over many years, through far-flung vales of unexpected disappointments to get to this day, and now they had come intimately up close with all of that, and this Manchester City had overcome it in the most spectacular of ways. Vincent Kompany said afterwards that when Agüero, shirt off and spinning it around his head, had run all the way back over the centre circle and collapsed on the pitch, and all his team-mates had piled on top of him, several of them were actually crying, right there and then. All around them, Manchester City supporters were roaring and hugging and crying and bouncing up and down, then the whistle went and they had won the Premier League.

Lads ran on to the pitch at the end, poured on to it, like they know they're not supposed to, managed to grab some of the players for some euphoric hugging, let off blue and white smoke bombs, and stood in front of the Main Stand to sing. I looked on them and wished I was down there with them, feeling it as they were. Then they cleared the pitch and played 'We Are the Champions', by Queen, which sounded as naff as it always has, but hearing it meant that Manchester City really were the champions. While nobody blue in Manchester had wanted to even talk all week about the possibility that they might win it, preparations had had to be made, the route of Monday's victory parade worked out with the police, fireworks readied to go off the top of the stand. And the boards came out which said: 2011–12 champions of the Barclays Premier League.

City had arranged that all the surviving players of 1968 who could be traced were invited to go on to the pitch, that Tony Book, Skip, would walk out holding the trophy with Mike Summerbee, and hand it to the team of 2012. Say what you like about all this buying the title and ownership by a faraway sheikh contravening the traditions of football, it was another classy touch. To pay such respect to the local heroes of the past when the new regime could be entitled to relish the present they had bought and fashioned. It was so wonderful to see the former greats walk out, and there was Franny, where he belonged, in a row of ex-players of which he was one, not barmily roared back by us in desperation, to run the whole show.

So Skip handed the trophy over and Vincent Kompany raised it and the players went delirious. I had a strange thought that after all that drama, such high athleticism and skill too, so much emotion, so much connecting of people with their lives and families and memories, for it all to be crowned with the handing over of a silver cup seemed a little childish. Then the players brought their wives and girlfriends on to the field, and their kids, and ran around and showed the cup to all the fans, who could not believe they were really here.

I stood out there for as long as I could, taking it all in. Again I was surprised by how emotional it was. I too had clenched my fist and roared when Agüero's goal went in. I'd wanted it for all these people; I wanted them all to go home happy just this once, and for a great football story to happen, however compromised by all the money. The way the team had done it, so close to failure for so long, had reminded people who City really were, the fallible Manchester team, and made it feel more that Manchester City had won the Premier League, rather than Abu Dhabi United. I was glad for all the people who still felt the same about it, as I did not, who had been everywhere with City and had the club, still, as the backbone of their lives, and now had this as the moment they would talk about for ever. Young boys were singing, but I couldn't help wondering what moral this actually sent to them: reach for the stars, work hard, always keep going to the very end – and get a sheikh to put in £1bn. I was welling up for all the times I had watched City as a boy, with my dad, my cousin, scrounging all the lifts, the bus rides from Grand Lodge, the terraces in the 1980s, the great escape of football.

Whichever smart guy was responsible for the music ran through a well-judged repertoire, playing 'Wonderwall', an anthem for the 1990s generation and chippy, lippy Manchester defiance – Liam Gallagher popped up on the big screen, acting silly. The stadium was finally starting to empty, and the players with their Premier League title, which ultimately they deserved to win, thinning into a straggle. Perhaps they had run out of tracks, but on the sound system they played the song then which used to signal the players running out at Maine Road in the 1970s. I think the players themselves had recorded it, as they did then. Nobody ever sang along with it at Maine Road, and some thought it cheesy. It reminded me more than anything of the old North Stand, high and cantilevered, and grey, cold afternoons watching City, my club, my team, to which I unquestioningly felt I belonged:

> *City,* [it went] *Manchester City,*
> *We are the lads who are playing to win,*
> *City, the boys in blue will never give in.*

I had loved it so much, as a boy.

CHAPTER 21

CHAMPIONS

Khaldoon Al Mubarak agreed to meet me for an interview the day after City had won the Premier League just four years into the ownership of the club by Sheikh Mansour bin Zayed Al Nahyan. We met at the Lowry Hotel again, in the same suite on the sixth floor he had stayed in three years earlier. Outside, City fans were descending on Albert Square and the planned route around Manchester city centre for the players to parade the Premier League trophy from an open-top bus. He, Simon Pearce and the Abu Dhabi entourage were not staying for the parade. They were flying back to Abu Dhabi, and the following day, Mancini and Brian Marwood were coming out to meet Sheikh Mansour and start to plan for the summer, for the next phase of player signings and an assault on Europe.

Al Mubarak seemed more thrusting without glasses; he was obviously still excited by accomplishing such a landmark achievement, and so was a little more bullish than the thoughtful leader I had encountered before. We sat down on the comfortable couches, and the highlights of the game, culminating in Agüero's grace under pressure and whirling celebration, was playing on Sky on Khaldoon's TV. He was cool, though; while the players had hired the Town Hall function room for a party where they went mental, he'd had a more restrained celebratory dinner at the Lowry – no alcohol for him. So I surprised myself by the first question which his relaxed bearing prompted me to ask:

'Are you actually used to this kind of thing?'

And he replied: 'Honestly? I would be lying if I said this was not genuinely a plan, that we would win the Premier League at the end of the fourth year. We did not just write a letter to set out a dream, we genuinely had a plan, which needed clear milestones and implementation and many things to be introduced.

'We were very clear that year one was to learn the ropes and manage change; year two, to up it a notch, compete for a Champions League position while improving the infrastructure and culture of the club. Year three: be in the Champions League, continue the evolution of the business side and academy, and win a cup to give us the winning feeling. Year four was about going for it, win the Premier League and go as far as we can in the Champions League.'

These are people charged with building impossible pipelines across the Gulf, racetracks in the desert, and crafting an image for a whole country. They have all the money in the world and great expertise and they are used to getting things done.

Al Mubarak was still puzzled by the dread and defeatism of the City fans: 'We want to have fans roaring the team on,' he said. 'As soon as there is any adversity, they get so nervous, they think it is going to be Typical City and end in failure. We have to eradicate that, and I very much hope that the manner of this victory, where the team kept going until the very end, will change the mindset. When I look at the next five years, the fans have to be with us, every step of the way.'

He was adamant, looking back, about his two most difficult challenges overcome at City: the sacking of Mark Hughes, which had been so badly received in the December sleet of 2009, and the stand-off with Tevez. On Hughes, he insisted even now it had been the right thing to do, to line Mancini up, then allow Hughes to manage the team through the home game against Sunderland, because otherwise it would have disrupted the players too much and affected results.

'I don't want to be apologetic to Mark,' he said, more hard-edged than I'd seen him before. 'It was not a good episode. I told him he had to evolve. From a business perspective there is no question in my mind it was the right thing to do. The manager was not going in the direction we wanted.

'We were criticised for talking to Roberto first – of course: I'm not going to fire the guy running the ship without having a replacement in place. People looking at it say we were cold-blooded and harsh, but for me it is business. I'm going to do whatever it takes for the journey. We had targets.

'I hope the results have shown that it was the right thing to do.'

On Tevez, which he argued was an 'unnecessary' battle to have to fight, he was convinced that they had been right to taken a stand, that it had been vitally important for them not be manipulated into backing down, and allowing him to leave at a loss. When he had given the interview to *The National* in Abu Dhabi on 25 January, saying AC Milan should stop 'congratulating themselves,' he believed they thought they could wait until the 31st, and City would cave in on the last day of the transfer window and just let Tevez leave cheaply.

'So I said to Galliani I was not prepared to go to January the 31st, and he should come back to me with a firm offer on the 25th or the deal was off. If I'd budged, allowed AC Milan to have him at a huge loss to us, every agent would think we could be pushed around and it would affect every deal.

'It was a landmark,' he continued. 'We cannot allow ourselves as a club to be mucked around. It was a hell of a gamble for me, not to let him leave for AC Milan in January, because he could have sat out all year, not played for us and lost his value. But I was firm that we are not rich people to be taken advantage of, to give him what he wants and let the market screw us.'

He would not say how much they were asking for the player who came back in the end and won yet another league championship, but £40m seemed around what they were insisting upon. AC Milan baulked, and once the transfer window closed, Tevez had just two options: play or fester. So he came back, and Al Mubarak felt they had set a mark of seriousness. He said both Tevez and Mancini had been 'extremely pragmatic' to set aside their grievances and for Tevez to play in Mancini's team.

Al Mubarak said they believed they could and would continue to invest and would still meet Uefa's financial fair play rules, by driving up income to £350m eventually, shedding the fringe players from the wage bill, and relying on a core of quality. I feel they are over-estimating how far they can make City a global entity. Its support, it seems to me, has boiled down over the years to a 45,000 core. They had some empty seats even for the first ever Champions League game against Napoli, in September. They are not Manchester United. Plus all their sponsorships from Abu Dhabi companies will fall to be investigated by Uefa as to whether they represent 'fair value', or are really another way for the owner to put money in to subsidise excessive spending. But what do I know? They are people used to bringing projects to dazzling fruition.

I asked him about Sheikh Mansour. Why does he never come to a game at the club he bought? Al Mubarak smiled and said: 'His highness is very discreet.'

I asked what that meant, and he said Mansour does not really like being seen in public, and the whole operation which surrounds an outing. 'He enjoyed the Liverpool game when he came, but it was a lot of fuss for him to be in the public eye; he isn't going to be left alone when he does.'

'He genuinely prefers to watch it at home on TV,' Al Mubarak said.

I asked him if this were not a little strange, to put so much money in and never come, as if City are some hyper-real home entertainment game – 'Premier League Club Owner' or something, in which he buys the best team and gets to sit at home and watch it win a championship.

Khaldoon didn't think so: 'He loves it, he is over the moon. I spoke to him five minutes after the whistle blew. He watched it on his own, as a fan. And afterwards he got 2,500 text messages.'

I asked him about what he had said three years earlier, that he hoped the project would lead to improved understanding between the Muslim world and the West, England.

In March 2012, Human Rights Watch had issued another report on workers' conditions on Saadiyat Island, acknowledging that 'notable improvements' had been made there since its 2009 report, including workers being paid regularly, having proper rest breaks, and most significantly, all of them being covered by medical insurance. However, based on interviews with forty-seven workers, Human Rights Watch argued there was further to go because too many were still having to pay large lump sums to recruitment agents before they arrived, which 'frequently trap them in debt'.

This time, reflecting a new confidence that the issues were being addressed, the Abu Dhabi authorities had issued a robust defence. They argued HRW's findings were based on too small a sample of workers interviewed many months previously, and that the report 'is not an accurate reflection of the current situation on Saadiyat'. The Tourism Development and Investment Company, responsible for the huge projects, which have been re-committed to after a review, said that as recruitment fees were paid by workers in their country of origin, not Abu Dhabi, they were very difficult to police. However the fees had been outlawed and, if proven to have been levied on workers, now had to be reimbursed. The TDIC emphasised it took workers' welfare seriously, and had appointed an independent monitor to report regularly, although the reports have not yet been made available to the public.

I said to Al Mubarak that I had thought a lot about whether the rebuilding of Manchester City had increased understanding between Manchester, England and the Muslim, Arab world. Actually, I said, I did not think that had happened. The Manchester City fans were very grateful for the money spent and the transformation of their club, but I wasn't sure it had enhanced comprehension of the Arab world. I'd come to think it reinforced the idea in people's minds that some Arabs were very rich. Elsewhere there was chaos we had seen on our televisions, political upheaval, the Arab spring revolutions against unelected dictators, to which the Al Nahyans, in a country not divided by different strands of Islam, and where they had kept the Emiratis wealthy and mostly content, had not been vulnerable. And most of the ways in which they were interacting with the West and welcoming visitors were via the buying up of our culture: the Premier League football club, the Grand Prix, soon the Louvre and the Guggenheim. I wondered if their Manchester City project had driven home the reality that they had a great deal of money in Abu Dhabi, because of oil, while we are sunk in dreadful economic problems, the consequence of allowing our industries to collapse. Talking in the Lowry Hotel in Salford the day after winning the Premier League, he said actually he hadn't thought about that aspect much at all.

'We're a small country, everything we do is a reflection of where we come from, and I hope it reflects well on us,' he said.

They were checking out, flying back, and moving on to the next stage of their plans.

'Enjoy it,' he smiled as we shook hands and said goodbye.

I went from there to try to catch up with the victory parade of the open-top bus, but the City fans were streaming back from the parade by then, some carrying inflatable bananas. They had seemed just a laugh then, but now the bright big yellow things seemed like they had all along been 1980s standard bearers for the return of success, who knew when, who knew how. I walked across the new bridge over the Irwell, just along from where the famous picture of the stinky river was drawn, which features on the cover of Engels's classic book on the inequality of Victorian Manchester. I saw Bridge Street, where the restaurant was in which I served some time, then Parsonage Square, where I'd done happier work for a while, then turned into Deansgate. There it was: Manchester, so great and proud a place to be from, if not always the greatest place to live.

It was still full of City fans, ecstatic, although by the time I got there, the parade had been and gone. The first fan I saw was a bloke about my age, roaring the song about City being the best team in the land and all the world, with one son sitting on his shoulders and the other running along beside, holding his hand. It was getting late and the 100,000 people who had turned up for the parade, decked in blue and white, still disbelieving, were heading home. I walked up Market Street, where people were walking to Piccadilly for buses, trains and Metrolink. In the middle of that pedestrianised street, under the overhang of the brutal Arndale Centre, which has squatted on Manchester since the 1970s, swagmen were selling T-shirts and flags, hastily printed on rough material and attached to thin and splintery sticks.

The flags were blue and white, and on them it said: CHAMPIONS.

Manchester City's victory parade, May 14 2012

BIBLIOGRAPHY

Manchester City

Manchester The Greatest City: The Complete History of Manchester City Football Club, Gary James (Polar 1997)

I'm Not Really Here: A Life of Two Halves, Paul Lake with Joanne Lake (Century 2011)

Colin Bell: Reluctant Hero, Colin Bell with Ian Cheeseman (Mainstream 2005)

Blue Blood: The Mike Doyle Story, Mike Doyle with David Clayton (Parrs Wood Press 2004)

Thank God for Football!, Peter Lupson (Azure 2010)

Blue Moon: Down with the Dead Men at Manchester City, Mark Hodkinson (Mainstream 1999)

Niall Quinn: The Autobiography, Niall Quinn with Tom Humphries (Headline 2003)

Trautmann's Journey: From Hitler Youth to FA Cup Legend, Catrine Clay (Yellow Jersey 2010)

Manchester and General Histories

The Condition of the Working Class in England, Friedrich Engels (Penguin Classics 1987)

Manchester: A History, Alan Kidd (Carnegie Publishing 2008)

The Victorians, A. N. Wilson (Arrow Books 2003)

Crime City: Manchester's Victorian Underworld, Joseph O'Neill (Milo Books 2008)

Manchester, England, Dave Haslam (Fourth Estate 2010)

Indices of Multiple Deprivation 2010: Analysis for Manchester (Manchester City Council 2011)

No Such Thing as Society: A History of Britain in the 1980s, Andy McSmith (Constable 2011)

Fantasy Island: Waking up to the Incredible Economic, Political and Social Illusions of the Blair Legacy, Larry Elliott and Dan Atkinson (Constable 2007)

One of Us, Hugo Young (Pan Books 1990)

Abu Dhabi

Abu Dhabi, Oil and Beyond, Christopher Davidson (Hurst and Co 2011)

A Diamond in the Desert, Behind the Scenes in the World's Richest City, Jo Tatchell (Sceptre 2009)

The Abu Dhabi Economic Vision 2030 (Government of Abu Dhabi 2008)

Plan Abu Dhabi 2030 (Abu Dhabi Planning Council 2007)

The Island of Happiness: Exploitation of Migrant Workers on Saadiyat Island, Abu Dhabi (Human Rights Watch 2009)

The Island of Happiness Revisited (Human Rights Watch 2012)

Abu Dhabi: The Complete Residents' Guide (Explorer 2006)

Football General

100 Seasons of League Football, Bryon Butler (Queen Anne Press 1998)

The Official History of the Football Association, Bryon Butler (Queen Anne Press 1993

The Ball is Round: A Global History of Soccer, David Goldblatt (Riverhead Books 2006)

Sky Sports Football Yearbooks, Glenda Rollin and Jack Rollin (eds) (Headline various years)

Uppies and Downies: The Extraordinary Football Games of Britain, Hugh Hornby (English Heritage 2008)

Alan A'Court: My Life in Football, Alan A'Court with Ian Hargreaves (The Bluecoat Press 2003)

Shot! A Photographic Record of Football in the Seventies (When Saturday Comes 1994)

Football in the Digital Age: Whose Game is it Anyway?, Sean Hamil, Jonathan Michie, Christine Oughton and Steven Warby (Mainstream 2000)

The Hillsborough Stadium Disaster: Inquiry by Lord Justice Taylor, Interim Report (HMSO, 1989)

The Hillsborough Stadium Disaster: Inquiry by Lord Justice Taylor, Final Report (HMSO, 1990)

Blueprint for the Future of Football (The Football Association 1991)

Manchester United

Manchester United Official Illustrated History (HarperCollins 2011)

Manchester United: The Betrayal of a Legend, Michael Crick and David Smith (Pelham Books 1989)

The Day a Team Died, Frank Taylor (Souvenir Press 1998)

The Lost Babes: Manchester United and the Forgotten Victims of Munich, Jeff Connor (Harper Sport 2006)

Johnny the Forgotten Babe: Memories of Manchester and Manchester United in the 1950s, Neil Berry (Brampton Manor Books 2007)

Thaksin Shinawatra

Thaksin: The Business of Politics in Thailand, Pasuk Phongpaichit and Chris Baker (Silkwork Books 2004)

Not Enough Graves (Human Rights Watch 2004)

Financial Accounts, Offer Documents and other official Companies House filings of Manchester City, Manchester United, Liverpool and other football clubs.

The *Guardian, Telegraph, Independent, Daily Mail, Manchester Evening News*, BBC website and other online sources.

www.soccerbase.com is invaluable for official player, club and manager records

www.wikipedia.org is a remarkable resource, now more thoroughly citing original and official sources

ACKNOWLEDGEMENTS

As this book partly tells my own journey in football as well as Manchester City's, I have too many people to thank individually for all the friendship, help and encouragement over so many years. A life of playing and watching football and supporting a club is a story of a mum and dad enabling it all in the first place, friends, teammates, teachers, friends' dads, older players and coaches who drove us everywhere, encouraged us to play, taught us a lot and made us crease up laughing, lifelong friends made supporting City and many other mates along the way.

At Manchester City, I am grateful to all the people working at the club, managers, players, directors, 'owners,' professional advisers, fans and fanzine editors whom I have spent time with or interviewed over many years, for all their help and insights. I am particularly grateful to the new senior people following the takeover by Sheikh Mansour of Abu Dhabi, who have been so open to my inquiries and prepared to answer questions from the beginning.

In journalism I feel I have been very lucky to have had great encouragement from editors and colleagues throughout, and the generous spirits of more senior and experienced writers, including some legendary people. At the *Guardian*, Paul Johnson is always supportive and was very understanding at a difficult time last year. Ian Prior, Mike Adamson, Mark Redding, Mike Herd, Matthew Hancock and others with whom I have worked closely over the years have always been greatly encouraging. I will always be grateful to Ben Clissitt for originally asking me to write for the paper. All my other colleagues and fellow writers at the *Guardian* are brilliant at their journalism and great to work with. Particular thanks to Rachael Hayes and Jack Harrington for looking after us, and Yvonne Fletcher who did that unforgiving job with such good cheer for so long.

Since 'coming of age' in my knowledge of football and how it works, that the clubs are not clubs and in fact have 'owners' who are too often self-seeking, I have always found the leaders of the alternative view inspirational. Andy Walsh and Adam Brown have been in the engine room and think tank of the collective effort that is FC United of Manchester. After Brian Lomax, the founding father, Dave Boyle led Supporters Direct with great energy and insight. Malcolm Clarke, Steve Powell, Michael Brunskill and others at the Football Supporters Federation fight the good fight ceaselessly and always perceptively.

At AM Heath, thanks to Bill Hamilton for his help and support, as ever. I am very grateful to Richard Milner at Quercus for believing in this book and for all his advice, encouragement and hard work on it.

Although I cannot mention all the friends with whom a life in football has been shared, I can't leave out Andy Press, Ric Demby, Sean Thorpe and David 'DJ' Michael. Writing about it, from Drinkwater Park on, brought many memories back.

One night in the pub, the guys at Thursday night football demanded a mention, so here you are: Dave Bradley, Matt Shepherd, Pete Bradley, Andrew Bradley, Andy Bradley, Andy Freeman, John Whittaker, Steve Wilson, Steve Peel, Rich Downey, Stuart 'Batty' Simpson, Miles Sutton, Chris Shepherd and Ryan Dunn. Thanks for having me in the game.

David Conn, 2012

INDEX